PURE
LUCK

PURE
LUCK

ALAN BRAMSON

THE AUTHORIZED BIOGRAPHY of
SIR THOMAS SOPWITH, 1888-1989

FOREWORD BY
HRH THE PRINCE OF WALES

Patrick Stephens Limited

First published in 1990

British Library Cataloguing in Publication Data

Bramson, A. E. (Alan Ellesmere)
Pure luck: the authorised biography of Sir Thomas
Sopwith, 1888-1989.
1. Great Britain. Aircraft industries, history
I. Title
338.476291300941

ISBN 1-85260-263-5

*Patrick Stephens Limited is a member of the
Haynes Publishing Group P.L.C., Sparkford, Nr Yeovil, Somerset, BA22 7JJ.*

Typeset by Harper Phototypesetters Limited, Northampton, England.
Printed in Great Britain by: J.H. Haynes & Co. Ltd.

3 5 7 9 10 8 6 4 2

Contents

Acknowledgements

WITHOUT THE HELP of those who knew Sir Thomas Sopwith it would have been impossible to write this book and I am grateful to all who sent me information in response to my many letters. I want to thank Sir Peter Masefield for his constant support and encouragement. John Crampton managed to persuade Sir Thomas that I should write his biography, and but for his influence this book may never have progressed beyond few thoughts on paper. And it was due to my old friend, John Scott, that I met John Crampton.

I must particularly thank Don McClen, Director of Corporate Relations at British Aerospace, for steering me in the right direction for many of the interviews and to the Earl of Gowrie, Sir Arnold Hall, Sir John Lidbury, Mr Jim Joel, Mrs J. McLean Snr, The Hon Richard Beaumont and Sir George Edwards, one time business rival but always a friend and admirer of Sir Thomas Sopwith, for their important contributions. Thomas Edward Sopwith has greatly supported me by reading the manuscript and checking the accuracy of facts relating to the family and Lt Col. Derry St J. Radcliffe devoted a great deal of his time to finding old material as well as recounting his experiences as Sir Thomas's right-hand man over a great many years.

Most of the information concerning Sir Thomas's marine activities was provided by Frank Murdoch who was personally involved in the design of the 'J' Class yachts and who acted as an adviser while the motor yacht, Philante, was under construction. To the many who kindly sent me information the fact that I am unable to mention all names does not diminish my appreciation.

In obtaining the various photographs I have enjoyed the help of the Sopwith family, Mike Goodall of the Brooklands Museum Trust, also Peter Shoebrook and his assistant, Pauline Guest of British Aerospace at Kingston.

Finally I want to acknowledge the support I have had from Mr Patrick Stephens, the publisher and my wife, Miriam, who has adopted her usual role as valued critic and proof-reader.

Foreword

by HRH The Prince of Wales

THE LIFE OF Sir Thomas Sopwith spans the entire history of aviation. Sir Thomas, during his lifetime, *was* British aviation. The value of his contribution to military flying during the Great War of 1914-1918, World War Two and in the years since, cannot be over-estimated. The risks he, his companies and his colleagues took for the good of their country must never be forgotten and can never be underestimated.

His talents as a yachtsman, a sportsman in the field and as a host won him many friends throughout the world. And his personal qualities earned him the greatest affection from those who worked in his many companies.

I count myself as incredibly fortunate to have known him and to have been able to listen to his stories about the early days of flight. As a pretty keen aviator myself, it always fascinated me that in those early days, if you wanted to fly, you climbed into an aeroplane and taught yourself!

Sir Thomas Sopwith was always especially quick to recognize and embrace the technology of the times. Yet his great achievements on water, in the air and as an industrialist of international status were matched by exceptional modesty.

I am very proud to have been asked to contribute this Foreword and I believe it fitting that Alan Bramson, the biographer of the remarkable Sir Thomas, is himself a pilot of wide experience as well as an established aviation author.

I am sure this book will be a worthy memento of one of the great men of our time. It should be read by all who aspire to follow in his footsteps.

Preface

OVER THE PAST 10 to 15 years any author with thoughts of writing a biography of Sir Thomas Sopwith would have met with a polite but firm refusal from the man himself and his family. It was not that he wished to be discourteous, far from it; no greater example of the classic English gentleman, ever lived. But this same gentleman had another rare side to his character, a true modesty allied with a genuine surprise that anyone should wish to be interested in his long and varied life.

There had been a book, published in 1970, entitled *Sopwith—The Man And His Aircraft,* which gave a good account of his aircraft during the Great War and, although it recorded some of his personal exploits, it was not a biography of the man, something a number of publishers have been wanting to print for a long time. Interest in the possibility of a Sopwith biography was reawakened after his hundredth birthday, and, although new approaches were made at regular intervals, the answer was always the same—Sir Thomas does not want his biography to be written.

To have the most superficial knowledge of Sir Thomas Sopwith— sportsman, pioneer aviator, yachtsman, industrialist—is to realize that it would be quite unthinkable for the life of this great centenarian to go unrecorded. Through the gentle persuasion of several family friends, among them Sir Peter Masefield, Lord Waterpark and John Crampton (who was Technical Sales Manager of his favourite aircraft, the remarkable *Harrier*) Sir Thomas reluctantly gave his consent to my writing this book with the words: 'Can't think why—who'll read it?'

If you walk into a room full of people and ask: 'Who was Tommy Sopwith?' the answers will depend on the interests of the person being questioned. To the motorsport fan, he was Sopwith the pioneer racing driver (although researches reveal that he did very little racing); to the yachtsman, he was Sopwith who challenged the America Cup and came near to winning;

9

to the power boat enthusiast, he once held the world waterspeed record; to the aviation buff, he was a pioneer pilot; and if the question is directed to someone from the City, he will probably say: 'He founded an industrial empire'. All these answers are true, all relate to the same man.

It is because of Tommy Sopwith's prowess in so many widely differing activities that writing his biography is such a daunting task, one that seemed to assume growing and alarming proportions as more and more information on this remarkable Edwardian, indeed late Victorian, was revealed. That he was versatile is obvious; that he was a great sportsman is clear; that he was a gifted engineer is certain, but his grasp of financial matters is perhaps unusual in one enjoying the other talents mentioned. But Sopwith's secret weapon was his great personal charm and an unfailing talent for persuading the right people to work with him, then letting them get on with the job without too much control. Having got his man to join the team he would encourage him to produce a masterpiece, and of those there have been plenty. It was a policy that worked well enough, for Tommy Sopwith's little aircraft business of 1913 grew from a 10-man workshop to an industrial empire which, at one time, employed 127,000 people.

History is punctuated by famous men and women who made their name in all walks of life. Sometimes we discuss such a figure and gain the response: 'I know he was a great person, but on the way up the ladder he did . . .; and he was very unfair to . . . as well as . . . in the process'. During my many interviews with people who were personal friends of Sir Thomas Sopwith, or who worked for him at various levels, not once did I hear a critical word. Without exception, he was regarded with deep affection by all who were fortunate enough to know him. He was the prime example of how to build up a great business of international standing without driving the staff and being ruthless with the management.

In the course of writing about Sir Thomas Sopwith I have tried to confine myself to the man. If some parts of the text appear to be more of a history of Hawker Siddeley than a biography, it is because the great aircraft group was so much a part of the man; Hawker Siddeley *was* an extension of Tommy Sopwith, his invention, his achievement, and a reflection of his very special personality. Originally, I wanted to call this book *101 Years of Tommy Sopwith,* but the publishers and a number of others who have helped me gather information thought *Pure Luck* typified the man; that was the answer he gave when asked to explain his phenomenal success throughout a very long life. The canvas is vast and my writing is inadequate, but if it reflects a little of the subject's greatness something will have been achieved. Certainly, it has been a great privilege to have Sir Thomas Sopwith's approval for this book. It is a responsibility I have accepted with great circumspect.

Alan Bramson, London, 1990.

CHAPTER
1

Another Thomas

IN 1590, ABOUT the time King Henry VII was laying siege to Paris, there was a Sopwith family in the Northumbrian city of Newcastle. Birth certificates, or indeed public records as we understand them today, were yet to be invented, so it is difficult to trace the earliest members of the family.

A starting point that can be authenticated would be Matthew Sopwith who, in 1735, opened up a lead mine near Hexham in partnership with a Mr Ennington.

Lead mining was to become an activity favoured by several generations of the Sopwith family in the years ahead.

Matthew Sopwith had four sons, Jacob (born 1709), Matthew, Nathaniel and Francis. The four boys each had a farm on the Angerton estate of the Earl of Carlisle. Jacob, the eldest, married and, in 1741, had a son Thomas. He later set up a cabinet-making and building business in Newcastle.

There are so many Thomas Sopwiths in this great family that it might be helpful to append dates whenever the name is mentioned. Thus, builder Thomas Sopwith (1741) fathered a son Jacob in 1770 who eventually married Isabella Lowes. They, in turn, had a daughter Mary and a son Thomas who arrived on 3 January, 1803. This was about the time when Napoleon sold Louisiana to a United States that had been an independent country for only 27 years. It was a very different Britain in those days. Total population was less than eleven million, half of its subjects died before reaching the age of 17, and one in ten of the male population was in the armed forces.

Thomas Sopwith (1803) is of particular importance to this biography because of his remarkable grasp of many diverse subjects, both practical and intellectual. He was also grandfather of the subject of this biography, and, in the wonderous ways of nature, probably responsible for passing on talents that emerged to such momentous effect in the grandson he never saw.

A biography, written by Benjamin Ward Richardson, and based on 171 beautifully compiled diaries written by Thomas Sopwith (1803) between 1822 and 1879, was published in 1891. In it he describes Sopwith as 'practical, scholar in men, events, things; and Northumbrian to the backbone'.

At a time when youth was firmly kept in its place, Sopwith, then only 19, was quickly recognized by the City Fathers of Newcastle and retained on various survey projects, among them a new gaol. That same year, he was admitted a free Burgess of the Corporation of Newcastle and issued with a musket for the defence of the town. Through hard work and a quest for perfection Thomas Sopwith (1803) improved his modest education to such effect that, in 1845, he was elected a Fellow of the Royal Society and, in 1857, Durham University awarded him an Hon MA.

Thomas Sopwith (1803) MA, CB, FRS, was a talented pianist, an astronomer, a meteorologist, and sufficiently skilled as a practical engineer for the great Sir Joseph Whitworth (1803-1887) to claim in public that '. . . I was quite as good with my hands, when I was young, as Tom Sopwith'. This was praise indeed; Whitworth pioneered standard screw threads in the days when every factory used its own pattern of nuts and bolts. Later a partnership was formed with a rival company founded by William George Armstrong, one-time solicitor turned engineer, and the Armstrong Whitworth concern made an international name for itself building ships, guns, knitting machines and, eventually airships and aeroplanes. If only Sopwith (1803) could have looked into the future he would have been astonished to learn that, half a century later, this large company would be taken over by his grandson. Among Sopwith's eminent friends were George Stephenson, builder of *Rocket,* the first practical steam locomotive, and McAdam, the pioneer road builder.

In October, 1829, Sopwith (1803) was employed by Parliament to survey routes for several new railway lines. This was a period when the new steam-powered carriages were revolutionizing travel in Britain. Steam was the jet engine of the times and its impact in the early 1800s was perhaps even greater than that of the gas turbine which, a century and a half later, would alter the face of aviation. For example, in the days of hand presses, newspapers were printed at a rate of only 250 copies per hour. The arrival of steam power increased the printing rate tenfold.

In 1830 Thomas Sopwith (1803) made his first journey to London, a horsedrawn coach trip of 273 miles covered in 33 hours. You paid extra to travel inside the coach and the fare cost £4 10s (£4.50) with 17s 6d (87p) for guards and drivers, 2s for breakfast and 7s for cooked meals *en route.* Much as he loved travelling in a coach-and-four, Sopwith embraced the steam train and recognized the effect it would have on transport. Today his observations on the future of railways make amusing reading. In 1834, he said:

'Horse or engine travelling at ten or twelve miles per hour is probably the most economical speed, and is sufficiently quick for most purposes; but the march of intellect will never rest satisfied with this, and they are now scheming a velocity of forty miles an hour'.

Among the diaries, written by Thomas Sopwith (1803), is a reference to local schools in the Newcastle area. He deplores the way letters to school governors from government officials, often on quite trivial matters, started with the words: 'My Lords disapprove . . .' or 'My Lords require you . . .' and so on. His dislike of pomposity in any form would, in the years ahead, be inherited by his grandson.

From 1 July, 1845 to 1871, he was principal agent for the world's largest lead mines operated in Northumberland and Durham by the W.B. Lead-Mines concern which had its headquarters at Allenheads, near Hexham, Northumberland.

The owner of W.B. Lead-Mines was Thomas Wentworth Beaumont and, on 6 November, 1845, Thomas Sopwith (1803) met him in London to discuss plans for the new house that was to be built for him at Allenheads. As he noted in his diary:

'I had made the building of a new house, with spacious garden and ornamental ground, the sole condition on which I would accept the agency of the W.B. Mines. All other matters, such as amount of salary, arrangements as to time of residence, and, in short, all other details, I was willing to leave either in the sole disposition of Mr Beaumont, or, at all events, as matters to be considered and discussed, but the new house was of the very essence of the agreement'.

Sopwith (1803) seems to labour the matter of the house in his diary, almost as though he were stating his case in a court of law. Perhaps this is because he anticipated trouble when his employer saw the finished building. Whether it was because, from the plans he was shown, Mr Beaumont was unable to visualize what kind of house was going to be built is not clear, but when he saw the almost completed building he claimed that Sopwith had no right to have ordered such a grand residence. At first he wanted it to be pulled down but Sopwith drew his attention to the cost of such an exercise and he was allowed to have the house completed. It is believed that eventually Beaumont himself used the house as a shooting lodge; certainly it is in use to the present day. Sopwith (1803) makes no reference to these differences, but when Thomas Wentworth Beaumont died in Bournemouth on 20 December, 1848, he was described in his diary as 'a kind employer and generous friend'.

Sopwith's years of intellectual and material successes had been punctuated by sadness. On 28 July, 1829, soon after their son Jacob was born, his wife Mary expired in her bed. The son was of a difficult temperament and a source of anxiety to his family, and some years later he died in India. In 1831 Sopwith (1803) married Jane Scott, but she passed away 24 years later, and Sopwith married his third wife, Anne Potter, in 1858. However, it is from among the nine children of his second marriage that the story is continued by another Thomas Sopwith who was born on 2 July, 1838, within a few days of Queen Victoria's coronation. He went to schools at Allenheads in Northumberland and Bruce Castle before becoming articled to Sir W. Armstrong and Co at Elswick, Newcastle-on-Tyne. Then, in true Sopwith tradition, the lure of the lead mines enticed him to join the Beaumont company which traded as 'W.B.' Lead Mines.

In 1862 Sopwith (1838) made a tour of the principal mining centres on the continent of Europe and, several years later, he and his father (Thomas Sopwith 1803) spent the months of April and May setting up The Spanish Lead Co at Linares in southern Spain. The following year Thomas Sopwith (1838), by then 27 years old, was put in charge of the enterprise.

On 1 March, 1866, Thomas Sopwith (1838) married Lydia Gertrude Messiter from Wincanton, Somerset, and, in the custom of Victorian times, raised a large family. In 1867 their first daughter, Violet, arrived followed by Daisy. Then in 1870 came the twins, Rosamond and Lilian. May was born in 1874; Olive 1876; and then Iris.

The most important date in this story is 18 January, 1888, because that was the day when Thomas Sopwith, by then 50 years old, and his wife, Lydia, became parents of the only boy of the family. And as this baby was the eighth child, they named him Thomas Octave Murdoch Sopwith. He was born at 92 Cromwell Road, Kensington, West London, then a smart residential area of large terrace houses. Today most of these have been converted into small hotels, although number 92 stands in pristine condition as the Bank of Credit and Commerce International.

To put the year 1888 in perspective, Thomas Sopwith was born five years before King George V, then Duke of York, married Princess Mary of Teck who later became Queen Mary. In 1894, when he was six years old, the Manchester Ship Canal and London's world famous Tower Bridge were opened.

Although business commitments entailed Thomas Sopwith Senior spending much of his time in Spain, he was very much a family man. During the school holidays he would lease an estate on the Scottish Isle of Lismore from the Duke of Argyle and relax there with his wife, Lydia, and the eight children until he had to return to Spain.

Spending his childhood holidays mainly in the company of his mother and seven sisters, the young Tommy Sopwith must, at times, have felt like the only boy at a girl's school.

Without a doubt he was very much loved by his sisters and holidays on the island were to have a profound influence on him, developing an enthusiasm for country activities and, above all, a passion for sailing—interests that remained with him throughout a long and active life.

On 30 July, 1898, the most appalling tragedy struck. Thomas and his father were out shooting on the Isle of Lismore with a friend. They were in a boat when a sporting gun that was lying across Thomas's knees accidentally went off, killing his father. Whether or not there was a faulty safety catch has not been determined, but it was an horrendous experience for the 10-year-old boy, and one that marked him for life. Father was brought back to England and buried at Brookwood Cemetery on 4 August, 1898.

At the turn of the century most written accounts describe the Sopwith family as being wealthy, but Tommy Sopwith always disputed this. In fact, Thomas Sopwith Senior left a gross estate of £51,721, quite a lot of money in those days but certainly not in the wealthy class. Tommy Sopwith's description of his family as 'comfortably well off' is more appropriate.

By 1898 most of his sisters had married well and his father's will divided much of the estate between Tommy and his mother. The eldest girl, Violet, was the wife of E. Burd Grubb, an American she had met while staying with her father in Madrid and who, later, attained the rank of General. They met at a tea party during 1890 when he was American Minister to Spain in the days before the USA had an embassy in that country. The Sopwith talent for decision-making must have been inherited by Violet because three weeks later they were married. The next sister, Daisy, married Frank Green-Wilkinson, and then Lilian became the wife of Rear-Admiral Freddy Morgan who was, for a time, Captain of Queen Victoria's yacht, *Britannia*. From all accounts her twin sister Rosamond was a very sweet but somewhat frail girl who suffered from such ill health that she remained single. Following a number of operations, she was afflicted by uncontrollable depression and, in 1937, when Rosamond was 67 years old, she committed suicide.

May, who was four years younger than the twins, was Tommy Sopwith's constant companion during his early flying days. At a period in British society when love affairs were considered very *risqué* May had a liaison with a married man. When the relationship terminated it was such a shattering experience for her, that consequently she never married. May, who was known within the Sopwith family as 'Hettie', had a wonderful sense of humour; and whenever there was a party she was invariably the centre of hilarity.

Olive married Jack Joel, a member of the famous South African gold and diamond mining family. Although the Joel's business interests were in Africa, the family was actually born in England. From a previous marriage Jack Joel had a son, Harry (widely known as 'Jim'), and later to become a racehorse owner who enjoyed the distinction of winning both the National and the Derby. Iris, next in age to Tommy Sopwith, married Edward Raikes who was a King's Messenger. At first Olive and Jack lived in Grosvenor Square, London, not far from the present-day American Embassy, and they were forever entertaining the other Sopwith girls to lunch. As a lad, Jim Joel often suffered from earache and it was to May Sopwith that he would turn for help; she seemed to have the magic touch. The relationship between the Sopwith and Joel families was on a particularly happy basis.

When he was 11 years old, Thomas attended Cottesmore School, then situated at Hove on the south coast of England. It had been founded in 1896 by its headmaster, Davison Brown (who was known as 'The Baron'), so Thomas must have been among its earliest pupils. By then the Sopwith family had moved from Cromwell Road to nearby 5 Queen's Gate Place and, when he was at the family's London home, Tommy would cycle down Gloucester Road, across Fulham Road and Kings Road before crossing Battersea Bridge and making for that important centre of a boy's life in the 1890s, the cycle shop where all wisdom reigned in the world of brakes, saddles, sprockets and chains.

Among his many boyhood interests, school featured low on Tommy Sopwith's list. There was the occasion when the thought of parting from the holiday delights of Lismore and returning to Cottesmore proved too much for the boy. The boat was due to leave for Oban, but Thomas had locked himself in the lavatory and, since words of persuasion had no effect, they had to break down the door. Cottesmore was a boarding school and this did not suit the future Sir Thomas Sopwith at all. There was another incident when he ran away and had to be retrieved by the headmaster. No records were kept at Cottesmore until 1900, but an entry that year shows that he weighed 4 st 10¾ lb and stood 48¼ in tall. He managed to make the top form and play football in the school team, but if Thomas Octave Murdoch Sopwith did not have a high opinion of his school the feeling was mutual; of his sporting activities a report on his character read:

Very slow and timerous. Does not take sufficient interest in practice games and will make little progress till he does.

This seems to indicate that young Sopwith belonged to that select band of which Winston Churchill was a prime example—no good at school but outstanding in life!

In 1907 Olive's husband Jack Joel bought the 3,000-acre Childwick Bury Stud estate near St Albans, north of London. Here some of the finest racehorses were, and indeed continue to be, bred and the Sopwith girls would be entertained at the great house. Now the mansion is owned by a film producer but the estate belongs to Jack Joel's son Jim, an active 94-year-old who remembers his stepmother Olive and her sisters with affection; the Sopwith girls were all outstanding in their different ways. His mother had died when he was seven and when Olive Sopwith became his stepmother she was just 19 years older than him while Tommy Sopwith, the baby of the family, was only seven years his senior. Although in later years they would enjoy many a happy day shooting together, Tommy Sopwith never shared Jim Joel's love of horses.

When the Boer War started on 10 October, 1899, Tommy was an 11 year old schoolboy. His stay at Cottesmore School came to an end in 1901 when he reached the age of 13. It was always intended that he would go from Cottesmore to the Royal Naval College, but the senior service had other ideas. To quote Tommy's own words: 'They didn't think I was clever enough, and they were probably right', a self-depreciating comment, which illustrated the modesty of the man.

As the Royal Navy had closed its doors on him, other plans had to be made and, after leaving school, he joined the Seafield Park engineering college at Lee on Solent not far from Portsmouth on the south coast of England. The college conducted its activities in a series of country mansions set in beautiful grounds. In the workshop, lathes, drill presses and milling machines were driven by leather belts which descended from overhead power shafts. There was a laboratory, and the college generated its own electricity via a 22-hp gas engine. Several cars and motor cycles of the period were provided to give students practical experience of mechanical engineering. Seafield Park's founder and owner was Herbert Mansel Jones and he was obviously a very progressive educationalist because there were few cars on the roads at the turn of the century. The training at Seafield Park was more practical than academic, but this suited the young Thomas and laid the foundations for a future which few could have contemplated at the time, least of all the young man himself.

When Orville Wright made the world's first controlled flight in a heavier than air machine on 17 December, 1903, Sopwith was nearing his sixteenth birthday. The internal combustion engine was still in its crawling, or perhaps one should say, spluttering stage but it was as fascinating to him as the computer is to today's youngsters. As an enterprising young man from a successful family, it is perhaps natural that his first business project on leaving Seafield Park engineering college was to set himself up, in partnership with a Mr Phil Paddon, a boyhood friend, as a consultant to the fledgling motor trade. Later they opened a showroom at 1 Albemarle Street, off London's Piccadilly, and sold Rolls-Royce cars. Even at that tender age a combination of business success and the inheritance left him by his father allowed Tommy Sopwith to follow many interests—yachting, speedboats and a little motor racing. For example, on 27 September, 1906 he was the youngest driver in the Isle of Man Tourist Trophy Race when he competed in a two-cylinder Peugeot belonging to Charles Friswell (later Sir Charles). A year or two later he was driving a Mercedes racer at 100 mph and almost came to grief at Brooklands:

When I was coming under the Member's Bridge, the front pair of cylinders broke in half and knocked the bonnet over my head and deposited itself on the left front wheel. Somehow or other we stayed the right way up.

Even earlier, in November, 1904, was the 'Hatfield 100 Mile Reliability Trial', an event held for three-wheelers. Although Tommy Sopwith was yet to reach his seventeenth birthday he won the event in a Pearson, beating nine older and more experienced drivers. *The Motor* magazine of 8 November that year managed to get his age wrong, but their comments make interesting reading:

'Mr. Sopwith is but 18, but he looked, as he sat [in] his powerful machine, four or five years younger than that, and his apparent youthfulness rather astonished most of the onlookers'.

Certainly, at that period of his life, Tommy Sopwith had a round, rather serious face and was small for his age. His 'powerful machine' was all of 6½ hp and, while this was double the power of most other vehicles in the trial, he was also the best driver taking part. He completed the course in 5 hours 1 minute at an average speed of 20 mph. The driver who came second did not finish for another 13 minutes.

Tommy Sopwith's early flirtation with motor cycles started around 1904 when he was sold his first machine by a man called Wilkinson who, by strange coincidence, was later to become Jack Joel's chauffeur. That first motorbike was not an unqualified success because the young Sopwith managed to fall off it at the bottom of Cricklewood Hill.

An introduction to the air

By the time Tommy Sopwith was in his teens the sport of ballooning was well established and fashionable, and the idea of ascending in a wicker basket had a special appeal for the technically-minded young Thomas. Soon he was engaged in the activity with such distinguished people as The Hon Charles S. Rolls (of Rolls-Royce fame), a young Mr Brabazon, who later became Lord Brabazon of Tara, and Frank Hedges Butler, founder of the Aero Club (later to become the Royal Aero Club).

In 1906 Tommy Sopwith (then only 18 years old) and Philip Paddon, bought a rather untidy secondhand balloon which they named *Padsop*. It was purchased from the Short brothers who were manufacturing balloons under railway arches at Battersea, London. In those days the Shorts had an arrangement with the local gas company. They even laid on a special pipeline to cater for the growing sport and, for a very modest charge, would fill a balloon and have it ready for flight within an hour or so.

Earlier that year, in fact on 24 June, Thomas had made his first flight with Charles Rolls in the balloon *Venus*. His first ascent at night followed on 5 July.

One had to be at least 21 years old before a balloon pilots' certificate could be issued, and, as a result, Tommy never had one because, by that age, he was directing his energies to other interests.

Rolls had a reputation for being 'careful' with his money and, when his balloon came to earth and had to be deflated for the return home by road, he was reluctant to open the rip-panel and release the gas because there was a modest charge for it to be re-stitched before the next flight. Instead, he would ask some local lad to hold open the spring-loaded gas valve. Some of the locals naturally wanted to see what went on inside a balloon and after breathing in coal gas they spent the next half-hour on their backs!

At the height of the ballooning craze it was considered fashionable for two, three or four enthusiasts to pack a hamper, complete with suitable liquid refreshments, before casting off on a clear, starlit night to destinations unknown. As the champagne flowed spirits rose while the climbing balloon drifted silently over the countryside, the aeronauts peering from their creaking basket, straining to recognize the moonlit features passing below. At intervals the hoot of an owl, or the screech of a fox, would drift up to the balloon and punctuate the silent night. One balloonist used to amuse himself by blowing a bugle in the early hours of the morning as he drifted over a sleeping village. A bugle in the sky! It would set the dogs barking, while frightened countryfolk hid under the bedsheets!

Of historic interest was the two-and-a-quarter hour flight from Chelsea to Eynsford, Kent, made by 18-year-old Thomas in his balloon *Padsop* on 8 September, 1906. With him, as passenger, was the then unknown Mr Grahame-White who was nine years his senior. Less than three years later, on 6 November, 1909, Grahame White would make a first, untutored take-off from the military parade ground at Issy-les-Moulineaux, the main flying field at Paris, in his Bleriot monoplane *White Eagle*. It was not long before the world was reading about the famous record-breaking Claude Grahame-White. Within a few years Thomas and Claude were firm friends and friendly rivals on the airfields of Britain and the USA.

The tranquillity of drifting across London in the early hours of the morning, watching the gaslit streets sliding below, was a source of inspiration for young Thomas and his friends, but, on 4 November, 1906, he and his balloon partner, Paddon, almost came to grief when foolishly they took off in an easterly gale. As Sir Thomas recalled some 80 years later:

'We shot across Battersea Park, and in less than a couple of hours we were somewhere between Bath and Bristol. We'd averaged more than 60 miles an hour over the ground, and there was not a lot of land left between us and the Atlantic Ocean. So we ripped the envelope, and down we came; and it took us three fields to stop after we'd hit the ground'.

While the balloon was dragging its aeronauts through fields and hedges, a little girl, no more than five years old, tried to help by grabbing the runaway basket. Sopwith, fearing that they might all be lifted into the air again by the gale, warned the child not to hold onto the trail rope. This life story could well have ended with a newspaper report of 'two balloonists killed in a gale' but, by some miracle, there were no injuries. Eighty-two years later, the following letter was received by Sir Thomas Sopwith on the occasion of his hundredth birthday:

'*Congratulations from the little girl who obeyed your order "Don't Touch the Rope" from the balloon flight in 1906. Now, in my 87th year I am enjoying good health. I am the proud owner of the signed picture of the Camel and Pup planes. I very much value it and thanks so much for giving it to me*'.

(Mrs) H. D. Lear, Hawkhurst, Kent

Long after Tommy Sopwith had departed the motor trade, on 27 April, 1946, Phil Paddon wrote to him to say that, for reasons it was refusing to disclose, the Motor Agents Association had refused to renew his membership and that that was likely to put him out of business. Paddon Brothers Ltd were established in 1905. After the Paddon and Sopwith days at Albemarle Street the business had moved to premises in Brompton Road where it had been bombed out during the war. Now it was selling Rolls-Royce and other cars from a temporary address in Dorking, a country town south-west of London. Tommy Sopwith's reply must have made the Motor Agents Association think again:

'*My dear Phil,*
I take it almost as a personal insult to be told that you are not in the motor trade, in view of the fact that you and I together founded your present business more than 40 years ago. I am beginning to wonder if I really make aeroplanes! I have done £4,880 worth of business with your firm during the war, and I shall continue to do business with you'.

Although 40 years had passed since, as youngsters, they had shared a balloon together, Paddon Bros Ltd were still using PADSOP as their telegraphic address.

Even during the ballooning days, perhaps four years before Tommy Sopwith had sat in an aeroplane, sister May was his constant companion and supporter. They took off on 12 September, 1906, in *Padsop* and, after about four hours, landed rather untidily at Dunmow, Essex, under anything but ideal weather conditions. Scores of excited local people turned up and May Sopwith, who had only come along for the balloon ride, was told off by the crowd for taking a mere boy up in a balloon. She was 14 years older than her brother.

The sporting man was soon to reveal itself in Tommy Sopwith's character, and so was his sense of humour. He once bet his friends £5 each that he could lay down for five minutes at the junction between Piccadilly and Bond Street, two very busy roads even then, without being moved by the police. In those days cars could be parked in the centre of the road and Sopwith lay underneath his, pretending to adjust something. He won his bets—and gave them all a splendid dinner with their own money.

One might have expected that the combination of motoring and ballooning would have led Tommy Sopwith to the aeroplane. But it was his other passion, a love of the sea, that set him on the path to heights of achievement that no one could have considered possible at the time.

CHAPTER
2

Early Flights

THE BALLOON FIXATION was to die hard in the British press and when, on 17 December, 1903, the Wrights made the first controllable flight in a heavier-than-air machine this internationally important news appeared as a small paragraph in the *Daily Mail* dated 19 December, 1903.

BALLOONLESS AIRSHIP
(from Our Own Correspondent)

Messrs. Wilbur and Orville Wright of Ohio, yesterday successfully experimented with a flying machine at Kittyhawk, North Carolina. The machine has no balloon attachment and derives its force from propellers worked by a small engine.

In the face of a wind blowing at twenty-one miles an hour the machine flew three miles at the rate of eight miles an hour, and descended at a point selected in advance. The idea of the box-kite was used in the construction of the airship [sic].

Although Tommy Sopwith was a mechanically-minded youngster and involved at the earliest possible age in ballooning, cars and motor cycles, news of the Wrights' epic first flight made little impact on him. At the time, he was far more interested in sailing and country activities.

Not many years after the Wright brothers' first flight Thomas and his friend. V. W. Eyre, became the owners of a 166-ton schooner called *Neva*. At one time this had belonged to Princess Henry of Battenberg. They had bought it in a somewhat dilapidated state and, being enchanted by the internal combustion engine from its earliest days, Thomas had ambitions of fitting one in *Neva*. A Thornycroft paraffin engine had been selected for the purpose, but its installation in the old hull was no minor task and he needed the help of a practical engineer. Someone recommended a talented mechanic, named Fred Sigrist, who worked at the Parsons' Motor Company in Southampton. Bill Eyre engaged him and he was paid a salary of £2-14s (£2.70p) per week. Sigrist left his job at Parsons in 1910. And such were his fortunes after joining

Tommy Sopwith that when a return visit was made some years later to his old employers, Sigrist was driving his own Rolls-Royce car. Within a few years the Sopwith-Sigrist relationship was destined to rock the aviation world.

On 18 September, 1910, Sopwith learned that a Mr J. B. Moissant (an American architect of Spanish parents) had flown in his Bleriot monoplane, with his mechanic, Albert Filieux, from France and landed at Willows Wood, Tilmanstone. Not content with being the first pilot to fly a passenger across the English Channel, Moissant was also the first to carry livestock; on that Bleriot monoplane was his kitten which rejoiced in the name of Mademoiselle Paree. Sir Thomas makes the point that the name was often spelt Moisant but when, later, this pioneer pilot continued his flight to a cricket field near Beckenham, Kent, and signed his autograph with a double 's' for a young lad, he commented: 'That's how *I* spell it, son'.

The flight from Issy, near Paris, to Beckenham in the Greater London area, did not inspire businessmen looking to the new flying machines as a potential time-saver—it took all of 22 days because of high winds and heavy rain! Also Moissant kept breaking undercarriages and propellers and these had to be sent by surface transport from Paris. Nevertheless, Moissant's accomplishment was important because it was the first cross-Channel flight while carrying a passenger. Unfortunately, this great pioneer pilot was killed at the end of December, 1910, while preparing for the American Michelin Trophy. This was awarded for the longest non-stop flight by the end of 1910.

Although Thomas had visited the military parade ground at Issy a year previously to watch some of the early French aviators performing in the air, the Moissant flight fired his imagination and he lost no time in visiting Brooklands, the famous motor racing track, where early aviation was enacted from the area within the straights and banked curves. There, Mrs Maurice Hewlett was running an aviation business offering pleasure flights. She later made aviation history by teaching her son to fly. Mrs Hewlett had a Henri Farman 'flying machine' piloted by a Frenchman, named Gustav Blondeau, and in Sopwith's own words:

'I went down to Brooklands where Maurice Hewlett had brought a Farman over from France and was giving joyrides around Brooklands at a fiver a time. So I thought I would have a fiver's worth which consisted of two circuits inside the track at Brooklands. And I think that was the start of the bug'.

'The start of the bug', he called it, the flying bug that afflicts the majority of people once they enjoy the privilege of flying in a small aircraft with an unrestricted view of the land below and the sky above—an experience as far removed from sitting in an airliner as yachting is to travelling by car ferry! This new enthusiasm was to drive the young Sopwith along paths destined to influence the histories of Britain and, indeed, some other nations. But for his influence on events during the Great War of 1914-1918 and World War 2, which followed some 21 years later, the world would have been a very different place today.

Sopwith's first aeroplane, which he bought new for £630, was a Howard T. Wright Avis monoplane powered by a 40-hp ENV engine. Howard and his brother, Warwick, were highly regarded motor car engineers at the time and they manufactured their frail aircraft under a Battersea railway arch. They were not related in any way to the famous American Wright brothers, but Howard had at one time assisted an American-born British subject, Sir Hiram Maxim, in some of his early flying experiments before the turn of the century. Working for the Howard Wright concern at the time was Jack Pollard and, many years after the event, he recalled the afternoon when Tommy Sopwith visited the small works where the aircraft were being built. There was an Avis monoplane hanging from the ceiling and Sopwith must have been on his way to a show of some kind because he was in evening dress and carrying one of those collapsible opera hats which he kept squashing flat, and allowing to spring out again.

Around 1910 motorized carriages were beginning to replace horse-drawn cabs and some idiotic officials decided to name them 'Taximeter-motor cabriolets'. D. G. Gilmour, a famous pioneer pilot of the day, abbreviated the term and applied it to aircraft manoeuvring on the ground. The word 'taxi' has been used ever since. In those days pilots under training were taught to taxi at increasing speed until they had gained sufficient confidence and directional control to chance a first take-off. This was known as 'rolling'. As Tommy Sopwith once explained:

'That consisted of rolling along the ground and making it go more or less where you wanted it to go. That took a certain amount of time, but eventually one made friends with it [the aeroplane]. Then you started to roll it along in a straight line and go a little bit faster each time. As happened in several cases, one's first flight was by mistake, because you looked over the side and found the ground had gone—so you had to try and get back again'.

Although Sopwith had had no previous instruction, after only a few trial rollings he flew his Avis at Brooklands on 22 October, 1910, covered 300 yards, then pulled back on the stick, raised the nose too high and, while trying to land, stalled and caused serious damage to the Avis in the ensuing crash. *Flight* magazine reported the incident thus:

'After a few straight runs he guided the machine into the air in great style. But after 200 or 300 yards it rose suddenly to a height of 40 feet or so and, for a moment, looked like falling backwards—so steep was the angle. Fortunately, he righted it but, in landing, came down sideways, smashing the propeller and chassis and damaging one wing'.

Six days later the monoplane was repaired, and Sopwith spent the day practising 'rolling'. His flying skills rapidly improved until, on 4 November, he was able to make a complete circuit of the airfield. It is interesting to note that, from his first encounter with the early flying machines, Tommy Sopwith had an instinct for assessing handling qualities. This is the more remarkable since he had no previous standards for comparison. Previous standards or not, after only a week as a self-taught pilot he came to the conclusion that his 40-hp monoplane was under-powered and replaced it with a Howard Wright biplane fitted with a 60-hp engine. On 21 November, 1910, he practised 'rolling' in the morning, straight hops before lunch, and complete circuits in the afternoon, all in time to be tested by Harold Perrin of the Aero Club which issued him with Aviator's Certificate No 31. That evening Tommy Sopwith took up his first passenger, W. O. Manning, designer of the Howard Wright monoplanes and biplanes, although only a few hours earlier he had not even done a turn in his new machine. Much had been achieved during the two months that had passed since seeing the Bleriot after Moissant's first crossing of the English Channel with a passenger.

When Tommy Sopwith gained his Aviator's Certificate, King Edward VII had only recently died of bronchitis, King George V was newly on the throne and, following the revolution in Portugal, the Portuguese King had been deposed and Britain's oldest ally was proclaimed a republic.

Viewed against the standards of the day, the general lack of flying experience and the limited capabilities of those frail aircraft, the test for an Aviator's Certificate was no easy task. Candidates had to make three circular, three-mile flights, each one terminating in a landing within 150 yards of a marked spot on the aerodrome. The exclusiveness of aviation in those days is illustrated by the fact that, by the end of 1910, there were less than 50 qualified pilots in Britain. The Royal Aero Club had only been issuing Aviator's Certificates since 8 March, 1910. No 1 went to J. T. C. Moore-Brabazon and No 2 was gained by the Hon C. S. Rolls who was killed in July that year when his aircraft broke up in the air at the Bournemouth flying meeting. Furthermore, only 18 pilots had been trained in Britain during the year when Sopwith gained his certificate. Many years later he recalled:

'I seized every opportunity to get into the air and by the time I had ten hours flying behind me I began to feel I was a really experienced pilot'.

Today, the average pilot has at least 50 hours experience before gaining a Private Pilot's Licence.

Fifty years later to the day, on 21 November, 1960, while giving a lecture to the Royal Aeronautical Society entitled *My First Ten Years in Aviation,* Tommy Sopwith (by then Sir Thomas) told the audience:

'Well, as you can imagine, my first efforts at flying, including crashing the monoplane and buying the biplane, cost me quite a bit, so I decided to try and get some of it back by having a go for the big prizes'.

First there was the Michelin Cup for the longest non-stop flight by a British pilot in a British machine. Although he had only ten hours solo flying experience, on November 24 Sopwith flew non-stop over a closed circuit for a distance of 107 miles which he covered in 3 hours 12 minutes, celebrating his recent achievements by taking his sister, May, on her first flight. During the Michelin Cup competition May was on the ground, counting the circuits, providing in-flight catering in the form of hot beef tea carried in a thermos flask and generally looking after her brother's wellbeing. In the background, too, was Fred Sigrist, a wizard with the temperamental engines of the day.

Then there was the £4,000 Baron de Forest prize for the longest non-stop flight from any point in England to anywhere on the Continent. The aircraft would have to be manufactured in Britain and the competition was intended to stimulate powered flight in the UK which, at the time, was lagging behind other countries, particularly France.

Sigrist believed that an aero engine was most likely to fail during the first minutes after take-off. So the Howard Wright biplane was taken by road to Eastchurch. This would allow 30 minutes overland flying prior to the Channel crossing and so ensure the engine was 'settled'. In those days the pilot sat in the open on the lower wing, totally exposed to the elements and without the safety of even a lap strap to prevent falling off. The human species may have been clever enough to invent the aeroplane but it seemed unable to visualize the risks and consequences of falling from the aircraft in flight! But there was some protection: to help Sopwith keep his feet warm Fred Sigrist made a simple 'fuselage' for the Howard Wright biplane by fitting it with the hood off a baby's pram.

Shortly before Christmas, on 18 December, 1910, the weather seemed ideal so Sopwith took off at 8.30 a.m., pointed towards Dover and flew over Canterbury at 1,000 feet. Even in those days there was a 'wireless' station at Dover and it reported that Sopwith had passed overhead at a height of 1,200 feet, flying at a speed of 50 mph. Somewhere over the English Channel his compass decided to point north-west wherever he turned, so he used the sun as a guide until it became obscured by cloud; then it was a matter of steering by intuition. He wanted to aim for the Paris area, but a combination of poor visibility and a rogue compass decided otherwise.

After 22 minutes he became the sixth pilot to cross the English Channel at a point on the French coast unknown to this day. By then, the wind had strengthened and his feather-light machine was being violently thrown about. As he later recalled:

'Soon I crossed the Belgian frontier and it got so rough I was nearly thrown out, but hung on with one hand under the seat. We had no seat belts in those days; nor did we have such luxuries as a airspeed indicator. The only instruments were a rev counter which worked, a compass which did not and a barograph—a very sensitive one which Cecil Grace had given me, 6 in in diameter and reading to only 2,000 feet'.

With hilly terrain ahead and a violent wind to contend with Sopwith was, for the first time, beginning to lose his nerve. So, although there were another 11 gallons of fuel in the tank and the engine was running faultlessly, conditions forced him to land at Beaumont in Belgium (about nine miles from the French border). The aircraft touched down and rolled to a halt. Standing nearby, the only witness to the landing, was an old Belgian peasant working in his field. When Sir Thomas was 96 years of age he was interviewed on television by Raymond Baxter and, although 74 years had passed, he clearly remembered this rather deflating reception:

'The old man turned, looked at me, then turned his back and went on hoeing his bloody potatoes'.

Discussing his reception on an earlier occasion he said:

'The apathy of the villagers, although they had never seen an aeroplane before, was indeed remarkable. Two old women, to whose cottage I went, did not appear at all astonished that I should have appeared out of the air. All they wanted to know was what the weather was like in England'.

Apathy or not, he had flown a distance of 169 miles in 3 hours 40 minutes and established a record. (In 1990 terms the £4,000 prize money was worth £120,000).

While Tommy Sopwith was flying to Belgium, his sister May, stood anxiously on watch at the Lord Warden Hotel, Dover. After landing, Tommy sent a telegram to her instructing Fred Sigrist to come across, dismantle the machine and ship it home. Even in his exhausted state Sopwith was planning another flight in case a rival pilot managed to beat his 169 miles before the end of the year. In the event he had nothing to fear; the weather changed and gales grounded all flying machines. Nevertheless, the great Claude Grahame-White did take off from Dover only to crash soon afterwards and gratefully accept a lift back to London in Sopwith's car.

Among the pioneer aviators of the day 22-year-old Sopwith was very much the youngest. Moore-Brabazon was 26, de Havilland 28 (in September, 1920 he formed de Havilland Aircraft Co Ltd.), Claude Grahame-White, 31, Roe (who founded the Avro company) 32, the Hon C. S. Rolls, 33, and the impressive Samuel Franklin Cody was a 49-year-old grandfather.

On 31 January 1911, Sopwith was awarded a Royal Aero Club prize for the Belgian flight by the Duke of Atholl, an enlightened aviation enthusiast who was far-sighted enough to tell the gathering that future aircraft would have a parachute device for saving pilots. In the speech that followed, Major Sir Alexander Bannerman generated some hostility by claiming that aircraft had not improved since the Wright Flyer of 1903 and that they would never influence the conduct of war, opinions that revealed a total lack of aeronautical knowledge and the Army's fear of competition from the air at the time. True to character, Sopwith made the most relevant comment of the occasion by lamenting the lack of suitable British aero engines.

The years 1910 to 1914 could perhaps be described as the flamboyant days of aviation when some of the over-confident aviators engaged in antics that pushed their flying machines to the limit, for little was known about aerodynamics or lightweight structures at the time. Judging by some of the articles that appeared in 1911, even the magazine *Flight* had not grasped that, when an aircraft flies, the air flows around it from nose-to-tail, irrespective of the wind direction relative to the ground. The engineers of the day knew all about building large bridges or ocean-going liners, where weight was a secondary consideration, but the design of airframes that were both strong and light represented new and practically unknown technology.

Inspired by a confidence born of ignorance, some of Sopwith's contemporaries used to delight in diving on the airfield and pulling up at the last moment in a manner that must have stressed their frail machines to within an ounce of breaking point. One worthy by name of Graham Gilmour, who seems to have made a name for himself as a 'stunt' pilot in 1911, once took off in his Bleriot monoplane while wearing a bowler hat. Finding it not to his liking as an item of flying clothing, he flew low over his little hangar at Brooklands, flung his hat into the crowd below and then pulled up into a steep climbing turn.

Tommy Sopwith was quick to regard the primitive flying machines as a means of transport, not just as a replacement for the balloon which, in the main, was no more than a device for getting into the air and admiring the view below. An example of his practical application of the aeroplane was during 1910 when he flew in for lunch with his sister, Olive, and brother-in-law Jack Joel. For this occasion, a large field on the Childwick Bury estate had been selected as an 'aerodrome'. Unfortunately, Sopwith damaged his Howard Wright biplane while landing, and it was ten days before a suitable workshop lorry could be obtained to make the necessary repairs. Jack Joel was not fond of aeroplanes, partly because he felt they might frighten his horses. To make matters worse, when the lorry arrived it damaged the main gate to the estate. Jim Joel, then a youth of 15, was told by his father: 'See him off, see him off; I want to get rid of his bloody aeroplane'. Talking, during 1989, of Tommy Sopwith's eventual departure from Childwick Bury, Jim Joel said:

'It was a very misty, murky sort of day. The 'plane went up and I held my breath and thought "Oh my God"—he just managed to clear the top of the trees as he waved at me to say goodbye'.

By 1911 Tommy Sopwith had formed the habit of flying from Brooklands to Datchet golf course, two miles east of Windsor, in order to have coffee with his sister, May, at the nearby Manor Hotel. It is hardly surprising that these occasions attracted local crowds. The two long-distance flights, and his use of the aeroplane as a means of transport for social occasions, came to the attention of King George V who asked if Sopwith would fly to Windsor. On 1 Feb, 1911, Thomas took off from fogbound Brooklands in the knowledge that only a few miles away the sky was clear at Windsor. First he landed at Datchet, then motored the two miles to Windsor Castle where Sir Charles Cust of the Royal Household helped him select a suitable landing area within the castle grounds.

By the time Sopwith was circling the castle in his Howard Wright cheering crowds, among them many Eton boys, had gathered. He landed on the East Lawn to be met by the King and his sons, Prince Henry, Prince George and Prince John, who were shown over the aircraft by Sopwith, while May Sopwith, Mr and Mrs Raikes (that is his sister Iris) and Fred Sigrist were presented to the King.

After the occasion, Tommy Sopwith flew back to Datchet golf course and landed. There, watching with a keen eye, was an 18-year-old boy, named Sydney Camm, who had recently been elected Secretary of the Windsor Model Aeroplane Club. Who could have imagined that 12 years later young Sydney, the model 'plane enthusiast, would be working for Thomas Sopwith and eventually become the finest designer of fighter aircraft in the history of aviation.

By now Tommy Sopwith was a dedicated pilot and for £1,100 he bought a Martin & Handasyde Type 4B monoplane with a 50-hp Gnome rotary engine. Then he acquired a 70-hp Bleriot monoplane in France. At this rate, the funds of the well-off young man were starting to decline so it was with some enthusiasm that he learned of the prizes to be won at the various flying competitions in America. The challenge appealed to him and offered an amusing method of replenishing his bank balance.

The American competitions

William R. Hearst, the famous American newspaper proprietor, inspired a competition for the first east-west trans-American flight, starting from New York. This generated interest from pilots in many countries and resulted in something of a European invasion.

Many of the pilots taking part were very experienced measured by the standards of 1911, but this was hardly likely to intimidate the young Tommy Sopwith. From an early age, those who knew Sopwith recognized in him a quiet professionalism. He set up a team with Dudley Sturrock as manager while Fred Sigrist looked after the maintenance with Harry England and Jack Pollard, another early pioneer who had only recently been employed at the Howard Wright Company, manufacturers of Sopwith's first aeroplane. The 70-hp Bleriot and the Howard Wright biplane were shipped out while Sopwith and his sister, May, crossed on another liner. They met up with their eldest sister, Violet, who had married General E. B. Grubb of the US Army. Sopwith was a good-looking young man, one of the tallest pilots flying at the time, reserved in many respects but nevertheless good at public relations. He was rapidly accepted by the Americans as the typical English sportsman. Under a two-column heading which said:

THOMAS SOPWITH, FAMOUS ENGLISH AVIATOR,
NOW HERE FOR FLIGHTS

the *New York Herald* of 7 May, 1911, carried a picture of Sopwith wearing a bowler hat with sisters May on one side and Violet on the other, followed by a history of his record flights in England and mention of him landing in the grounds of Windsor Castle at the invitation of King George V.

The Bleriot was made ready at Hempstead Plains airfield on Long Island, but the following day Sopwith crashed at Mineola in severe turbulence while taking Nelson Doubleday of the famous publishing firm for a flight. Fortunately, neither was seriously injured. The event, however, was no novelty to Doubleday—he had experienced four crashes during five previous flights! Sopwith, being a man of means, immediately ordered another Bleriot from France, but, meanwhile, the Howard Wright biplane had arrived and on it he gave one outstanding performance after another. In particular, he stunned the citizens of Philadelphia by circling the tower of their City Hall. The Philadelphia *Telegraph* of 17 May, 1911 carried the following story, printed in red, no less!

EXTRA!
ENGLISH AVIATOR MAKES CIRCLE
AROUND CITY HALL IN BIPLANE

Thomas Sopwith, the English aviator, in his biplane, made a flight of several miles this afternoon. He ascended from the race track at Point Breeze and flew up Broad street to the City Hall at high speed, to the delight of the thousands of pedestrians who watched the birdman.

On reaching the municipal building he came down until he was no more than 100 feet above the crowd. He then circled around the Hall and made a return to the starting point without mishap.

In the eyes of the American press, the act of circling the Philadelphia City Hall had turned him into a superman, and the story was featured in daily newspapers all over the USA. Typical of Tommy Sopwith's character was the interview he gave to a paper called the *Press* the following day. The headline and text were as follows:

SOPWITH FLIES OVER CITY HALL AND CIRCLES TOWER
Thousands stare and Wonder as Airman Circles Penn Statue.
Sopwith Tells of His Flight Around City Hall

'*So many aviators have promised great things when they went aloft, and then failed to keep their promises, that I never announce what I intend doing when I start*' *said "Tom" Sopwith following his flight about City Hall. 'In that way I save myself from what you in American call "four-flushing", I believe. I went up with every intention of circling City Hall, but if I had announced it and then failed, I should have felt very foolish, and I would have disappointed a lot of people.*

Later in the same report the newspaper told its readers:

A PERILOUS FLIGHT

Flying over built-up cities in heavier than air machines is a feat that aviators usually shy at. The smoke from the city and the resulting atmospheric disturbance makes a flight over a large city perilous in extreme.

Such newspaper reports may seem laughable today but one must remember the frail nature of aircraft in 1911 and the fact that there was often a difference of only 7-to-10 mph between maximum and stalling speed. Apparently neither May Sopwith nor her elder sister, Violet, were aware of what brother Tommy was about to attempt. Indeed, they were engrossed in watching a 25-mile motor race at the time. Then the 'Round-the-Town-Hall' flight was announced by megaphone from the judge's stand (electric public announcement systems were yet to appear) and, after the near-hysteria died down among the crowd, May later told the newspapers that she had tried to persuade her brother not to fly over towns:

'If Tommy had done that in London', she said with a smile, 'he would have lost his licence. It is not allowed over there, you know'.

Soon after the Philadelphia City Hall episode Tommy Sopwith gave his sister, Violet, her first flight. He was 23 years old at the time and she was 44. The newspapers were full of such headlines as:

MRS. E. BURD GRUBB MAKES FLIGHT IN AIR

While one is tempted to ask if there is any better place to fly than in the air, she was, nevertheless, the first woman in the city to fly in an aeroplane. Seventy-eight years later her daughter, who is also named Violet, recalled that father (General Grubb) was very concerned about the prospect of his wife going up in a flying machine and, to keep the peace, her mother withheld news of the flight with kid brother, Tommy, until the General read about it in his morning paper.

The following column, which appeared in the *Philadelphia Record* on 20 May, 1911, seems to indicate that America may not have been quite the classless society it was fond of portraying to the outside world:

Mrs. E. Burd Grubb and Miss May Sopwith at Point Breeze
Every Day to See Brother in Air

Smart Set Has Given Itself Over to Outdoor Enjoyments.

Society was interested in aviation this week. At least one or two members of the smart set went up in the air, and the rest journeyed down to Point Breeze in the dust to witness the air evolutions of young Mr. Sopwith. Fashionable persons here had more to interest them in Mr. Sopwith's flights than they had in Grahame-White, because of the relationship which he bears with Mrs. E. Burd Grubb who is very popular with the social leaders.

From Philadelphia the Sopwith team moved to Columbus, Ohio. By then Tommy Sopwith had his eyes on William Hearst's trans-America competition, and to provide the necessary range for the long flight, a 35-gallon fuel tank was ordered from a local engineering firm. This would also be used for an attempt on the World Endurance Record, at the time held by Henri Farman, a wealthy Englishman born and settled in Paris who spoke perfect French but only a few words of his mother tongue. The *Columbus Dispatch* of 18 May proclaimed:

SOPWITH IS AFTER WORLD ENDURANCE FLIGHT RECORDS
Is Master of Biplane

Another newspaper told the good folk of Columbus:

SOPWITH EXPECTED TO ARRIVE THIS MORNING
His Mechanics Already Here

Such was the novelty of heavier-than-air flight in those days that some of the newspapers seemed unsure of what to call the early aircraft. Some used the word 'car', others referred to 'airships', while the more enlightened called them aeroplanes (instead of the term airplane now used in the USA). The *Columbus Dispatch* was clearly trying to hedge its bets when it reported that:

At 3:30 Tom Sopwith, the Englishman, got away with his big air boat, a Howard Wright machine.

Sopwith's enterprise left the Americans breathless. Here was a modest, self-effacing young man of the English upper set who was highly organized, very competitive and not averse to a little self-promotion. On one occasion he flew in formation with the Oyster Bay to New York express, while his sister, May, waved her handkerchief at the astonished passengers looking out of the train. Then there was the incident when a Mr W. Atlee Burpee, sailing from New York to Britain on the new liner, *Olympic,* discovered that his reading glasses were broken as the great ship pulled out of New York harbour. A new Marconi wireless station had been set up in the Wannamaker department store and a message was sent from the ship urgently requesting that a replacement pair of spectacles be sent on the next steamer. Within an hour the package had been delivered to Sopwith and he took off with ambitions of dropping the package on the *Olympic* as it steamed away from New York. Smoke belching from its funnels spoiled his aim and the package fell into the sea. Nevertheless, it was a good try and, for his exploits, Sopwith was presented with a fine silver cup by the Aero Club of New York.

In 1911 the idea of a pilot trying to drop a package on an ocean liner was a good enough story in its own right, but under the banner heading:

BIRDMAN DROPS PACKAGE FOR THE OUTBOUND OLYMPIC

was an even greater flight of fancy on the part of the reporter who claimed that the parcel drop was only a practice run and when the spectacles were delivered from the Wannamaker Store 'Sopwith gazed seaward, where the *Olympic* was already a black speck. 'Oh, I've had enough for once', he said. 'Besides, it's time for tea'.

Such behaviour in the face of a challenge would, of course, have been totally out of Sopwith's character.

To supplement expenses and help pay the wages for his competition team Tommy Sopwith flew joyrides. One of his passengers was Henry Taft, brother of the then US President, and this led to many others clamouring for flights. On 25 June, 1911, one of the New York newspapers described the event in these terms:

PRESIDENT TAFT'S BROTHER TAKES HIS FIRST FLIGHT
Spends ten minutes in Sopwith's
aeroplane and says at the end
'Great! splendid! but once
is enough'.

Henry W. Taft, who is not as heavy as his brother, the President, went up with Tom Sopwith yesterday in Tom's aeroplane. It was the chief event of a record-breaking flying exhibition for Long Island. Seven aviators made flights during the afternoon at Nassau Boulevard and in all fully a dozen passengers were carried, probably the record for one day in the United States. Round trip tickets were sold for the first time in this country.

Mr Taft at first said he would not enter an aeroplane for a million dollars, but after seeing the English aviator's masterful way of handling his Howard-Wright biplane, pulled himself together and said 'By George! I will try it'.

Describing the landing the newspaper went on to say:

With a gentle glide Sopwith brought his big biplane gradually to earth and the landing made was so easy that if a basket of eggs had been carried not one of them would have cracked. Mr. Taft climbed out of the machine with a broad smile on his face.

Some of the American newspapers, no doubt taken aback that an Englishman should make more money out of flying than most of the US pilots, wrote complaining that he was charging $50 for a few minutes in the air, conveniently overlooking the cost of bringing aircraft by sea from England and the wages that had to be paid to the three mechanics. A particularly ill-natured column in the New York press was supposed to have been based on interviews with Americans who had just returned from holidays in England:

To their disgust they found that aerial joy riding in England had become so common that it was almost vulgar. All over London there were placards advertising a taxiplane service at Hendon and Brooklands, guaranteed to be safe, for rates as low as ten shillings. This is equal to $2.50 American money.

From this report it seems that aviation in those early days was a little more advanced in Britain than America, but the newspaper column ended with these rather barbed words:

It is a nice, clean, sportsmanlike business that pays well. For this reason it is rather remarkable that our American aviators don't engage in it. Their laggardness is a mystery. When they take up a passenger they do it, almost without exception, purely for the pleasure it gives them.

Even the Wright brothers joined in the witch hunt by filing a Bill of Complaint in the court, aimed at preventing Sopwith from further flights in America on the grounds that his British-designed-and-built Howard Wright biplane infringed their patents. One newspaper reported:

WRIGHT BROTHERS AFTER SOPWITH
*Allege aviator is injuring their
business*

The relationship was put on a friendly basis after Sopwith ordered an American Wright machine. This was a peace-making gesture because, by 1911, events were overtaking the Wright Flyers and there were more advanced aircraft on offer. Indeed, during an interview with one of the Chicago newspapers (which carried the headline Dislikes Wright Machine) in its August 12 issue Sopwith is reported as saying:

'Speaking from a mechanical standpoint, I think the Wright machine is a monstrosity. I don't see how it could be any worse and still it seems to fly very reliably. As you say in this country it seems "to get there" but that chain from the motor to the propellers is a very bad arrangement.'

Speaking of the Wright brothers to Peter Masefield many years later Sopwith said:

'You know the Wright brothers were a very curious pair, quite different—Wilbur the thoughtful, imaginative man who did all the hard work and had all the ideas. Orville, rather brash, not very nice, who I had a lot of trouble with. When I went to America in 1911, Orville came storming around to me and said "You can't fly here because you are breaking all our patents." '

These early air displays drew quite enormous crowds and it was not uncommon for perhaps 300,000 people to descend on the airfield. One of the fashionable events of pre-Great War days was the 'Quick Start' competition. The pilot stood by one wingtip, waiting for the starter's gun, then ran to his seat, the mechanic swung the propeller, hopefully the engine fired and an immediate take-off followed. The watch was stopped when the wheels left the ground. The Wright biplane that Sopwith had bought, largely to appease the splendid brothers, had massive wings and the ability to take off within a few yards at very low speed. These special talents were not lost on Sopwith and he asked the American judges if he could position himself at the same distance from his seat while standing *in front of* the machine instead of to one side, a request that was granted although they must have thought the young Englishman was quite mad. There were, after all, no parking brakes on aircraft in those days so, unless chocks (large wedges) were placed before the wheels, the aircraft moved forward as soon as the engine started. By using to his advantage the potential danger of being run down by his own aeroplane Tommy Sopwith managed to achieve some very quick starts, the best being an astonishing nine seconds. It is, perhaps, not surprising that no other pilot tried to copy Sopwith although the procedure won him a lot of prize money.

There were, of course, many flying accidents during those early meetings, some of them due to mechanical failure, others to lack of flying experience. Talking of these accidents more than 70 years later Sir Thomas said:

'But you see we never travelled very fast. Seldom more than, I suppose, about 45 or 50 mph. So when you hit the ground it wasn't anything like it is today. You could do quite a lot of crashing without hurting anybody at all.'

Of course, Sopwith had his narrow escapes and suffered minor bruising from time to time.

The Chicago Aviation Meeting which started on 12 August, 1911, attracted more than 300,000 spectators on the first day. Pilots from Europe and the USA took part. By now Sopwith had his replacement Bleriot and, on it, he won the speed trials, a spot landing competition in which he had to arrive as close as possible to a marked area on the airfield, a point-to-point race and a rate of climb contest. He also came first in the bombing contest in which the pilots had to drop oranges on a target. In fact, he won more events than any other pilot at the Chicago event and this earned him $14,000 in prize money.

Unfortunately, there were two fatal accidents during the nine-day event and voices were raised demanding that no more flying should be allowed to occur. However, May Sopwith wrote a letter to one of the Chicago newspapers strongly supporting the competitions and pointing out that all activities had their risks. In her letter she said:

'I am sure there isn't any reason for the meet stopping now. The people have come here to see the machines demonstrated and there isn't any reason for stopping the programme.

Some one says that the machines should not be flown until they are perfected, so that the accidents will not be so frequent. How on earth do we know when they will be perfect? We may not live to see it. We want to know what is being done, and what has been done, and the men want to show us their machines and how to manage them. It's all fair and honest and even if accidents do happen, they are expected and should be accepted as the inevitable.

People who understand aeroplaning and what it means aren't foolish enough to want to call the meet off now. I want it to go on and I am willing my brother shall fly and I want him to. We may not have another chance for some time to have the world's greatest aviators, and the world's greatest machines, before us. It may be the last chance for some of us and it's the greatest wonder of the age.'

Coming from a fit and healthy young woman the plea that 'it may be the last chance for some of us' might be regarded as a little melodramatic, but May Sopwith's passionate support for the flying fraternity of 1911 was something of which brother Thomas could be proud. It also made her many friends among the other pilots, British and American.

From triumphs at Chicago the Sopwith 'air circus' moved to Squantum Field, Boston, to take part in a big flying meeting in September, 1911. In its day Squantum Field was a fine aerodrome built on reclaimed land with grandstands and proper hangars. Claude Grahame-White, by that time regarded as a veteran racing pilot, came over from England to compete in the event which he had attended with considerable success the previous year. He had sailed from England in the old *Mauretania,* stopping *en-route* at Cherbourg to load on board the latest 70-hp Nieuport monoplane which he had ordered. At the time it was the fastest aircraft flying, and a combination of brilliant pilot flying an outstanding aircraft represented a formidable challenge to Tommy Sopwith. Many regarded Grahame-White as one of the finest and most experienced display pilots of the day; certainly his airmanship had astonished the Americans during the meetings of the previous year when he saw off challenges from their best aviators, among them the Wrights and Glenn Curtiss. Claude Grahame-White used to call Tommy Sopwith 'Long Tom'.

Like Sopwith, Grahame-White was accompanied by his sister and when the Americans made good-natured fun of the two brother-and-sister teams he said: 'A fellow can't have a better champion and guide than his sister'.

Tommy Sopwith had ordered racing wings for his Bleriot, but these had yet to be delivered. A standard Bleriot was clearly no match for the Nieuport racer, or, for that matter, several other aircraft at the meeting. But Sopwith was a sportsman and it was not in his nature to withdraw from some of the speed events, even if he had little chance of winning.

Sadly, the 1911 meeting at Squantum Field, Boston, was a shadow of the 1910 event. It had degenerated into an exhibition of stunt-flying, the prize money was one tenth of the previous year's and many of the great pioneers, such as the Wrights and Glenn Curtiss, were not attending. In their place came, with few exceptions, a motley crew of opportunists who had little to contribute to the advancement of aviation. Consequently, it is not surprising that, between them, Tommy Sopwith and Claude Grahame-White cleaned up the prizes. The big event was a timed race from Squantum Field to the Boston Light and, having won the event the previous year, Grahame-White was favourite to take the prize. Out of the five aircraft taking part one went around the wrong lighthouse and another made a forced landing after its radiator had burst.

Sopwith had learned how to take advantage of the wind while air racing. He kept low while flying into a headwind, thus allowing ground friction to reduce its effect, but climbed higher in a tailwind so that it added to the airspeed and increased the groundspeed (that is, speed over the ground). Hugging the ground he passed two of the American pilots battling against the wind 800 feet above. Although Grahame-White beat Tommy by 28 seconds, the great aviator had failed to comply with all conditions of the race by flying a final circuit of the airfield. The judges disqualified him, leaving Sopwith the winner. Meanwhile Sopwith continued to win prizes for quick starts and bomb-dropping with the usual oranges.

During September, 1911, Tommy Sopwith returned to New York to continue giving exhibition flights and joy rides from Brighton Beach airfield which was actually on a racetrack near Coney Island. On 10 September, only 12 months since his first close look at an aeroplane, when Moissant visited Folkestone, Sopwith took up another pilot named Lee Hammond and had the misfortune to suffer an engine failure while flying over the sea in his American Burgess Wright biplane. Gliding towards the safety of a nearby beach, one wing was hit by a wave and the aircraft turned over trapping the two pilots underneath. Many years later, when he was Sir Thomas, he recalled:

'Well, after quite a struggle, I came up and looked around for my chum—and he wasn't there. So I thought: crikey—this is no good. And I started trying to get back under to look for him. Then suddenly up he came, all covered in seaweed. And he said to me: "Tom, what time is it?" And I said, "What's the time got to do with it?" I thought he'd gone off his head. But he said: "Hell! I've got a train to catch", and all he was worried about was the time because he had to catch his train to go and fly in another meet the next day'.

The Burgess Wright biplane was a write-off and, much as Tommy Sopwith disliked many of its design features, he nevertheless bought another one to replace it. However, on his return to England the Wright's engine was immediately replaced with a French-built Gnome which was probably the best available at the time.

It was an eventful meeting at Brighton Beach; another pilot caused mayhem by losing control after starting the engine. His aircraft charged the crowd which wisely scattered as he hit the fence. Then Claude Grahame-White, intent on entertaining the spectators, ran his Nieuport into soft ground causing only minor damage but stirring up mosquitoes by the million.

The American competitions had been a happy venture for Tommy Sopwith. He had won a large, appreciative audience, had competed against some of the finest pilots in the world and, on many occasions, won. He had broadened his flying experience and his substantial winnings were able to recharge his flagging bank balance. He returned home with every reason to be well satisfied with his own performance and that of his hardworking team.

Back in England, the aviation scene was beginning to look a little more encouraging. This was almost entirely as a result of private enterprize for the State exhibited a calculated indifference to the rapid development of aeroplanes. One of the most effective entrepreneurs was Claude Grahame-White. Early in 1910 he had founded the London Aerodrome at Hendon and, over a period of time, it became a fashionable weekend place of entertainment for the public. It was, after all, little more than six miles from the centre of London and there most of the famous pilots of the day could be seen performing. There were joyrides, aerobatics and exciting air races, often around a closed circuit marked by black-and-white pylons; what they lacked in speed those pioneer pilots made up for by flying only a few feet above the ground. Passengers by the hundred were flown without incident and a billboard proclaimed:

A. PASSENGER FLIGHT	Two circuits of the Aerodrome	£2 2 0
B. EXTRA FLIGHT	Two very high wide circuits of the Aerodrome	£3 3 0
C. SPECIAL FLIGHT	Outside the Aerodrome, in the direction of Edgware, returning towards the Welsh Harp	£5 5 0

Although they were rivals at many of the competitions, Tommy Sopwith and Claude Grahame-White were good friends. After Claude was married on 27 June, 1912, in the parish church of Widford in Essex, a reception for the 200 guests was held at the nearby country residence of Sir Daniel (of Great Western Railway fame) and Lady Gooch. Sopwith and others of the flying fraternity took off from the lawns in their formal cloths and gave an impromptu air display.

Grahame-White instigated a round-London race which he called the 'Aerial Derby', an event starting and ending at Hendon with turning points at Sunbury, Esher, Purley, Purfleet, Epping and High Barnet, a distance of 81 miles. It would be an annual event to rival the more established sporting occasions. The 'Aerial Derby' got off to a fine start when Lord Northcliffe donated a *Daily Mail* gold cup for the winner. Additional cash prizes were offered by the Grahame-White Aviation Company for the first, second and third places.

The first race was flown on 8 June, 1912, and a list of well-known French and British pilots entered. One of them, Jimmy Valentine, rapidly put himself at a disadvantage by dropping his compass into the Thames. There was also a pilot who flew so far off course that he found himself over the English Channel, while another had an engine failure. This left the race to Tommy Sopwith and a Frenchman named Guillaux, with the famous Gustav Hamel trailing third. At the moment of victory Guillaux ran out of fuel and landed short of Hendon, so the race went to Tommy Sopwith. Moments later a message came through from the turning point at Purley. According to the observers stationed there Sopwith had turned short of the pylon. In fact, they had not seen him because he had turned rather wide. At first he was disqualified and the cup was awarded to Gustav Hamel, then an appeal was lodged, supported by a great number of eye-witnesses who confirmed that he had flown around the pylon, and Sopwith eventually got his cup. To this day, however, it has a model of Hamel's aeroplane on the lid.

While the appeal was dragging on for five months, Sopwith reached an understanding with Gustav Hamel that whoever was awarded the cup would lay on a dinner for the others flying in the race. After Sopwith was finally declared winner the dinner that followed at the Café Royal in Regent Street, London, must have been a great success because 'Colonel' Cody fell asleep in the train taking him back to Farnborough and awoke in Bournemouth to stagger from the train in his tails!

Sopwith School of Flying

The money that Sopwith won during the various competition flights in Europe and the USA enabled him to set up the Sopwith School of Flying. This was started at Brooklands in 1912 and first advertised in February of that year. Talking about those days, Sir Thomas once admitted that he was '. . . teaching people to do something I knew very little about myself'. The fleet consisted of his Howard Wright biplane and the American Burgess Wright, both fitted with dual controls for elementary instruction. There were also a Howard Wright and a Bleriot monoplane for advanced training. Fred Sigrist looked after the day-to-day engineering, while Sopwith and the pioneer pilot, Fred Raynham, gave the flying lessons.

Although both the Admiralty and the War Office showed very little interest in the development of aviation, and perhaps even wished it would go away, the Army did at least set up an Air Battalion in 1911. Officers wishing to fly were first required to gain their Royal Aero Club Aviator's Certificate at one of the private schools. Standard charge for the course was £75, and the fee was reimbursed by the War Office on satisfactory completion of training. Then the officers were accepted at the elite Central Flying School which had just been established at Upavon, an historic military airfield on Salisbury Plain. Some of the officers taking the CFS course actually took their own 1911-1912 vintage aeroplanes with them; indeed they were encouraged to do so.

Perhaps the most famous student pilot to pass through the system was Major Trenchard, later to become the virtual founder of the Royal Air Force. Viewed internationally, Major Trenchard was one of the most significant figures in military aviation, because it was he who later demonstrated to the world the advantages of having a separate air arm. Trenchard wanted to become a pilot in the Royal Flying Corps which was formed in April 1912. After much opposition from his commanding officer, who considered the Major too old for the task, he was grudgingly allowed to take up flying.

Brooklands, historic home of motor racing and one of the first to feature a track with banked turns, has equally historic connections with early aviation. Trenchard, who had taken a room in nearby Weybridge, walked to this Mecca of petrol engines, both ground and airborn, where a number of small flying schools, operating out of modest huts, were jockeying for position. Looking at the various schools, standing closer together than semi-detached houses, Trenchard must have been spoiled for choice. However, on the recommendation of one Lt Colonel Frederick Sykes (later Chief of Air Staff), who had himself learned to fly at the school, he visited Sopwith at his cottage near the Brooklands' racetrack. Knocking on the door, he said: 'You Sopwith? Can you teach me to fly in ten days?' Sopwith agreed to enrol him as a student pilot. The fee of £75 was for flying lessons and insurance covering breakages and third-party risks. Many years later Sopwith recalled:

'Trenchard impressed me the moment he walked in. He said the War Office had given him a fortnight to get his Aviators' Certificate, and that if for any reason he missed the test by then he would be over age. I promised to do my best for him'.

Trenchard was at Brooklands, awaiting his instructor at four a.m. on the misty morning of 18 July, 1912, when Copland Perry, who was to teach him the mysteries of flight, arrived to say that he understood the urgency and the first flying lesson would start without delay. The short trip that followed was enlivened by Perry pointing to the sewage farm and remarking that trainee pilots seemed to end up in it instead of on the airfield. After a total of 1 hour 4 minutes flying, dual and solo, Trenchard obtained his Royal Aero Club certificate No 270. It was his ticket to the exclusive Central Flying School. As Sopwith later recalled:

'It was no light accomplishment, but Major Trenchard tackled it with a wonderful spirit. He was out at dawn each morning. He was dead keen to do anything that would expedite tuition—a model pupil from whom many younger men should have taken a lead'.

However Sopwith had reservations about Trenchard's skill at the controls:

'When he died he was known as the "Father of the Royal Air Force". But I think it was just as well he didn't go on flying himself for very long; he would never have been a good pilot'.

Many years later Sopwith described Hugh Trenchard as:

'A great leader of men, yet he was almost illiterate. He hardly ever wrote a letter'.

Another trainee pilot of note was an army officer named Smith Barry who was later to develop a method of flying instruction, civil and military, that was adopted worldwide and has remained in use ever since. There were famous names in the making at Brooklands in those days—Howard Flanders who later designed some famous monoplanes. Jack Alcock who, after the Great War, became the first to fly the Atlantic, George Handasyde who designed the very successful Martinsyde aircraft during the First World War, Geoffrey de Havilland who later set up his own world-famous aircraft manufacturing concern, Rex Pierson who became a famous designer with Vickers, Keith Davis (the first man to fly in India) and a character known as 'Daddy' Sassoon (later Sir Victor) who shared ownership of a Bleriot monoplane with Otto Astley.

Sassoon's eyesight was suspect and he made a habit of trying to land 20 feet above the ground. After one particularly bad crash when several weeks were spent repairing the damage, Astley is alleged to have told his partner: 'Now, Daddy, fly the bloody thing right into the ground before you flatten out'. He did — and it took weeks to repair the damage again.

Another outstanding early aviator of the day was Howard Pixton who was an instructor at the Bristol school based at Brooklands. Within a few years he was to bring glory to the name of Sopwith. But it was the arrival of four Australians that was to have the most profound influence on Tommy Sopwith and his enterprises. Two of these learned to fly at the nearby Bristol school. The others were Harry Kauper, who became works manager when Sopwith started building aeroplanes, and Harry Hawker, star trainee pilot at the Sopwith school, who eventually gave his name to one of the most famous aviation concerns in the world.

The importance of Hawker to the Tommy Sopwith story cannot be over-estimated. Harry George Hawker was born on 22 January, 1889, at South

Brighton, Moorabin, Victoria, Australia. Like Sopwith he disliked school and left at the age of 12. His father ran a small blacksmith/general metalwork business at Balaclava, a town north of Melbourne, and this must have influenced his natural engineering ability. Harry's first job was with a motor firm called Hall & Warden. It had been led to believe he was 14 years old, and Hawker was paid 5 shillings (25p) a week. The training led him to become an expert motor engineer and soon he obtained a good position looking after the maintenance of a number of cars belonging to a Mr de Little of Melbourne. For this he was paid the then quite considerable salary of £200 a year.

In 1911 he met up with a young Australian by the name of Harry Busteed (later Air Commodore). Busteed had seen a Bleriot monoplane in Australia and, fired with enthusiasm for aviation, was intent on visiting England with ambitions to fly. Subsequently he realized his ambitions at the Bristol school. From his generous salary Harry Hawker had managed to save £100, a lot of money in those days, and he decided to journey with Busteed. However, life proved difficult for Harry Hawker in England where, by tradition, it was not easy to get a job without previous references. Eventually he worked at Commer Motors for little more than £3 a week but, through another Australian friend, Harry Kauper, was taken on by Fred Sigrist at Sopwith's flying school at Brooklands. There he started working on 12 July, 1912, at a salary of £2 a week.

Harry Hawker had saved money for his return ticket home to Australia, but the working atmosphere at the flying school suited his temperament and he desperately wanted to gain his Aviators' Certificate. The going rate for tuition leading to the all-important piece of paper was £75, but that was beyond him, so he enlisted the help of Sigrist who told Sopwith 'Hawker here wants you to teach him to fly'. A figure of £50 was suggested. At first the boss was not very keen and, at that point, Hawker rolled up his trousers and took a wad of £5 notes out of his socks. Many years later Sopwith said he produced the money '. . . like some old tart from the top of her stockings'.

Hawker gained his Aviator's Certificate (No 297) on 17 September, 1912, and it was not long before his talents were being recognized; he was making a name for himself as a test and competition pilot. With his customary modesty Sopwith said of Hawker '. . . he was a much better pilot than I ever was'. By 1913, although he had been flying for barely 12 months, Harry Hawker held the British speed, altitude and endurance records.

It was less than two years since Tommy Sopwith had taught himself to fly and gained his certificate. In that time he had won many competitions and set up one of the earliest flying training schools at Brooklands. During 1912 there were 16 civil flying schools operating in Britain and, over the 12-month period, they managed to train 181 pilots. Largest and most successful of these early schools was operated by the Bristol Aeroplane Company with branches at Salisbury Plain and Brooklands. The Sopwith school produced 11 new pilots that year and gave many short flights to those who had not been in the air before.

By 1913 letters of complaint were appearing in the aviation press about unscrupulous elements cashing in on the flying craze. Bogus flying school operators were taking money in advance for the training course, then spending it on lessons for themselves so that they might learn to fly and eventually teach others. But by this time a chance remark of Fred Sigrist's had induced Tommy Sopwith to cease flying training and turn to aircraft manufacture. The events that followed were to sow the seeds of an engineering empire and make Tommy Sopwith an internationally-known figure, both within and outside the world of aviation.

CHAPTER
3

Sopwith Aviation Company Ltd

WHILE OTHER NATIONS were advancing the frontiers of aerial knowledge, the British Government seemed determined to ignore aviation. In contrast, Germany was spending £1,500,000 annually on aircraft research, and the French were holding a number of competitions aimed at encouraging aeronautics. In 1911, for example, there was a competitive fly-off at Rheims where no fewer than 29 different aircraft types flew, all of them French designed and built.

Under pressure from the public, the newly-formed British Air Battalion sent along two captains and a lieutenant as observers. Conditioned as they were by official disinterest at home, the three officers were naturally staggered at the level of France's support for aviation, and the enormous progress that was being made in that air-minded country. Following their report of the Rheims meeting, several British manufacturers set up a deputation and, in November, 1911, it met at the War Office with Colonel Seely, Secretary of State for War, to warn the General Staff that Britain was not only being left behind by France and Germany—it was not even in the race.

The deputation must have rung some alarm bells in the dusty corridors because, within a month, it was announced that military trials would be held on Salisbury Plain during 1912. Following the trials suitable aircraft would be ordered for the purpose of training 100 officers as pilots. At the time, Britain was the wealthiest nation in the world, but such was the parsimonious nature of its leaders that the total prize money for all the winners was only £11,000. In contrast, the French authorities had, the year earlier, made awards totalling £53,000.

By now Tommy Sopwith had been recognized by the authorities as a first-class test pilot and he was one of the 'experienced' aviators to be retained for the trials (in those days a pilot with 100 hours flying was regarded as the equivalent of a 10,000 hour man of today).

Those who had been following early developments in aviation with an intelligent interest were not in the least surprised when the Military Trials, at Larkhill on Salisbury Plain, confirmed the extent to which Britain had fallen behind in aeronautics. For example, Sopwith flew two versions of the Coventry Ordnance Co biplane—one powered by a 100-hp Gnome, the other with a 110-hp Chenu engine. These grotesque and, frankly, quite revolting aircraft were so unsuccessful that the engine in one of them refused to run at all. From the military point of view the only practical machine was one designed and flown by Geoffrey de Havilland, but since he was working for the Royal Aircraft Factory his Government-built aircraft was not allowed to take part in the trials.

The competition was finally won by S. F. Cody, although none of the aircraft distinguished itself. It was during the Military Trials that the newspapers confused S. F. Cody with another American, Colonel Cody of 'Buffalo Bill' fame. Consequently, when King George V sent him a telegram of congratulations on winning the trials, it was addressed to Colonel Cody. From that day, he was known as Colonel Cody.

It could be claimed that the Rheims meeting of 1911 was the making of Tommy Sopwith, because reports of aeronautical progress in France precipitated the Military Trials in Britain. There, surrounded by undistinguished aircraft from a number of manufacturers, Sopwith came to the view that he could design something very much better himself.

At the time of the Military Trials, Fred Sigrist, the outstandingly talented mechanic who looked after Sopwith's yacht engine, had been sent to overhaul aero engines at the Sopwith School of Flying. It is more than possible that the great aeronautical events of the next 75 years started with the modifications that Sigrist made to the American Burgess Wright biplane that Tommy Sopwith bought to appease the Wrights during the American competitions. With Sopwith's agreement, Fred Sigrist proceeded to improve the stick-and-wire flying machine by building a streamlined nacelle for the occupants who, hitherto, had sat in the open. It was in this improved Burgess Wright biplane that Harry Hawker, Tommy Sopwith's Australian pilot prodigy, won the British Michelin Cup, together with £500, for a duration flight of 8 hours 23 minutes, a British record at the time. Tommy Sopwith was very much the boss of the little aviation concern at Brooklands but, at an early stage, a team spirit had emerged. Collectively, as ideas flowed from one active mind to the next, Sopwith, Hawker and Sigrist were the right mix for success.

Good ideas on their own are rarely certain to succeed. But when such ideas arrive at the right time and are developed by people of talent, undreamed of success can follow. So it was that Tommy Sopwith returned to his flying school at Brooklands, depressed by the line-up of inadequate aircraft that had taken part in the Military Trials, and toying with the idea of designing something better. The spark that then ignited the creative process came from Fred Sigrist in the form of a chance request: 'Let me take the engine out of the Bleriot and the wings of a Burgess Wright biplane', he said, 'and I will add a fuselage that will make it a better aircraft than either of them'. In fact, they made the wings themselves but based them on the American Wright design.

Plans were chalked full-scale on the floor of the Brooklands shed and the aircraft that emerged was called the Hybrid. Unfortunately, during one of its early flights, Harry Hawker damaged it in an accident. Re-built, the Hybrid flew well, if rather slowly, at an undistinguished maximum speed of 55 mph, but it displayed such a talent for weight-lifting that the Admiralty bought it for £900. In later years Thomas Sopwith would say that the Hybrid was '. . . an exercise in one-upmanship on the Wright Brothers'.

So it was that Sopwith Aviation was formed. The sewing machine used by Sopwith's sister, May, to make up fabric covers for the early aircraft, is now preserved at the Brooklands Museum. Sopwith once said: 'It is difficult to give an exact date to the start of the Sopwith Company—like Topsy "It just growed". However, it is reasonable to say that the Hybrid project was the beginning of an aviation empire.

When the Navy bought the Hybrid, Sopwith asked Oliver Swann, a senior official at the Admiralty, if his account could be settled without delay since there were wages to pay at the fledgling Sopwith concern. Swann, a man of means, sportingly agreed to fund the £900 from his own pocket and claim it back from the Admiralty if the need arose, but 'My Lords in Navy' were quick to settle the account.

The Hybrid went to Eastchurch where it was based on a private airfield owned by Frank McClean, a patriot who, from his own resources, was helping to finance the Navy's entry into aviation. In those days Eastchurch Aerodrome was used as a training base by the Royal Navy, although the Hybrid seems to have earned its keep flying in oysters from Whitstable for the Officer's Mess.

With ambitions raised by his first sale, Tommy Sopwith gave thought to building an improved Hybrid. There were also several other designs at the back of his mind, including one capable of operating from water as well as land. However, even quite small aircraft occupy a lot of space and the little shed at Brooklands was not large enough for constructional work. It so happened that at the corner of Canbury Park Road, in nearby Kingston-upon-Thames, was a disused roller-skating rink with a floor area of 16,000 sq ft. and Sopwith bought this for a few hundred pounds. 'The Rink', as it was called, used to charge admission rates of a few pence and, for that, people used the floor with the backing of a 'Full Military Band', as it was described in the advertisements. However, the local newspaper misreported the story by claiming the premises were rented. The following headlines appeared in the *Surrey Comet*:

AEROPLANE FACTORY IN KINGSTON
Mr. Thos. Sopwith Rents the
Central Hall Rink
Skating to Terminate Tonight

Sale of the Hybrid went through on 21 October, 1912, and on that day Sopwith's first draughtsman was put on the payroll, one R. J. Ashfield, previously employed at Tiffins School as a £60-a-year teacher. As a schoolboy, Ashfield and his friends had a passion for model aeroplanes and, at one time, they even built a full-size glider that was big enough to carry a boy, although it never did. Commenting on his glider 60 years later Ashfield said: 'We didn't kill ourselves, a fact I have often wondered at'.

When Ashfield became Sopwith's one-man drawing office he was on a salary of £3 per week—an above-average rate of pay at the time when you could buy a three-bedroom detached house for little more than £400 in the Kingston area, while two- and three-bedroom flats could be rented for 8s 6d and 13s 6d per week respectively. Ashfield often used to recall how excited Tommy Sopwith was when he came into No 1 shed at Brooklands and announced the sale of his first aeroplane to the Admiralty.

In Kingston Sopwith recognized an ideal location for aeroplane construction. There were plenty of skilled carpenters and other trades people. It was near to the aerodrome at Brooklands and, since he contemplated designing seaplanes, the nearby River Thames was an added bonus. Transporting the aircraft from Canbury Park Road to the aerodrome at Brooklands, or the river, did at times earn him the displeasure of the law. In 1912 there were few motor cars on the road, but horse-drawn vehicles abounded. At times the local police did not take kindly to the sight of Sopwith towing his latest aircraft behind a car, and it was often necessary for Sopwith to send out 'scouts', so that a route could be planned to avoid the local Bobby.

Although the Hybrid had been 'designed' by Sopwith and Sigrist it was not long before Harry Hawker was brought into discussions on future projects. He had already developed into a talented test pilot, and the enterprise rapidly gathered pace. Jack Pollard was responsible for aircraft construction at the Kingston skating rink and, as various projects began to materialize, Ashfield took on several assistants who were to form the nucleus of a drawing office.

By now the Sopwith Aviation Company was well and truly in business. It was largely run on enthusiasm with Sopwith leading the team. An enquiry from the Army or the Navy would be discussed with Sigrist and Hawker. The three men would argue the details, then Ashfield, the chief draughtsman, would be brought into the picture and expected to produce drawings within a matter of hours. Converting the drawings into hardware was the responsibility of Jack Pollard in the experimental shop, but Sopwith was always there, questioning, suggesting, encouraging. The spirit, generated from Sopwith at the top, was remarkable. In later years Sir Thomas often referred to his little company of 1912 as 'The Gang'. Asked to list the 'gang' members he said:

'Well, I suppose, first of all, me. Then our ex-engineer from the schooner, Fred Sigrist, who was boss of the construction gang. There were only about half-a-dozen all told. Harry Hawker by this time, of course, and there was one called Reggie Carey, who tried to look after the finances; he could almost do it in a pocket book.

'The first aeroplanes weren't built to drawings at all. They were built to sketches. Our first proper designer—alleged—was called Ashfield, a schoolmaster, who did all his sketches in what I think was originally a washing book.'

In addition to Sigrist and Hawker, Bill Eyre, who shared the schooner *Neva* with Sopwith, was also part of the team in the capacity of engineer and 'interested party'. By 1913 the staff of Sopwith Aviation Ltd included six carpenters and metal fitters. Jack Whitehorn, the original 'Buttons' from roller-rink days, was retained as tea-boy. He remained with the company and its successors to become its longest-serving employee, and Secretary of Hawker's Sports Club, eventually retiring at the age of 74.

In 1913 Mr R. O. Cary, who had previously organized a number of early flying displays, was appointed as General Manager of the tiny concern. In that year Mr Frank Spriggs joined the company as office clerk. Forty-four years later he retired from the business as Sir Frank Spriggs, having held a number of important directorships in Sopwith Aviation's successor companies— enterprises which had attained proportions way beyond the imagination of all concerned, including Tommy Sopwith.

The Hybrid was largely inspired by parts of other aircraft but on 7 February, 1913, the Three-seater, a totally Sopwith design of remarkably modern appearance, made its first flight in the hands of Tommy Sopwith with Harry Hawker as an observer. It created a sensation at the Aero Show held at the Olympia Exhibition Hall, London, during February, 1913. In the Three-seater the pilot sat behind a side-by-side two-seat passenger cockpit. This was good weight-lifting on an engine of only 80-hp. To improve downward visibility three large Celluloid windows were let into the fuselage sides. Almost immediately the Sopwith Three-seater began to win competitions and establish records. For example, on Whit Monday, it won a cross-country race at Brooklands, and on 31 May Harry Hawker established a new British altitude record by climbing it to 11,450 feet. On 16 June he beat his own record by reaching 12,900 feet, and on 27 July he climbed to 8,400 feet with three passengers on board as well as himself. The Three-seater cost £1,185 and was ordered by the Army as well as the Navy which used them for coastal patrols.

Sopwith Aviation was able to deliver them at a rate of one per week from November onwards.

Having sold its first aircraft to the Admiralty and, bearing in mind Tommy Sopwith's love of the sea, it is hardly surprising that he and his team should turn their attention to marine aircraft. As a speedboat-enthusiast Sopwith had been a customer of S. E. Saunders Ltd for some years. This old-established boat builders had a unique system of lightweight hull construction which went under the patent name of Consuta. Planking consisted of laminated wood strips cross-sewn with copper wire. This enterprising firm was engaged in on-going research into hull design. It was even experimenting with the ejection of air bubbles under the hull to reduce water friction.

Using the Consuta method, the Saunders company built a 21-ft long hull with side-by-side seating for a pilot and one passenger. To the top of the hull were attached 40-ft biplane wings designed by Sigrist and drawn by Ashfield. Between the wings was a 100-hp Green engine and the tail surfaces were carried behind on a structure consisting of wire-braced booms. It was also fitted with a mechanically-retracted undercarriage to allow operations from land as well as water, a very advanced feature at the time. They called it the Bat Boat and it is generally regarded as the first truly successful British flying boat. In the hands of Harry Hawker it won the £500 Mortimer Singer Prize for amphibian aircraft. In 1913 it was bought by Winston Churchill on behalf of the Admiralty for £1,500.

During 1913 one of Tommy Sopwith's sisters gave him a pet bear cub named Oonie. It would visit the workshop with him, clamber over the wings and, unless restrained, eat the fabric for which it had developed a liking, possibly because in those days the material was painted in boiled sago to make it smooth and airtight. A photograph of Oonie once appeared in a publication which described him as a monkey. Tommy Sopwith was very put out about this. He was even sadder when, after about a year, he had to donate Oonie to a zoo because he was becoming so large and unmanageable.

Up to 1913 most of the pioneer aircraft firms designed by intuition. Aerodynamics were only partly understood and few, if any, design offices employed a stressman to ensure that the hardware would not fold up in the air. Much ingenuity was, and still is, devoted to keeping the structure as light as possible because obviously every pound or kilogramme saved was a pound or kilogramme of extra payload. Monoplanes had earned a bad reputation. They lacked the box-like rigidity of biplanes in which upper and lower wings were linked by vertical inter-plane struts cross-braced by strong wires. Following a number of structural failures in the air, the Government set up that typically British institution, a committee, to find the reason why. This produced the *Departmental Committee's Report on Accidents to Monoplanes*, and one of its totally sensible recommendations was that firms building aeroplanes should employ a qualified stressman.

Tommy Sopwith took on Frank E. Cowlin, BA, a young mathematics graduate from Cambridge who had since turned his attention to engineering. After a short period at Vickers he joined the Sopwith concern alongside Ashfield and a tracer. His first task, with Tommy Sopwith always in the background supervising the designs, questioning this feature and suggesting improvements for that, was to send stress calculations for Sopwith aircraft to the War Office and the Admiralty. Such was the pace of aeronautical development under Sopwith's leadership that soon there were four assistant designers working on different projects, each with a draughtsman and an apprentice. The assistant designers were specialists in one particular field— Burgoyne was an expert on seaplane floats; Alston's field was mechanical design, while another was in charge of cockpit layout. A close working relationship existed between Tommy Sopwith, Harry Hawker, Fred Sigrist, a test pilot, called Victor Mahl, and the design office. Everyone was expected to express opinions and the team spirit was outstanding—an extension of Sopwith's remarkable personality. R. J. Ashfield, who for a short while became chief of design during the early days of the company, said of his boss:

'Mr Sopwith was always a joy to work for, giving praise for a good job, and not mincing words over a bad one. But after the storm it was all over.'

'Pop' Ashfield, as he became known, claimed in later years that after Sopwith, Sigrist and Hawker had debated a new project, his boss would walk into the drawing office, hand him a scrappy piece of paper with an almost incomprehensible sketch on it, and say: 'Make something out of that Ashfield' and leave him to get on with it. This was part of Tommy Sopwith's character and greatness; from his earliest days as an employer he believed in giving his staff scope for initiative. Given the right people this policy was bound to succeed because it brought out the latent talents of seemingly quite ordinary folk.

Tommy Sopwith was the youngest and certainly one of the shrewdest aircraft manufacturers of his day. It was his recognition of the Navy's insistence on having a navigator in every aircraft that enabled him to offer the Admiralty suitable designs and clinch an order for six of his aircraft in the face of stiff competition. However, events were moving fast and the short but remarkable reign of Sopwith-the-Pilot was coming to an end. Even relatively small businesses have to be managed and, by late 1913, Sopwith was so committed to running his growing company that he was forced to give up flying except on the odd occasion. He is proud of saying that he started and finished being a pilot before the airspeed indicator was invented. Thereafter, test and demonstration flights were undertaken by Harry Hawker and Freddy Raynham, another famous pioneer test pilot of the period.

The year 1913 was very eventful for the Sopwith firm. Harry Hawker broke the British duration record with a flight of 8 hours 23 minutes, gained various altitude records with and without passengers and won the Mortimer Singer prize for amphibians with a Sopwith Bat Boat.

Less successful was the attempt to win the *Daily Mail* £5,000 prize donated by the late Lord Northcliffe for the Seaplane Race around Britain. The event, which started at Southampton, had to be flown over a 1,540-mile route taking in Dover, Yarmouth, Scarborough, Aberdeen, Inverness, Oban, Dublin and Falmouth, finishing at Southampton. It was restricted to British pilots flying British aircraft fitted with British engines, and the winner had to complete the flight in 72 hours. It was an event that strongly appealed to the sportsman in Tommy Sopwith. Unfortunately, it got off to a bad start because, shortly before the race, the universally-popular Cody was killed when his aeroplane broke up in the air. Then, one by one, for various reasons, the other competitors dropped out, leaving Harry Hawker the only starter. He was flying a Sopwith 100-hp Tractor Seaplane accompanied by fellow-Australian Harry Kauper acting as mechanic.

The Sopwith team took off on 16 August, but by the time Yarmouth had been reached Hawker was in a state of collapse from exhaust fumes and sun exposure. An extended exhaust pipe was fitted and, after returning to the starting point, a new attempt was commenced on 25 August; 495 miles were flown on the first day. There was no intercom between the two seats and the only way that Hawker and Kauper could communicate with one another over the roar of the engine and the general clamour of the wind through the wires was to pass written notes back and forth. Harry Hawker had pasted his maps on cardboard and these now reside in Australia. On them is written such comments as 'The engine is kicking', 'The exhaust pipe nut is loose', and, of fundamental importance, 'Which way is north?'

It was while approaching Dublin, later in the event, that the engine began to fail and Hawker decided to alight on the water so that the problem could be rectified. Unfortunately, his foot slipped off the rudder bar as they were alighting, a wingtip entered the water and the seaplane crashed. Hawker got away without a scratch but Kauper suffered cuts about the head and a broken arm. The event was postponed until 1914 but, by then, the assassination of an obscure royal in a Balkan state was to trigger the Great War and the race faded away. Although Harry Hawker had not completed the route Lord Northcliffe sportingly awarded him a special prize of £1,000 for his fine attempt—one of the most impressive seaplane flights to that date. Once again, a Sopwith aircraft had excelled.

In March, 1914, Tommy Sopwith turned his little aircraft manufacturing business into The Sopwith Aviation Company Ltd. Share capital was £26,000 and, although it has been recorded in another publication that the new company was partly financed by Jack Joel (the South African gold and diamond mining millionaire who had married Sopwith's sister, Olive), this is without foundation.

The skating rink had become inadequate and, by now, they had bought additional premises in nearby Canbury Park Road. The first directors were named as Thomas Sopwith, his sister Gertrude May Sopwith and Reginald O. Cary, the General Manager. Director's fees were £50 per year and the future looked good—there was an encouraging order book and the staff were working overtime. The company's first export order, a number of seaplanes for the Greek Naval Air Service, was just about to be delivered and the smell of sawdust, glue and newly-introduced dope (Cellulose-based paint in place of the boiled sago) pervaded the factory.

Steps towards a Sopwith fighter

In 1913 Harry Hawker wanted to visit his parents in Australia and it was decided that while he was there, he should conduct a sales tour for the Sopwith concern. For ease of transport the smallest possible two-seat aircraft, with a pilot and passenger sitting side-by-side, was designed. Although the design was Harry Hawker-inspired, Tommy Sopwith and Fred Sigrist also took an active part in it. The tiny biplane was known as the Sopwith SS, but it rapidly collected the nickname 'Tabloid' after some small tablets then being manufactured by the medical firm, Burroughs Wellcome. This highly-respected pharmaceutical concern was not amused, and threatened to sue Sopwith Aviation for using its registered trade name. However, Tommy Sopwith insisted that he and his directors regarded the new design as their model SS and if people wanted to call it 'Tabloid' there was nothing they could do about it.

The 'Tabloid' was a remarkable little aircraft, years ahead of its time and with an outstanding all-round performance. Among other distinctions, it was the world's first single-bay biplane (that is, there was only one pair of struts on each side of the fuselage, each pair of wings being braced by a single set of crossed bracing wires). It had a top speed of 92 mph and it could fly at 37 mph, a speed range unheard of in those days. On 29 November, 1913, it astounded officials at Farnborough by climbing at a rate of 1,200 feet/minute with its pilot, a passenger and a full fuel tank. For an aircraft of only 80 hp such a climb performance would be regarded as outstanding today. The 'Tabloid' set new standards and inspired several rival manufacturers to build similar aircraft. It was to father the first Sopwith fighter but, before that, it would bring glory to Britain as a racer.

The second of the famous Schneider Trophy races was held at Monte Carlo on 20 April, 1914. Aircraft had been entered from Germany, Switzerland, the USA, Britain and France. The French had taken aviation seriously from the start; their progress had been remarkable in terms of airframe and engine design and, not unnaturally, they expected to win. Most of the aircraft taking part were monoplanes and that included the other British competitor, Lord Carberry with his French-designed Morane-Saulnier. So, when Sopwith decided to enter a biplane, most of the other competitors thought this was some kind of a joke; no biplane could race a monoplane and expect to win, was the general feeling.

For the race a single-seat version of the 'Tabloid' was fitted with one wide float in the centre and two small ones under the wings. The 80-hp engine was replaced by a new 9-cylinder, 100-hp Gnome which Sopwith brought back from Paris, virtually with his baggage. By now Harry Hawker was involved in the tour of Australia, so for the race Tommy Sopwith retained the services of an experienced and very reliable pilot called Howard Pixton. Preparations were not without their last-minute dramas as the following account narrated by Tommy Sopwith illustrates:

'In its original form this aeroplane had one central float which was installed too far aft. Three days before we were due to ship the aeroplane to Monte Carlo it had not flown. Howard Pixton was the pilot and on the first attempt to fly, at Hamble, the machine cartwheeled over on to its nose and sank. At daylight next morning we salvaged the aeroplane, took it to Kingston by road, sawed the single float into two, built two new sides and installed a twin-float chassis. We then took the aeroplane to Teddington and, without permission, flew it off, this time successfully.

From the time it was at the bottom of Hamble river until it was airborne again was less than three days. You could not begin to do things like this today; in fact you could hardly get the design work started. In those days all you had to do was rough out a scheme on the back of an envelope, show it to those who were going to do the job and they then started right away without needing anything else.'

Sopwith travelled with the repaired and modified 'Tabloid' racer to supervise the challenge, and the aircraft was carefully tuned by Victor Mahl, a talented pilot-mechanic of the day.

Before the race had even started the field began to thin out. Lord Carbery crashed his Morane-Saulnier while practising, and so did the German challenger, Herr Stoeffler. The Schneider Trophy was not so much a race as a speed competition because pilots were allowed to take off at any time between 8 a.m. and sunset, fly a demonstration lap and then alight twice on the water at designated positions. This was followed by flying the course while being timed. Two French pilots went up to do battle and they were soon joined on the circuit by a Swiss pilot, named Burri, and Pixton for Britain. Part way round the course, Espanet and Levasseur of France both had to retire with engine trouble, and the Swiss pilot ran out of petrol (although he refuelled and continued the course later).

In the hands of C. Howard Pixton, the Sopwith 'Tabloid' beat the best available opposition from the rest of the aviation world. Many years later

Tommy Sopwith was to recall that '. . . after the first 50 kilometres, the French were astonished to find the derided biplane lapping 23 mph faster than their best monoplane'. It was completing five laps for every four being flown by the opposition. The 'Tabloid' won the trophy for Britain at an average speed of 86.75 mph. Not content with that Pixton completed another two laps of the course at the then remarkable speed of 92 mph which became a world record for seaplanes. After seeing Pixton's performance, Roland Garros of France and the two American pilots, Weymann and Thaw, decided not to attempt the course.

In those days it was fashionable for the French to deride British pilots, even more so their aircraft, consequently the outcome of the 1914 Schneider Trophy race had a profound effect on their national pride. However, the French newspaper *Le Temps* was generous in its praise of Sopwith's little masterpiece in the hands of Pixton:

'This absolutely remarkable performance had, up to the present, never been accomplished on any hydro-aeroplane; that is why this English victory is particularly meritorious, all the more so because it was gained on a biplane specially constructed by the Sopwith Company.'

It is on record that Howard Pixton was a man of simple tastes and when Jacques Schneider offered to fill his trophy with the best champagne, 'Picky', as he was known, replied: 'Thank you; mine's a small Bass'. However, the important place in history of the 'Tabloid' is that when the First World War started, more than 130 were ordered and used for scouting by both the Royal Flying Corps and the Royal Naval Air Service. It was the forerunner of some very successful Sopwith fighters and probably the earliest single-seat, tractor-type fighter in the world. Yet Sopwith later admitted that neither he, nor for that matter any of his colleagues, recognized the significance of what had been achieved at the time, nor its likely influence on future Sopwith designs.

To obtain the best performance from the little seaplane they had calculated that it should be flown at a height of 300 feet. It was later found that there was a very considerable error on the altimeter and the course was, therefore, flown rather lower. But, as Tommy Sopwith once said of Howard Pixton:

'He was the sort of chap who did exactly what you told him to do. And I swear to God that if that altimeter had said 300 feet while below sea level, Pixton would have flown it straight into the sea.'

In 1914 Tommy Sopwith delivered a Bat Boat to Germany and, with a substantial order for floatplanes from the Greek Navy, his company had the makings of a good export business.

While Pixton was winning the Schneider Trophy, Harry Hawker was impressing his fellow Australians with the 'Tabloid', the fastest aircraft they had seen. He and Harry Kauper sailed on the RMS *Maloja* and arrived at Melbourne on 19 January, 1914. On board was the crated 'Tabloid' and the many trophies that Hawker had won in England. On arrival the little aircraft was kept at the C.L.C. Garage and Motor Works near his parents' home, and the first take-off was actually made from the street outside; fortunately there were fewer cars in those days. It was not long before people were paying Harry Hawker £20 a time for joyrides, although, to their great disappointment, he took none of his family flying. Although the tour was not without its minor accidents, some of them caused by over-excited spectators, the name of Sopwith was well and truly established by the time that Hawker was ready to come home.

Few Australians had done more than make brief hops by 1914 and *The Australian Motorist* of 2 February that year reported:

The outstanding feature of Mr. Hawker's flight on 27 January was the ascent from the street opposite the garage. Hitherto a wide open field was considered necessary for aviation and whilst this may be so to affect a safe landing, it is conclusively proved that in the hands of a capable aviator a modern aircraft can ascend from outside our front door. Hawker reached an altitude of 5,000 feet, but at times he came down sufficiently to permit his engine being heard. He covered the southern suburbs and descended by a volplane [the contemporary term used for a glide] into the golflinks. He touched earth and landed like a bird.

Tommy Sopwith's student pilot had come a long way. However, in commercial terms the tour was not a success and Sopwith Aviation received no orders, partly because the Australian Ministry of Defence regarded the 'Tabloid' as too advanced for its own pilots. Hawker's visit did, however, force the Australian Ministry to unpack their Bristol Boxkites and other elderly aircraft which had remained in their packing cases for 12 months or more. Harry Hawker had tried hard to interest the authorities in the 'Tabloid', which was the most capable aircraft flying at the time, but the finer points of Sopwith's masterpiece were lost on those who could barely understand the stick-and-wire designs that had remained in their wooden crates for so long.

During his stay Harry carried 40 passengers on local flights and broke the Australian altitude record by flying at 8,700 feet, but it was all to no avail. The much repaired 'Tabloid' was crated for the return journey, Hawker disembarked at Tilbury Dock, England, but instead of returning home to unpack he made straight for Brooklands and jumped into an aeroplane.

During this period of Tommy Sopwith's long life a strange transformation seems to have occurred. Between 1910 and 1912 Sopwith was the all-conquering, highly competitive, pioneer airman and he is on record as saying that, in those days, every opportunity was taken to fly. It was not just the attraction of winning trophies or earning considerable sums of money. He loved to get behind the controls and flying had captured him just as surely as it has countless other pilots of all generations. But events were dictating his everyday life and it is almost as though he had little control over the rapidly changing scenes at Brooklands and the Canbury Park Road premises. Prize money, won during the various British and American competitions, had enabled him to set up the Sopwith School of Flying at Brooklands and, going along with a suggestion from Fred Sigrist, the company had built the Hybrid out of a little of this and that aircraft, and its sale to the Admiralty had encouraged Sopwith to build new designs. What started as a small workshop with half-a-dozen staff soon began to grow.

In any expanding business a point is reached when managers are needed. Thus it was that Sopwith Aviation required a manager for the drawing office, a manager for the workshop, an office manager and so forth. The fast expansion of a business of any kind often requires additional finance and this was a matter for Tommy Sopwith to handle in addition to guiding numerous meetings with Sigrist, Hawker and Ashfield whenever a new design was under discussion. New designs were emerging from Sopwith Aviation at a rate that could not be achieved today when even light aircraft are relatively complicated to design and build. So it is hardly surprising that Tommy Sopwith had little time for flying—the need to captain his growing factory prevented this, and he was forced to entrust Harry Hawker with the important task of testing and demonstrating aircraft to prospective customers.

Although Hawker was regarded as chief demonstration pilot for the Sopwith company there were times when his health, subsequently diagnosed as a tuberculosis, gave cause for concern. There was a particularly bad episode during the London to Manchester and Back event of 20 June, 1914, when he had to retire at Coventry and come home. For some time after landing he was too ill to speak. Harry Hawker was a remarkably frail little man with the heart of a lion, and Tommy Sopwith thought the world of him. Apart from being very likeable, Hawker's contribution to Sopwith Aviation was not confined to demonstration, test and competition flying. He was also an 'ideas' man with sufficient grasp of engineering principles to convert thoughts into hardware. In the years to come when everyone was working under the pressures of war, Tommy Sopwith often had cause to worry about the frail health of Harry Hawker. This did not stop Hawker from pushing himself to the limit, although the aviation risks he took were usually carefully calculated.

A Hawker event that did go wrong was when he tried to do a loop in a 100-hp 'Tabloid' with the engine stopped. The manoeuvre was started at a height of only 1,000 feet, whereas he should have been at least three times higher since he was trying something new. He shut off the engine, entered a steep dive, pulled up into a loop and it all looked good until, just over the top, the aircraft flicked into a spin. The dynamics of a spin and the pilot technique required in resuming normal flight were not properly understood in 1914 but, even if they had been, there was insufficient height to recover and the aircraft spun into some trees before folding up like a cardboard box. Fortunately, Hawker got out unhurt and was flying again the following day!

The loop, first flown by the Frenchman Adolphe Pegoud in a specially strengthened aircraft, astounded the world of aviation. He demonstrated his skills in England in 1913, before the term 'aerobatics' had come into common use, and it was not long before others were trying to emulate the inventor of this manoeuvre. Today it is regarded as the simplest of the aerobatics to fly. First of the Brooklands' fraternity to try a loop, even before Hawker's ill-fated engine-off attempt, was R. H. Barnwell, one of the early test pilots. One day in April, 1914, an expectant crowd gathered, among them the young Sopwith, and many pairs of eyes were focused on Barnwell who was flying several thousand feet above the airfield. After the pioneer pilot had dived, pulled up with the throttle fully open and flown over the top of his loop, he landed and taxied in as the crowd ran to greet him. Tommy Sopwith asked him what he had just done and Barnwell replied: 'That's just what I have come down to ask you'.

Inter-service rivalry between the Army and the Navy initially resulted in a divided British aircraft industry with some manufacturers supplying one service exclusively, although, as aeronautics became more and more specialized, this was to be expected. Thus the RFC (Army) was largely supplied by the Royal Aircraft Factory at Farnborough supplemented by the British and Colonial Aeroplane Co Ltd (later to become the Bristol Aeroplane Co Ltd), Vickers Ltd and Handley Page Ltd, while Short Bros Ltd were designing and building exclusively for the RNAS (Navy). Sopwith Aviation Ltd. was originally designated a supplier to the Admiralty but, as the war progressed, Sopwith saw to it that his company had a foot in both camps. To a lesser extent so did A. V. Roe & Co Ltd, manufacturers of the famous Avro aircraft.

At the Royal Aircraft Factory a rather odd system of naming aircraft was in vogue. The word 'experimental' figured in most of them, thus some model numbers were given the prefix FE (Farman Experimental). These were designs broadly following the Henri Farman concept in which the engine was behind the pilot. Tractor aircraft, that is those with the engine and propeller in front, had the prefix BE (Bleriot Experimental); while others carried the letters SE in recognition of the tail-first layout originally adopted by the great Brazilian pioneer, Santos Dumont. Odd man out in the Farnborough letter-system of aircraft naming was the use of RE for reconnaissance designs, a famous example being the RE8 biplane which was widely known as the 'Harry Tate', after a famous comedian of the day. After a time, the system became confused and the letters bore little relevance to the design of the aircraft, a prime example being that excellent Royal Aircraft Factory-designed fighter, the SE5a, which was totally different to any of the Santos Dumont designs.

Although new aircraft were being designed and built by Sopwith Aviation at a rate that would be considered impossible today, we must remember that, unlike modern light alloy airframes, they were relatively simple machines, largely constructed of thin spruce strips held together with lightweight metal plates and braced with steel piano wire. The structure was, in the main, covered in linen or Egyptian cotton fabric which then received several coats of 'dope', a Cellulose-based paint which tightened the fabric and made it air- and water-tight. Nevertheless, much ingenuity went into these early aeroplanes and although Tommy Sopwith was closely involved in the overall design concept, he would be the first to acknowledge the essential contribution of Harry Hawker and, in terms of detail design, Fred Sigrist. Such was his natural genius that Fred Sigrist could 'see' where the stress would be in a fitting and where metal could be cut away for lightness. For Sigrist everything had to be simple—no complicated shapes or difficult-to-manufacture components.

Looking at Sopwith aircraft of the period and comparing them with those of other manufacturers, one is struck, however little may be known about aeronautics, by the advanced nature of their designs. While other firms were wedded to crude, 'stick-and-wire' concepts, Tommy Sopwith and his team were offering aircraft which could easily be mistaken for the products of 20 years later. It is easy to understand why other countries were anxious to place orders with his steadily growing company.

What makes the success of Tommy Sopwith so remarkable is his background. Coming from a family with few, if any, financial worries, the young Tommy was able to indulge his love of ballooning, motoring, yachting and flying on what used to be called a 'playboy' basis. Furthermore, his engineering training was practical rather than at the academic level of some of his competitors in the then fledgling aircraft industry. Indeed, several of these rival manufacturers had large vehicle, shipbuilding or armament concerns behind them. Unlike his father and his grandfather Tommy had only limited business experience. He was not familiar with the problems of staff management and his initial involvement with aviation was in the capacity of sporting aviator, intent in the main on having fun and winning prize money (in that order of priority). The first vestiges of turning his new-found recreation into a commercial undertaking came when he set up the Sopwith School of Flying at Brooklands. Then, barely two years later, he was running a fast-growing aircraft factory with all the problems of cost-control, quality-inspection, staff-management, selling in a small and very competitive market, and designing a new kind of flying vehicle that challenged the very frontiers of technology.

Faced with competition from other aircraft firms with a long engineering tradition, Tommy Sopwith took on the best with genius, leadership, a team picked as only he knew how, and a combination of qualities inherited from a long line of Northumberland Sopwith's, some of whom had distinguished themselves in engineering and other fields.

Simple as they were, Sopwith's aeroplanes embodied sophisticated engineering features that are a source of wonder to present day aeronautical engineers. In 1914, those faced with the task of making stress calculations for the frail aircraft of the day had little or no published information for guidance. Even less was understood of aerodynamics. So, when looking at the few Sopwith aircraft which have survived from that period, modern designers can only marvel at the genius of Sopwith and the hand-picked team he led. It is, of course, true that other manufacturers also designed and produced aircraft that were in advance of their time, but Tommy Sopwith did it more often and with frequently better results. When interviewed in 1949, Tommy Sopwith talked about designing and building aircraft before the start of the Great War in 1914:

'It is interesting that up to the time I received the first contract for the *Tabloids* for the Army none of my aeroplanes, and, so far as I know, no one else's, was ever stressed. All of them were built by eye and we had no idea of the factors—except that they were more than one! I have always maintained that if an aeroplane looks right, it generally is right, although at the same time this must not be carried too far. It was all a very different picture to a modern conception which has to go through the fine mesh screen of the design and stress offices. But bless you it *was* fun.'

A constant problem, faced by UK aircraft manufacturers before the Great War, was the lack of British aero engines. Along with other pioneer constructors, Tommy Sopwith often complained about the situation when he was asked to speak at various important functions. The Germans had some very reliable Mercedes engines and the French were able to supply a range of lightweight rotary units, such as the 110-hp Le Rhone, the 130-hp Clerget and various models of the Gnome, not to mention the famous Hispano-Suiza. It was not until the war had been in progress for several years that Lt Wilfred Owen Bentley (later to make his name as a car manufacturer) designed his Admiralty Rotary, and Rolls-Royce started producing engines suitable for bombers. These were, in the main, very reliable but other firms were building engines that were a source of constant trouble and, to the pilots of the day, a hazard akin to that of enemy action. In the main, Tommy Sopwith managed to avoid using these engines, although a few undesirables found their way into one or two of his prototypes.

With animosities being generated on the Continent—unrest in the Balkans, Germany flexing its muscles with an eye to world domination, and a tinder-dry Europe on the verge of bursting into flames at the first spark—it seems incredible that British firms were left free to trade with potential enemies. Yet only a few months before the Great War erupted Tommy Sopwith was in Germany leading a small team demonstrating some of his aircraft. The spark came, when on 25 May, 1914, the Archduke Francis Ferdinand (nephew of the Emperor Francis Joseph of Austria) and his wife were shot in their carriage by an assassin in Sarajevo, the capital of Bosnia. The fire lit and spread quickly through Europe with Austria declaring war on Servia, Germany declaring war on Russia, and Britain declaring war on Germany which, in turn, mounted a large-scale attack on France.

Sopwith and his team had got out of Germany only just in time. The war that followed drew in more and more nations and developed into one of the worst disasters human history has known. It placed Britain and its allies at peril, and presented a challenge which the young Tommy Sopwith met with his usual calm and decisiveness.

CHAPTER
4

The Great War

SEVERAL YEARS BEFORE the Great War Tommy Sopwith had become friendly with Alexander Hore-Ruthven whose sister, the Hon Beatrix Mary Leslie, was to become his wife. Alexander and Beatrix were remarkable members of a distinguished family. Their father was the eighth Baron Ruthven of Ireland and their mother a daughter of the fourth Earl of Arran. On 22 September, 1898, Alexander Hore-Ruthven (Sandy as he was known to his friends) won a VC at Omdurman in the Sudan and, many years later, he became Governor General of Australia from 1936 until 1944, an appointment he discharged with distinction and great popularity. He was very fond of his sister who was one year older than him. 'Trix', as she was known among her family and friends, was charming and beautiful but by no means a conventional lady of her times. In 1888 (the year Tommy Sopwith was born) she married Charles Orr Ewing, but they divorced six years later. That year she married Charles Edward Malcolm, but they too divorced in 1914. There were six children from the two marriages.

We tend to imagine that the Victorians were very prim and proper, but this was not always the case. Behind a facade of stern respectability sometimes lurked relationships fit for a lurid novel at worst or a Brian Rix farce at best. Even in those days some of the most respectable families had their colourful characters, as the following story of 'Sandy' Hore-Ruthven's marriage illustrates. 'Sandy' had met and wanted to marry a young lady by the name of Zara Pollock, but Zara's mother opposed the match on the grounds that the Hore-Ruthven family was not wealthy enough to keep her daughter in the manner expected. It would be stretching credibility to describe the Hore-Ruthven's as impoverished or even poor, but such was the opposition from her mother that Zara and 'Sandy' used to meet at remote railway stations in the centre of Ireland.

It was not until many years later that the true reason for the opposition to the 'Sandy'-Zara liaison became known. It appears that Zara's mother had a dashing lover named Jim Barry. At one time a titled Irish lady (name unknown) was also claiming his affections and the two women settled the matter by indulging in fisticuffs on the steps of a public building in Ireland. Naturally the incident hit the headlines at the time. In the event, Mrs Pollock (who is reported to have won the contest) married Jim Barry and they lived happily thereafter. But her subsequent opposition to the marriage of her daughter to 'Sandy' Hore-Ruthven VC had nothing to do with money; it was because at one time Hore-Ruthven's sister Beatrix was having an affair with Jim Barry, her future husband.

From all this we might be excused for believing that Beatrix was some kind of 'Scarlet Woman', but that was not the case. Indeed, most people who got to know 'Trix' admired and liked her very much, although there were times when her restless temperament and reckless adventures meant that she was not 'received in society', as they used to say. But whenever she was in trouble there was always the admirable brother 'Sandy' for moral support. Through him she met Tommy Sopwith, they fell in love and were married in 1914.

Beatrix, who was 17 years Tommy Sopwith's senior, was very much liked at Sopwith Aviation. It could not have been an easy start to marriage because such were the demands of war that there were times when Beatrix saw very little of Tommy. He had problems with existing aircraft, production schedules to be maintained and, if possible, improved, new designs to be built and tested, and future ideas to be sketched, discussed, refined and passed to the experimental shop where a prototype would be built.

However, even in times of war there had to be some relaxation, and shooting parties were arranged where Tommy Sopwith would preside, decked out in 'Plus Fours' and double-barrel gun, 'Trix' appeared in tweeds, and Harry Hawker wore a dark suit which really did not go with his gun. Among the beaters were the 11-year-old Jackson twins who were paid one shilling a day (5p) and given a lunch in the woods consisting of a massive beef sandwich washed down by a bottle of 'pop'. Later in the war when food-rationing made it impossible to provide the beef sandwich, the boys' fee was increased to half-a-crown.

In 1914 pilots were regarded as supermen and in Britain were not subjected to any social barriers. Since airfields were mostly situated in the country, service pilots were readily accepted within the gracious country households. Hospitality knew no bounds with fishing, riding and shooting for the asking, and an endless round of parties to attend.

When the Great War started in August of that year the entire British aircraft industry employed, at the most, only 1,000 people. Fortunately, the Sopwith company had no fewer than seven aircraft types available for war service, most of them suitable for the Royal Naval Air Service which had already taken delivery of six 'Tabloids'. A new factory was hurriedly built at Canbury Park Road, and Fred Sigrist was given the task of putting the Sopwith company on to a mass-production basis. He was a prime example of that rare breed, the intuitive engineer. Sopwith once said of him: 'Sigrist was all practical. No theory. I don't think he ever went to school'. But that did not stop him from becoming a senior director of several important companies. In fact, although Sigrist was one of thirteen children from a poor family, he was sufficiently bright at school to become a thorn in the side of his maths teacher. He would devise a problem to which he had previously calculated the answer before putting it to 'sir' in front of the class. When the poor man failed to provide an answer he would turn to his pupils and say 'Well it's obvious'. It happened every time and Fred Sigrist named him 'Professor Obvious'. For a short while after leaving school Sigrist trained with a local architect before his natural talent as an engineer lured him to the internal combustion engine.

It is a feature of war that when the belligerents are evenly matched, first one side gains a technical advantage, then the other. Holland was a neutral country and Anthony Fokker, the brilliant Dutch aircraft designer, having first offered his services to the Allies and been rejected, turned to the Germans who immediately recognized his talents. Indeed, such were his abilities that, early in the Great War, Germany had aircraft that were superior to anything the British or French were producing. Some of his fighters, notably the Fokker Triplane and, later in the war, the very capable Fokker DVII, became the scourge of the Royal Flying Corps. Tommy Sopwith had great admiration for Fokker, but it was not until many years after the Armistice that the two men met. According to Sopwith it is doubtful if in 1914 anyone really visualized the important role that aircraft were to play in modern war.

'I don't think we really looked on the importance of what aircraft were going to do in the future. I don't think anybody had the slightest idea as to how far they were going to be developed in a comparatively short time. In World War One we started by building aircraft without drawings, just to sketches. And then, of course, they gradually got more complicated and took longer to design.'

Aircraft manufacturing in Britain was on a rather eccentric basis during the war. Although there were the various firms, such as Shorts, Handley Page, Martinsyde and of course Sopwith, in Government circles, they were rather disparagingly referred to as 'the trade'.

Operating outside the vulgar environment of these talented but commercial concerns was the Royal Aircraft Factory at Farnborough. In 1914 aviation was in its infancy, and such were the unknowns, and the various obstacles facing manufacturers and pilots, that rival concerns tended to assist one another on a basis of 'disaster may come our way next'.

Looking back some 70 years, Sir Thomas Sopwith recalled that his relationship with the Royal Aircraft Factory was '. . . very good. We pooled ideas and information', and of the competing 'trade' manufacturers '. . . equally so. We were all in this thing together. In the factory, the squadrons—everyone'. But if ever he was asked about politicians and the Government he would answer with a decisive: 'Oh, I didn't have anything to do with them'.

The demands of war

Notwithstanding the need for high levels of production to meet the demands of war, there was no shortage of new ideas at the factory. For example, during 1915, Tommy Sopwith was granted Patent No 126,031 for his adjustable tailplane which could be set at different angles by the pilot, thus saving him the task of constantly exerting a pull- or a push-force on the control stick during the various phases of flight, such as climbing, cruising and descending. Under smooth conditions it enabled a pilot to fly his aircraft 'hands off' for short periods.

The Admiralty, in its wisdom, was so obsessed with secrecy that, to its cost, it refused to feed back operational information to its suppliers. A prime example of this ill-conceived policy was that, during 1915, a lack of suitable engines for Sopwith seaplanes resulted in their being so grossly under-powered that a number of them actually failed to take off and were wrecked in choppy seas. Yet it was 50 years before Tommy Sopwith knew of the problem. Had the Admiralty been more forthcoming with its feedback, the Sopwith company would have cured these problems.

Half-way through the Great War the Sopwith works was expanding so rapidly that cottages near the factory in Elm Crescent were being pulled down to make way for new workshops. The urgency of war set the pace, and as soon as the floors were laid work benches appeared. On these carpenters or metal-fitters could be seen making parts for the aircraft as the factory walls were erected around them. More and more skilled women were taken on for essential jobs, and Tommy Sopwith was probably one of the first employers in Britain to train women in the skill of oxy-acetylene welding.

Among those who had to move from Elm Crescent as the cottages came down and the Sopwith works expanded to meet the demands of war was the Brockwell family. Mr Brockwell was an experienced blacksmith by trade so he readily found employment in the metal fitting shop, while three of his daughters assembled wing ribs—strong but delicate looking components of airfoil shape that were about 4 ft 6 in long. These were made of thin wood strips glued together with small plywood reinforcing gussets at the joints. Daughter, Edith Brockwell, (later Mrs Harker) was a 17-year-old employee

92 Cromwell Road, London, where Sir Thomas Sopwith came into the world on 18 January 1888.

Above left Father of Sir Thomas Octave Murdoch Sopwith, Thomas Sopwith was born in 1838.

Above Lydia Gertrude Sopwith (nee Messiter), mother of Sir T.O.M. Sopwith.

Left Future sportsman, record-breaking aviator, world-class yachtsman and industrialist on the grand scale — Sir T.O.M. Sopwith as a child.

Students and teachers at the Seafield Park engineering school, photographed on 27 July 1903. The very young looking 15-year-old Tommy Sopwith is squatting in the front row, second from the left.

Some of the cars and motor cycles used for instructional purposes at Seafield Park, with Tommy Sopwith standing fourth from the right.

Violet Sopwith, Tommy Sopwith's eldest sister who married an American general.

May Sopwith, 14 years T.O.M. Sopwith's senior and his constant supporter during early flying days.

Ballooning days (left to right): Tommy Sopwith, Frank Hedges Butler (a founder of the Royal Aero Club) and the Hon C.S. Rolls of Rolls-Royce fame in the basket of *Padsop*, the balloon owned by Philip Paddon and Tommy Sopwith in 1906.

Scene of the action. An early picture of Brooklands taken from the air, with part of the banked motor race track behind the little sheds rented by some of the early aircraft firms.

Start of the flying bug. Frenchman Gustave Blondeau, who gave Tommy Sopwith his first flight at Brooklands for £5 in 1910. With him is Hilda B. Hewlett, owner of the company which operated from Brooklands. The picture was taken in 1913. (*Quadrant/Flight.*)

Tommy Sopwith in his Howard Wright Avis monoplane with which he taught himself to fly. Part of the Brooklands race track can be seen in front of the trees.

Twenty-two year old Tommy Sopwith in 1910, at the start of his flying career.

Royal Aero Club Aviator's Certificate No 31 issued to Tommy Sopwith on 22 November 1910.

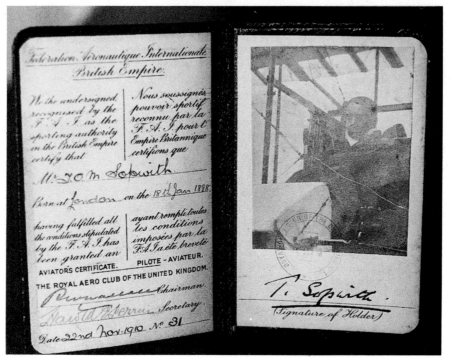

Tommy Sopwith and his Howard Wright biplane with which he won many competitions in Britain (notably the de Forest prize) and the USA. The little shield for the pilot's feet was made by Fred Sigrist from the hood of a baby's pram.

Tommy Sopwith with his sister May outside Victoria Station, London, after driving back from Dover on his return to England from the de Forest flight across the English Channel. Seated behind are Montague Grahame-White (brother of the famous Claude) and Miss Pauline Chase, the first actress to play Peter Pan.

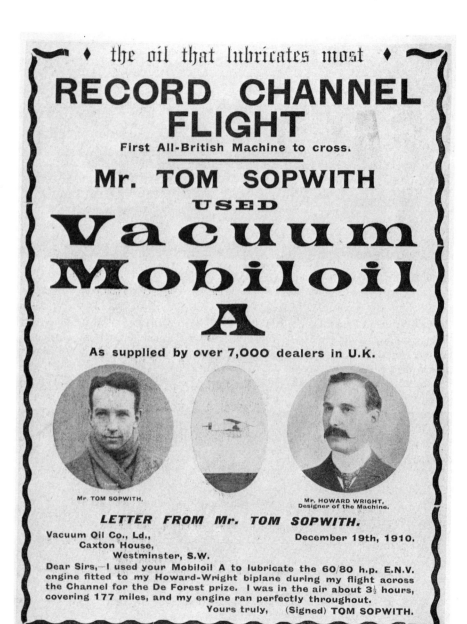

Vacuum Mobiloil advertisement which appeared in *Flight* magazine on 21 December 1910.

Sopwith in the Howard Wright biplane with which he won the de Forest Prize in December 1910.

Royal Command Performance, 1 February 1911. Sopwith and his Howard Wright biplane on one of the lawns at Windsor Castle. In the picture are King George V, and the young Princes Henry, George and John (dressed in light suits). The two men with a bucket of water on the right are there to fill the radiator, which was leaking at the time of the flight.

The Sopwith team during the 1911 American competitions. Seated left to right are J. Dudley Sturrock (team manager), a French mechanic named Pannier, Tommy Sopwith and Fred Sigrist.

Tommy Sopwith and his sister May, complete with veil to retain her hat while flying in the Howard Wright biplane.

Fred Sigrist and his wife, who is wearing the famous 'Monoplane Hat' which so intrigued the press during the 1911 competitions in the USA.

Sopwith in the American Wright Flyer which he bought to appease the famous brothers.

Tommy Sopwith breaking the 'Quick Start' record during the American competitions of 1911. From the starter's gun he was off the ground in under ten seconds.

The end of the Wright Flyer after ditching off Coney Island. Its wheels can be seen to the left of centre.

at the Sopwith factory in 1914. Edith knew the building well because, only a few years earlier, she used to visit the original Canbury Road works when it was a roller rink. When interviewed for this book she was an active 92-year-old. What was it like to work at Sopwith's during the Great War?

'We were all trying to do "our bit". We lived on one side of the road and the factory was on the other side. We made ribs for the wings—about a dozen of us—and the old boy in charge had white hair. He had retired but he came back. Mr Sigrist was a lovely, handsome man; he used to come round but never to talk [Fred Sigrist, by now 36, had become works manager]. We were a happy band and they used to get up these social things. We had a dance hall in Fife Road and we all used to go. One of the fellows, a mechanic, used to be the MC—keeping the ladies on their feet. All the Sopwith personnel used to stick together. The staff were very good; there was no bickering or anything.'

By then Harry Hawker was the chief test pilot, operating mainly from nearby Brooklands, and he believed in maintaining enthusiasm at the factory by showing the shopfloor staff that the product of their daily toil actually flew.

'He used to fly over the factory so we could all see him loop the loop.'

On 19 April, 1917, King George V and Queen Mary visited the Canbury Road factory.

'We were all told never to look up, just carry on. But I happened to notice that Queen Mary had long, narrow feet with pointed shoes. But she wore a lovely heliotrope toque with flowers on. When the Armistice was signed we all went up to the Witch Arms—and that's when I had my first Guinness!'

Discussing the royal visit with a friend in 1988, Sir Thomas Sopwith recalled that the King and Queen were intrigued by the line upon line of aircraft under construction. The Triplane contract was coming to an end, and next to these stood the first production runs of the Camel fighters that would replace them on the Western Front. On the spur of the moment, Tommy Sopwith turned to King George and said:

'Would you like to see this thing flying on your way back to Windsor? and they said, "Yes". I drove Hawker and they followed us. I remember when we were going through the gate, out of Brooklands and on to the road, I said [to the gate police] "Don't stop the car behind us—the King and Queen are in it!" '

At a dinner held to celebrate the first three years at Kingston following the move from Brooklands, Tommy Sopwith in his speech to the staff, gave credit for the success of his aircraft to Sigrist and Hawker. It was typical of the man.

Although this book is dedicated to Tommy Sopwith it would be incomplete without highlighting some of the outstanding aircraft that emerged from the Sopwith Aviation Co which, as a young man of 27, he was leading in times of war. The aircraft were, after all, an extension of his personality, although, as time went on and Sopwith aircraft became more complex, the design process had to be shared with others in the factory. Frank Spriggs had already been taken on to look after the bookwork and by then the drawing office was fielding a staff of 20, while the original skating-rink factory had been turned into the Experimental Department under the supervision of Jack Pollard.

The Sopwith Pup

In 1914 it was an advanced aeronautical concept to separate the development of new designs from those already in production. The first important design to emerge from the Experimental Department was the legendary Sopwith Pup which was destined to make history. Harry Hawker made the first flight in what was then rightly considered to be the most beautiful small aircraft ever built. When Colonel Brancker (later Sir Sefton Brancker) of the War Office visited Brooklands to see Tommy Sopwith's pride-and-joy, the little fighter was standing next to a much larger aeroplane and the man from the Ministry said: 'looks as though it had a pup'. The name stuck and the Sopwith Pup became a legend among single-engine fighters. Large-scale production started in 1916. As Tommy Sopwith recalled:

'The Pup was pre-Camel. It was a dear little machine with an 80-hp Gnome and, as a flying machine, it was the sort of machine you could give to anybody and he couldn't hurt himself. It did everything you wanted it to do—had no tricks and no vices.'

In the light of experience, Sopwith and his team had come to recognize that by keeping the weight of the engine, gun, pilot and fuel in close proximity the greatest possible manoeuvrability could be achieved, a concept that represented the collective Sopwith-Sigrist-Hawker intellect at its best. The Pup was based very much on the 'Tabloid' which, a few years previously, had won the Schneider Trophy race at Monaco.

The Pup took the aviation world by storm. Indeed, it was regarded by many pilots as the perfect aeroplane and its arrival did much to redress the balance during a period when RFC pilots flying on the Western Front were being outclassed by superior Fokker-built machines of the German Air Force. The Pup's particular talent was an ability to maintain height in a dogfight, something few other aircraft could do at the time. Furthermore, it could fly higher than the slightly faster German fighters and it was not uncommon for RFC pilots to achieve 18,000 feet. This was a remarkable altitude in 1916, and more than a little tough on the pilots because there was no oxygen, and not even the most rudimentary form of cockpit heating. On an average day the temperature at 18,000 feet would be minus 20°C, even colder in the winter. The draughts that filtered through gaps in the fabric covers of the fuselage, and around the open cockpit, cut through flying clothing like a knife. But as a fighting machine Tommy Sopwith's Pup was a masterpiece.

During the early stages of the war, before machine guns were fitted to aircraft, aircrew sometimes carried a shotgun firing chainshot—lead shot linked with wire. This somewhat crude weapon was intended to rip through the fabric of enemy aircraft, open up the wing covers and precipitate a ripping noise leading to loss of wing coverings and an end to natural flight. Chainshot, however, enjoyed little if any success.

It was only in the final years of World War 2 that rockets were fitted to some RAF aircraft for ground-attack duties, so it is perhaps natural that, during 1944-5, many people regarded these as a new form of weapon. Yet in 1917 Sopwith fitted Le Prieur rockets to the Pup for use against Zeppelins. Some of the little fighters were provided with flotation bags and flown off ships, because it was considered safer to ditch a landplane after action over the water, rather than attempt to land a frail seaplane in heavy seas—another concept that would be repeated during World War 2. Of particular importance, Tommy Sopwith's Pup was the only Allied fighter of the period capable of climbing high enough to attack a Zeppelin. On 21 August, 1917, Flight Sub-Lieutenant B. A. Smart took off from a 19-ft platform fitted over the 6-in guns of the light cruiser *Yarmouth* and shot down Zeppelin L23.

The Pup was so light that it needed the help of ground handlers while taxiing, even in a moderate wind. But it gave the RFC air superiority from late 1916 until the middle of 1917. By this time Tommy Sopwith and his team had one or two new surprises in store. In total some 2,000 Pups were built and they more than distinguished themselves.

Technology always advances rapidly under the impetus of war and none more so than aviation. There is a constant demand for more firepower, higher speeds, better fighting conditions and so forth. Another vital consideration is rate of climb—the ability to reach high altitude as quickly as possible to meet a threat which, during the Great War, might have been from enemy scouts, bombers or Zeppelins. Such was the rate of aircraft development during the 1914-1918 conflict that by 1916, little more than a year since it first appeared, the Sopwith Pup was being outclassed by some of the new German fighters, particularly when they were being flown by the legendary Richthofen Circus which had for some months been enjoying great success over the British Government-produced aircraft that formed a large proportion of the RFC's total strength.

The 1½ Strutter

During 1916, the Society of British Aircraft Constructors (now the Society of British Aerospace Companies) was formed, and Sopwith became a founder member. That was the year Sopwith's very successful two-seat fighter went into production. The 1½ Strutter, so called because of the unusual array of struts that emerged from the top of the fuselage to support the upper wing, was the first Sopwith design to be manufactured on a large scale by sub-contractors. In fact, the French built no fewer than 4,200 of them—more than were made in Britain. Strangely, the British Army was not at first impressed with the aircraft, although the Royal Naval Air Service ordered them in considerable numbers. Deliveries started in February of that year and soon demand was proving to be beyond the capabilities of Sopwith Aviation Ltd. As a result, large orders had to be placed with Vickers, and Ruston Proctor & Co Ltd of Lincoln. Another Tommy Sopwith innovation was the introduction of shift work to meet the demand for 1½ Strutters.

Some of the pilots who flew Sopwith aircraft were destined to reach fame and high command in the years to come. For example, one of the squadrons set up by Hugh Trenchard was equipped with the then very new Sopwith 1½ Strutter. The squadron formed part of a wing being commanded by Lt Colonel Hugh Dowding. Twenty-four years later, Air Chief-Marshal Sir Hugh Dowding, by then C in C Fighter Command, earned his place in history as 'leader of the few' during the Battle of Britain.

The Royal Naval Air Service operated the Sopwith 1½ Strutter off platforms mounted on the gun turrets of some big warships. The ship would steam into wind, the pilot would open the throttle to full power, then a quick release would be activated. Often the aircraft would leave the platform after a run of only 30 feet. This may surprise readers without a knowledge of aviation and perhaps it should be explained that it is the speed of the airflow over the wings that enables an aircraft to fly, not its speed over land or water. When an aircraft was sitting on its platform with the ship steaming at 25 knots (29 mph) into a 20-mph wind it had an airspeed of 49 mph, although it was stationary in relation to the warship. At 49 mph the warplanes of the day were more or less ready to take off.

Some of the Sopwith 1½ Strutters were fitted with a radio transmitter/receiver. This greatly extended the usefulness of the design because, for the first time, the Royal Navy was provided with long-range eyes and ears.

During the Great War ideas flowed between Sopwith, Hawker and Sigrist like the ever-changing currents of the seas, and the simplicity of wooden construction allowed new innovations to be translated from a sketch on paper to the real thing in a matter of weeks. For example, the 1½ Strutter was probably the first aircraft in the world to be fitted with airbrakes, surfaces on the lower wings that lifted upwards to help slow the aircraft. With a maximum speed of only 98 mph such a device may nowadays be regarded as a little ostentatious, but it was a very advanced feature at the time and some of the forward airfields on the Western Front and elsewhere were so small that airbrakes were a great advantage. There was also a bomber version in which the gunner's cockpit was converted for horizontal stowage of light bombs. These were dropped through spring-loaded trap doors in the floor of the aircraft.

The 1½ Strutter remained in production until 1923. By then some 5,500 had been made and operated by Britain, France, Rumania, Japan, Latvia, USA, Belgium and Holland. Tommy Sopwith always regarded the 1½ Strutter as one of his most successful projects during the Great War.

At one stage of the war it was rumoured among the squadrons that the Sopwith 1½ Strutter was under-stressed and likely to break up in the air if pilots threw them around in combat. Indeed, 43 Squadron lodged a formal complaint to the Commander of the RFC, Hugh Trenchard, who is reported as saying that: 'Forty-three Squadron should stop grousing and go home'. The squadron was commanded by Major Sholto Douglas (later to become Marshal of the Royal Air Force Sir Sholto Douglas) and he must have taken Trenchard's admonition to heart because, to dispel the adverse rumours about the aircraft, on 22 March 1917, he got his squadron on parade, then took off with his Adjutant, Thomas Purdey of the famous gunsmiths' family. It happened to be Tom Purdey's twentieth birthday, and to demonstrate his confidence in Tommy Sopwith's 1½ Strutter Sholto Douglas flew no fewer than 12 consecutive loops while the rest of the Squadron watched from the ground. The Squadron was 'suitably impressed'.

Safety measures

Crew protection in the event of an accident was virtually unknown during the Great War. This was partly due to lack of knowledge and partly to official stupidity. For example, although the parachute had long since been invented and proved to be a practical life-saving device, the War Office adopted a policy of stubborn refusal whenever a case was presented in favour of providing RFC aircrews with this relatively inexpensive equipment which could have saved many an expensively-trained pilot, air gunner or observer. True, the balloon observers had parachutes, but why not aircrew? Many senior officers were known to hold the unworthy view that if aircrew were provided with parachutes they might abandon the aeroplane at the slightest provocation rather than stay and fight. History, however, shows that such opinions were a scurrilous affront to the brave men who manned those early warplanes.

Few records exist but it seems clear that through attitudes that 'military men are paid to die for their country' General Henderson, General Commanding the RFC, was against parachutes while the RNAS view, as expressed by Commander Boothby, was: 'We don't want to carry additional weight merely to save our lives'. Brave words indeed, but spoken by men who did not risk sitting in a burning aircraft! It was not until the British public learned that German aircrew were enjoying the protection of parachutes that the War Office was forced to place an order for 500 of the so-called 'Guardian Angels' made by the Calthorp concern. Many of these life-saving devices were subsequently fitted to Sopwith aircraft.

Until standards of flying training were improved, largely as a result of a radically new system devised by the famous Smith-Barry, an ex-Tommy Sopwith student pilot of Brooklands days, life expectancy could be very short. At dinner times in the mess, pilots were on one side of the table while observers sat opposite. The table was arranged in the shape of a 'T' with the squadron commander and other senior officers at the head. As aircrew were killed, or taken prisoner, or went missing, everyone moved up the 'T' to make room for the replacements.

It was of course possible to be injured while on the ground. Aircraft hit obstructions while taxiing and crews were thrown forward, striking their faces on the sharp edge of the cockpit. Recognizing this problem, Tommy Sopwith introduced and patented the first padded coaming, a simple and inexpensive device that must have saved many a set of teeth and broken noses by the score.

The air gunner, sitting in the cockpit with his gun mounted on a large rotating ring, could aim in most directions (provided he avoided shooting off his own wings or tail). But the problems of arranging a forward-firing machine-gun so that it could be aimed by flying towards the target, loaded by the pilot and, equally important, positioned within the pilot's reach so that stoppages could be cleared, occupied the minds of designers on both sides of the conflict.

One solution was to mount the engine behind the crew and provide a cockpit for the gunner in the nose of the aircraft, but such arrangements were aerodynamically untidy; aiming advantages for the gunner were gained at the expense of aircraft performance. The efficiency of placing the engine in the nose of the aircraft and containing the crew in a streamlined fuselage which tapered towards the tail surfaces has, to this day, proved superior to any other layout. However, this raised the problem of how to fire a machine-gun that was within reach of the pilot without shooting off the propeller. An early and blatantly crude solution was the fitting of armour-plating to the blades. Bullets that hit the propeller were then deflected, but a proportion got away between the rotating blades.

The ideal solution was to provide a link between the engine and the gun so that it would only operate when the propeller blades were out of the line of fire. Such an arrangement was known as an interrupter-gear and several types were devised on both sides of the war. For his 1½ Strutter Tommy Sopwith used a system designed by H. A. (Harry) Kauper, the mechanic who had travelled from Australia with Harry Hawker to find work in the British

Aircraft industry. Almost 4,000 sets of the Kauper interrupter-gear were made.

The Triplane

In an effort to improve both rate of climb and the pilot's field of view Thomas Sopwith and his team devised the Triplane, irreverently known in the RFC as the 'Tripehound'. By spreading the lifting area over three wings it was possible to give them a narrow chord which intruded rather less into the pilot's field of vision than contemporary biplanes, an important requirement in a fighter and one that was somewhat lacking in the otherwise excellent Pup. Only 150 or so Triplanes were built, but the RNAS used them to good effect. During 1917 five examples from one squadron, named *Black Death, Black Maria, Black Prince, Black Sheep* and *Black Roger*, shot down no fewer than 87 German aircraft over a period of only three months. It is, therefore, hardly surprising that Anthony Fokker copied the design on behalf of his German clients.

The Sopwith Camel masterpiece

Probably the most remembered of Tommy Sopwith's achievements during the Great War was the Camel, a name immortalized by countless writers, factual and fiction, the famous *Biggles* stories by Captain W. E. Johns being a prime example. The Camel was developed from the Pup and generally regarded to have been the most effective fighter of the Great War. Although it was not the fastest scout of the day no German fighter could match its outstanding manoeuvrability which, in the right hands, could be almost unbelievable. However, in the wrong hands a Camel would eat its pilot for breakfast; it was no respecter of fools. 5,747 of all versions were built, most of them by sub-contractors, and Allied pilots flying this outstanding, top-scoring fighter shot down almost 2,700 German aircraft, including the legendary Baron von Richthofen, who had destroyed 80 Allied aircraft. From the first general arrangement drawing produced by Ashfield to the flight of the prototype took only six weeks and the little fighter was on operations with the squadrons within nine months.

The Sopwith Camel was so named because of the rather pronounced humped fairings over the two fixed Vickers guns that were mounted on top of the fuselage, directly in front of the pilot and within his reach. Some ingenious measures were taken to make the Camel a hard-hitting fighter, among them a speed-up kit, known as the Hazelton Attachment, which towards the end of the Great War, doubled the rate of fire to 1,000 rounds per minute.

Many years later Sir Thomas said of his immortal fighter:

'All our aeroplanes were built entirely by eye. They weren't stressed at all. The Camel was the product of a more scientific approach. We were just learning how to stress at the time of the Camel. In the hands of a competent pilot, who had made friends with the Camel, it could really play wonderful tricks. *But* it was a vicious little machine to fly and not easy; and it wasn't everybody's cup of tea. You had to be a good pilot to fly a Camel.'

By 1914 Herbert Smith had joined R. J. Ashfield in the drawing office and was responsible for collating on one sheet of paper the various ideas that flashed from Sopwith to Hawker, Hawker to Sigrist and Sigrist to Sopwith. The typical Sopwith philosophy of keeping together all heavy parts of the aircraft (engine, fuel, guns and pilot) gave the Camel unrivalled manoeuvrability, but this was not without complications. Like many aircraft of the day the Camel was powered by a rotary engine which revolved with its propeller and behaved like a large gyroscope. It is the perverse nature of gyroscopes that when they are forced to move out of their plane of motion, there is a reaction at 90° in the direction of rotation. So if you turned to the left in a Camel the nose shot up above the horizon and when you turned to the right it threatened to enter a dive. Of course, the pilot could counter these eccentric side-effects with his elevator control and, in the right hands, a Camel was capable of performing some very odd feats while baffling the enemy in the process. The legendary 'Bert' Harris, who flew Camels during the Great War, (later Marshal of the Royal Air Force Sir Arthur Harris who was head of Bomber Command during World War 2) once said of the capricious Camel:

'If you wanted to go into a left turn you put on full right rudder, and if you let go of the stick it looped!'

The Royal Naval Air Service placed a contract for the Camel soon after the first one emerged on 22 December, 1916, but in the cautious way of the men in khaki, it was not until May, 1917, that the RFC committed itself to the new fighter. By then Camels were already being delivered to the Navy. The first Camel to fire in anger was number N6347 which went into action on 4 June, 1917. Tommy Sopwith was able to offer the Camel with a choice of engines and it is interesting to compare the price of Britain's leading fighter in 1916 with that of the £20-million plus Tornado in 1989.

Type of Engine and Power	Price of Aircraft (excluding guns and instruments)
110 hp Le Rhone	£1,647
130 hp Clerget	£1,783
150 hp Bentley BR1	£1,519

A number of interesting and, at the time, quite astonishing experiments were made with Camels during the latter part of the Great War. For example, it seems hard to credit that all those years ago self-sealing fuel tanks were understood and actually fitted. Then there was the Calthorp Guardian Angel previously mentioned, an early form of parachute that, once it was accepted, saved many lives.

The Sopwith Camel was a versatile little aircraft and some versions were fitted with racks for four 25-lb or two 50-lb bombs. Ineffective as such a bomb load may seem in comparison with the 4,000- 10,000- and even 22,000-lb bombs that were carried by the RAF during World War 2, a Camel with its little bombs could inflict a surprising amount of damage on suitable targets. There was the raid of 19 July, 1918, when six of them took off from HMS *Furious,* one of the early aircraft carriers, and attacked the German airship sheds at Tondern. Zeppelins L54 and L60 were totally destroyed and another of the large sheds was seriously damaged. This was probably the first air attack to be launched from an aircraft carrier, and yet another Tommy Sopwith contribution to Allied victory.

Younger generations will no doubt find it hard to visualize the awe in which Zeppelins were regarded by the British public during the Great War but they were massive shapes in the sky, their bomb-loads were greater than those of any heavier-than-air machine flying at the time, and for a number of years they were able to fly higher than the defending fighters. British anti-aircraft guns were unable to reach Zeppelins flying at their operational altitude, so consequently they could attack London and other cities as they pleased. The little Pup was able to put up a brave defence, but its single gun was inadequate for the task of shooting down a large airship. Then along came the two-gun Camel which could almost match the altitude of a Zeppelin and the picture began to change. No wonder the name of Tommy Sopwith was so constantly in the public eye, for here was a good-looking young man of just 30 who was running the biggest aircraft company in the country and turning out the Spitfires and Hurricanes of the period. Such was his influence on military aircraft design that, in the latter stages of the Great War, half the total of all fighters operating on the Western Front were Sopwith Camels.

The Camel's potential as a Zeppelin destroyer was enhanced when it was able to operate from warships which could steam towards the expected flight path of attacking German airships and thus make best use of the little fighter's limited range. There were few aircraft carriers in those days but a simple, cheap and effective method of launch adopted by the Royal Navy was to tow a flat lighter behind a destroyer. On it would be a Camel shackled to the 'flight deck' by a quick-release device. When the fighting commenced some poor matelots would be detailed to start the engine of the Camel by swinging its propeller while trying to keep on their feet in the heavy spray. It was a hazardous occupation for those with ambitions to age gracefully.

The last Zeppelin to be destroyed before the Great War ended fell a victim of the Royal Navy and its lighter-borne Camels on 11 August, 1918. For several days a naval task force had been at sea transmitting misleading radio signals in an attempt to lure Zeppelins into the attack. It was an elaborate operation and, in many respects, a herald of things to come because it made use of the high technology of the day and was an early example of combined air/sea operations. The wireless signals had the hoped-for effect because, sure enough, one of the task force flying boats signalled that it had spotted a Zeppelin flying in and out of the clouds and heading towards the British naval ships.

Attached by a long cable to the destroyer HMS *Redoubt* was a lighter and on it stood Camel N6812 with Lt S.D. Culley seated in its cockpit. The signal was given to start up and take off as *Redoubt* went ahead at 30 knots into the prevailing wind. Culley was able to see the Zeppelin flying in and out of the clouds and he continued climbing until, at an altitude of some 18,700 feet, the Camel was at its ceiling with Zeppelin L53 a few hundred feet above. Positioning himself underneath the big airship he pulled up the nose and fired a burst on his two machine-guns. Vickers machine-guns could be temperamental and, true to form, one of them jammed after a few rounds but the other continued to operate. With its nose aimed high at the target and the airspeed needle rapidly moving towards zero, the thin air could no longer support Camel N6812. As it dropped into a stall, Culley was able to see a fire developing in the Zeppelin which broke in two, then fell past him and plunged into the sea below.

From contemporary reports in various journals it seems clear that the little Camel captured public imagination during the final year of the Great War, and for good reason. It had turned the tide of battle against the Fokker DVII and forced the Germans to discontinue Zeppelin operations. Yet Tommy Sopwith always regarded the 1½ Strutter as more significant, possibly because it enjoyed so much support in other countries. However, when peace returned in 1918, the Camel continued flying in Poland, Canada, and the USA as well as Britain. In that beautiful book *The Clouds Remember*, originally published in 1936, Major Oliver Stewart MC, AFC, described the Camel he knew so well in the following terms:

Gifted with a more strongly developed personality than perhaps any other aeroplane, the Sopwith Camel inspired the pilots who flew it with respect and affection. Once a Camel pilot, always a Camel pilot. And the very term 'Camel pilot' held a special meaning and was in itself regarded as a sort of commendation. For this machine was known to be at once difficult and yet responsive; wilful yet, with those who knew how to handle it, enthusiastically obedient. The Camel set a new standard in powers of manoeuvre, and even to-day it probably remains the most highly manoeuvrable aeroplane that has ever been built.

Pace of production

One might have thought that, having regard to the vital contribution it was making to Britain's war effort, those responsible for the nation's aircraft production should have been well satisfied with the Sopwith Aviation Company. Yet, during July, 1917, in one of those official misjudgements that are often the result of committee members who sit around tables trying to impress one another, the Air Board requested Tommy Sopwith to stop making complete aeroplanes so that his company could concentrate on spares. It was felt that a number of the sub-contractors had better facilities for assembling aircraft than those at Canbury Park Road, Kingston. Naturally the proposal was strongly resisted by Sopwith and his colleagues. Partly as a result of his opposition the Air Board did an about-turn and produced, like a rabbit out of the conjurer's hat, the National Factory Scheme which entailed building large new factories at Liverpool, Stockport, Croydon and Ham which is not far from Richmond. The young Thomas Sopwith thought better than the Air Board and decided not to join this expensive club which, as he predicted, ended in failure. However, the cloud had a silver lining because he managed to lease the new factory at Ham. Such was the pace of production ensured by Fred Sigrist that, towards the end of the Great War, 90 fighters per week were being completed by Sopwith's factory at Ham, in addition to those emerging from the other sites.

In recognition of his outstanding contribution to the war effort Thomas Sopwith was created a CBE in 1918. These were days of rapid and constant change but, fortunately, the simple wooden aircraft of the period could quickly be modified or new ones designed. Sopwith would visit the Western Front to discuss operational problems with the pilots and, within six weeks, a new design might emerge.

New aircraft were conceived by the Sopwith design team at a rate that would be quite impossible today. Some of the aircraft were very advanced at the time, exhibiting ingenious features aimed at increasing performance, improving the pilot's field of vision and carrying out specialist tasks. For example, there was the not very handsome Dolphin fighter of 1917 which gave the pilot much enhanced visibility in most directions by placing the upper wing behind the lower one, an arrangement known as backward stagger.

The Sopwith Snipe of 1917 was a splendid fighter which remained in RAF service until 1926. And one of Tommy Sopwith's most remarkable designs of the period was the Salamander which was fitted with armour plating for protection during trench-straffing, the purpose for which it was intended. This was a very advanced concept in 1918 and a specialist ground-straffing aircraft was not really produced again until 1970.

The pressures of war, however, were making heavy demands on everyone from Sopwith downwards. Gone were the days of design-by-enthusiasm with most of the work confined to Sopwith, Sigrist and Hawker. Now there were specialists who had to be welded into a team.

R. J. Ashfield, Sopwith's first draughtsman and eventually chief designer, was a quiet, retiring man who was good at his job but no leader of men. Perhaps he was a little too retiring for the cut-and-thrust of war and, by 1918, many of his responsibilities had been assumed by two of his staff, W. G. Carter and Herbert Smith. Ashfield decided to resign although later he rejoined the company and remained with it until 1962. By then 'Pop' Ashfield was 71 and he felt the time really had come to clear his drawing board.

In 1918 the Sopwith Aviation Co brought out the prototype of the 8F.1, a new fighter embodying modern constructional techniques in place of the stick-and-wire of most contemporary aircraft. However, due to pressure of work on other contracts, it took so long to be completed that the new fighter became known as the 'Snail', hardly a flattering name for a Sopwith fighter. Other designs continued to appear such as the Cuckoo torpedo carrier which was too late for the war. During the period 1914-1919 an average of rather more than six new aircraft types per year left the factory. While some were prototypes which never went into production, others were built in the hundreds and thousands.

By 1918, four years after the start of the Great War, Sopwith Aviation and its sub-contractors had built an astonishing 16,237 aircraft, comprising 1,847 Pups, 5,747 Camels, 5,466 1½ Strutters and various other fighters, such as the Triplane. Under Tommy Sopwith's leadership they had designed no fewer than 32 different types of aircraft during the four-and-a-half year period of the Great War and, at the end of that dreadful conflict, when the RFC and the RNAS had been amalgamated to become the present day Royal Air Force, the new service had more than 22,000 aircraft on strength, 25 per cent of them designed by Sopwith and his team.

When he was editor of *Flight* magazine, Mike Ramsden asked Sir Thomas if he had met any of the well-known fighter aces during the Great War and whether or not he had discussed the merits and demerits of Sopwith aircraft with them. Sir Thomas replied:

'Yes, I knew most of our best pilots in France. I remember Bishop, Ball, and the Canadian, Barker, very well. By and large, they were all fairly polite. Nobody flew at me in a rage!'

A man of property

From 1912 Tommy Sopwith had been living at Ordsall, near Chobham, Surrey but, five years after his marriage to Beatrix, he bought Horsley Towers, a magnificent Surrey mansion which stood in 2,750 acres. It was an enormous property for a young man to take on—he was 30 at the time—but the previous owner, Lord Lovelace, had returned from the war and decided to put the estate on the market. The auction took place in London and, within a matter of minutes, it was bought by Tommy Sopwith for the then quite staggering figure of £150,000. Horsley Towers very much needed to be brought into the twentieth century. Had the Romans who once occupied Britain been able to see the central heating system, they would have regarded it as old-fashioned. It needed a hot-water system, and a number of bathrooms were installed—prior to that domestic servants used to carry hot water to the bedrooms. A GPO telephone was connected for the first time. When eventually Tommy Sopwith had finished renovating Horsley Towers another £50,000 had been spent—enough money then to buy 40 or 50 nice houses in those days.

The estate included a private cricket pitch and the Sopwith's were forever inviting local school teams to play. Matches always ended with a tea-party funded by Tommy Sopwith and part of the ritual was a bunfight. Christmas parties for the local children at Horsley Towers were regarded by the youngsters as the event of the year, and, between times, pensioners received rabbits which the Sopwiths had shot on the estate.

By November, 1918, the Germans and their allies were retreating on all fronts, Austria sued for peace and on 9 November the Armistice was signed. The Sopwith company, which had operated from premises at Ham and Brooklands along with the factory at Canbury Park Road, employed some 5,000 people by the end of the war. Almost a third of these were women, although after the Armistice most of them left.

Only eight years had elapsed since Tommy Sopwith had taught himself to fly at Brooklands. Now, at the age of 30, he had become probably the largest aircraft manufacturer in Britain and the owner of Horsley Towers, a magnificent mansion set in the beautiful Surrey countryside. But very troubled waters lay ahead.

CHAPTER
5

The Traumas
of Peace

AFTER THE GREAT War Sopwith Aviation, like most of the other manufacturers, was faced with the most drastic contraction of its business. These were the days when 'Mum' stopped at home to run the house and look after the children, so most of the women, who had made up a third of the workforce, left soon after the Armistice was signed. However, because business was increasingly hard to come by, the company's staff had to be reduced even more drastically, from over 5,000 to 1,400. Great areas of the workshops lay empty and aircraft orders were few. As Tommy Sopwith said:

'It wasn't a question of winding down. It was turning off the tap. We had scores of sub-contractors. I really can't remember how many—and, suddenly, overnight, no one wanted any more aeroplanes.'

Although there was a glut of aeroplanes by the thousands, few of them were suitable for civil aviation and a Sopwith Camel could be bought, in good condition, for only £25. In a valiant attempt to keep the business going Tommy Sopwith started to make ABC motor cycles under licence; and, in the hope of boosting sales, a London office and showroom was opened, first at No 1 Albemarle Street, and then at 67 South Molton Street. These prestigious business addresses commanded high rents, so, to emphasize the aeronautical connection and make the point that the motor cycles came from the same firm that had built many of Britain's winning warplanes, a Sopwith Dove was displayed in the showroom. It was an attempt to capitalize on Sopwith Aviation's well-earned public esteem.

The Sopwith Dove, a two-seat civil version of the Pup fighter, was intended as a tourer and, as such, may be regarded as one of the earliest light planes offered to the public. The following remarkable story concerns Captain Barker, a Canadian serving in the RFC. During the war, while flying a Sopwith Snipe fighter on 27 October, 1918, Barker shot down a German two-seat aircraft. Almost immediately he was shot at and wounded by a German flying a Fokker DVII. Recovering from the ensuing spin he found himself in the centre of no fewer than 15 Fokkers flying in formation. Although wounded he attacked and shot down one of them. At this point he was wounded a second time and rendered unconscious, recovering in time to realize that he was being attacked again by the formation, yet another of which he shot down in flames. At that stage of the action he was badly wounded in the elbow and, as a result, fainted for the second time. Barker came round to find himself surrounded by German aircraft with smoke issuing from his Sopwith Snipe. Naturally he believed himself to be on fire, so he attempted to ram one of the Fokkers. When this failed he shot it down!

By now Barker was without the use of his legs and one arm so, with enemy aircraft surrounding him, this remarkable Canadian felt the time had come to call it a day. He managed to cross the British lines by hedge-hopping and made a controlled crash near some balloons. For his gallantry he was awarded a well-merited Victoria Cross.

Shortly after the Armistice the Prince of Wales and Barker were involved in an incident which, many years later, was recounted to the author by the ex-prince (for a short while he was King Edward VIII before abdicating in December, 1936, when he assumed the title of the Duke of Windsor). The event described by the Duke took place in 1918 at a time when Barker had not fully recovered from his epic dog-fight.

'I met Barker at some Canadian dinner in London—anyway we all had a very good time and he said: "Why don't you come and fly with me tomorrow morning. Let us renew our acquaintance with the air".'

It should be explained that Barker still had his arm in plaster so, not unnaturally, the Press appeared from nowhere and pictures of the Prince of Wales, about to be flown in a Sopwith Dove by a one-armed pilot, were given the usual front-page treatment. One of the pictures included a youthful Tommy Sopwith in a bowler hat, looking more than slightly anxious as the Prince and his pilot made ready for the flight.

'And my father [King George V] saw this in the newspaper and he gave me absolute hell. He said: "What are you doing flying with this man?" and I said: "Well you know, Father, he is a very gallant man and you gave him the Victoria Cross so I supposed it was all right for me to fly with him".'

All was not well at post-war Sopwith Aviation and the company was forced to scratch around looking for things to manufacture—anything to keep the factory going and bring in money for the still quite considerable wage bill. In this way, the company hoped to survive until such times as the great stock of wartime aircraft became obsolete and new designs were needed for the defence of the country. Much to the distaste of Harry Hawker, Sopwith

Aviation even made kitchen utensils. However, several prototype aircraft were built, including a quite large twin-engine triplane bomber called the Cobham. Twin-engine aircraft were not Tommy Sopwith's scene; he was essentially a single-engine fighter man and the Cobham was the only Sopwith design with two engines. Three were ordered, only two were built and one of these suffered from an unreliable type of engine, so the project did little to keep Sopwith Aviation in the aircraft business.

It is not widely known that, at one time, the giant Vickers concern offered Thomas Sopwith the job of running its company, but he was determined to remain captain of his own ship. In any case, a number of the Vickers directors felt that a man of only 30, however talented and whatever his proven success, was too young to be at the helm of so large an internationally-recognized company.

Harry Hawker

At this stage of the story it is opportune to centre on the remarkable Harry Hawker who progressed from junior employee to be one of Tommy Sopwith's closest friends, and who had such a profound influence on the Sopwith enterprise.

In 1915 Harry stopped to assist an 18-year-old girl named Muriel Peaty whose car had broken down. She, too, was very interested in mechanical things, they had a lot in common and two years later they were married. Muriel was a tower of strength to Hawker who was always frail although he never smoked or drank. By 1915 the first signs of Hawker's serious illness (a tubercular spine) were beginning to show. Although he retained his natural charm there were times when he displayed an uncontrolled impatience, and some of his colleagues were upset by what they regarded as his unreasonable, strongly held opinion. Nevertheless, even those who were sometimes critical of him were quick to acknowledge his talents. Ashfield, the chief draughtsman in the early days of Sopwith Aviation once said:

'As soon as Hawker started to fly, he had an angle we hadn't. He could tell where the shoe pinched. He was a damned annoying blighter, but he was *right!'*

Tommy Sopwith regarded his prodigy as a genius and many of the outstanding flying qualities of Sopwith aircraft have rightly been attributed to him. Hawker tested more fighter aircraft types during the Great War than any other pilot, and at the end of the war he was awarded an MBE.

The Atlantic crossing attempt

In 1919 Tommy Sopwith built a long-range aircraft, called the Atlantic, for an attempt on the first Atlantic crossing by air. He offered the opportunity of flying it to Hawker, and, although he had just become a father, his wife Muriel supported the idea. Harry Hawker chose Lt Commander Mackenzie-Grieve as navigator and they selected St Johns, Newfoundland, as the departure point.

The Atlantic was a large biplane powered by a 360-hp Rolls-Royce Eagle engine. These were the days before the advent of retractable undercarriages, but their value was nevertheless understood. On the Atlantic, the wheels and their supporting legs could be jettisoned after take-off, adding about 7 mph to the cruising speed. Another unusual feature was the top decking of the fuselage which, if a ditching became necessary, could be detached to become a small boat. There was also a wireless transmitter powered by a wind-driven generator.

They took off at 5.42 p.m., GMT on Sunday, 18 May, 1919, and for the first five hours flew in good weather. Then the visibility decreased and large clouds ascending to 15,000 feet or more made it necessary for Hawker to make his way through the gaps, thus deviating from the planned compass heading. Like most aircraft of the period there was no cockpit heating to fend off the bitter cold.

During the night Hawker noticed that the radiator temperature was rising dangerously until it reached 176°F. Eventually he throttled back and descended in a glide from 10,000 ft to 6,000 in an effort to cool the engine, but it threatened to boil as soon as power was restored. The weather began to deteriorate still further, forcing him down to within 1,000 feet above the water in order to see. Remember these were the days before proper flight instruments and, so that the pilot could maintain lateral and fore and aft level, some form of visual reference such as an horizon was essential. By now steam from the boiling radiator was freezing on parts of the top wing and it was only a matter of time before the engine over-heated and seized. They decided to fly alternate headings, south-east and south-west, in search of a ship. As dawn broke, two-and-a-half hours later, the SS *Mary*, a small Danish steamer, appeared below. After circling at 400 feet without provoking any signs of life they fired three distress signals and kept flying across the ship until a member of the crew appeared on deck.

Hawker ditched about two miles ahead of the *Mary*. Fortunately although 12-ft waves were breaking over it the aircraft floated well. Indeed it was still floating 10 days later when the Atlantic was found and salvaged by an American freight ship, the SS *Charlotteville*. By now the *Mary* was only 200 yards away but, due to the heavy seas, it was 90 minutes before the crew was able to lower a small boat to pick up Hawker and Mackenzie-Grieve. Fortunately, their life-saving suits kept them dry. The gallant pair was safe, but the Danish captain was unable to notify the good news because the *Mary* carried no radio.

The next morning, an early message that Hawker and his navigator had been picked up was reported to be false by some of the leading newspapers. The Sopwiths were living at Itchen Abbas, near Winchester, and they continually visited Hawker's wife, Muriel, to give her support. After five days, a telegram arrived from King George V expressing regret that '. . . the nation lost one of its most able and daring pilots to sacrifice his life for the fame and honour of British flying'. Although the telegram sounded a note of finality, Muriel never gave up hope.

Shortly before he left England for the Atlantic crossing attempt, Harry Hawker had prepared two motor cycles at the old skating rink in Canbury Park Road. They were entered for the 'Scottish Six Days Reliability Trial' and the services of Lewis Hunt Wells, a highly regarded competition rider of the day, had been retained for one of the machines, while Tommy Sopwith himself elected to ride the other. Part-way through the trial, when news came that Harry Hawker was missing, Tommy Sopwith immediately left for home, leaving Wells to continue on his own and, in the event, win the competition on the other Sopwith Aviation-built machine. For his fine performance he collected a gold medal from the Edinburgh & District Motor Club.

It was after a morning service at Hook church, in Surrey, that Muriel Hawker received an urgent message to contact the *Daily Mirror*. She was told the good news about the rescue. It had been an almost successful crossing of the Atlantic which had failed practically within sight of the Irish coast. Harry Hawker's feet had barely touched dry land before, in true test pilot fashion, he sent the following report to Tommy Sopwith:

'My machine stopped owing to the water filter in the feed pipe from the radiator to the watercock being blocked up with refuse, such as solder and the like, shaking loose in the radiator. It was no fault of the motor which ran perfectly from start to finish, even when all the water had boiled away. I had no trouble in landing on the sea. We were picked up by the tramp ship Mary *after being in the water 1½ hours. We are going to London from Thurso at 2 p.m. on Monday arriving in London between 7 and 8 p.m. on Tuesday'.*

The wreckage of the Sopwith Atlantic was later exhibited on the roof of Selfridges department store in Oxford Street, London. It was, then, that a proper investigation into the reason for Hawker's engine problems revealed a remarkable factor that was probably the true cause of the radiator boiling. Unlike car engines, those fitted in aeroplanes have to operate in air temperatures that can vary from sweltering heat on the ground to many degrees below freezing at altitude. Aircraft of the period were, therefore, fitted with radiator shutters, similar in concept to a Venetian blind, which could be adjusted in the air by the pilot. It was found that the lever controlling the radiator shutter in the Atlantic had been wrongly connected. Consequently, when Hawker saw the engine temperature rising and tried to bring it down by opening the shutter he was actually closing it. And when he thought it was wide open his radiator shutter was actually fully closed, cooling air was excluded and the engine boiled.

The seemingly trivial can mean the success or failure of an important air record. But for the incorrectly connected radiator shutter (or perhaps the wrong position of the OPEN and CLOSED labels in the cockpit—the cause has not been determined) Tommy Sopwith's Atlantic would probably have been the first to cross its namesake, and Harry Hawker would have received the distinction of being the first to fly the Atlantic.

Tommy Sopwith and his wife, Beatrix, went with Muriel Hawker to meet the train bringing the Atlantic flyers back home from Thurso in the north of Scotland where they had been landed off the *Mary*. The return to London saw remarkable scenes. Some 100,000 people greeted the two airmen at Kings Cross station, many of them Australians living in London. On the way to the Royal Aero Club, then located in Clifford Street, the car taking Hawker and Mackenzie-Grieve to a reception broke down! The Australians first pushed the car then actually carried it along the street until the police insisted on mounting the airmen on their horses for the rest of the journey.

The *Daily Mail* had offered a £10,000 prize for the first crossing of the Atlantic and it generously gave the two airmen £2,500 each for their all but successful attempt. On the insistence of King George V, Harry Hawker and his navigator were each awarded an AFC (Air Force Cross). Mackenzie-Grieve was an Air Force officer, but Hawker's award is believed to be the only occasion when a civilian was invested with this RAF decoration.

The demise of the Sopwith Aviation Company

The last design to be built by Sopwith Aviation was the Antelope which carried two people in a large, totally enclosed cabin.

From the end of the war until late 1920, only 15 aircraft were constructed, and it had been a very worrying few years for Tommy Sopwith and his colleagues. Then 1920 was upon them, bringing disaster, anxiety and hardship, all of which could have been avoided.

The Government seemed unable to comprehend that the safety of Britain and its then massive Empire largely depended upon the air. Through sheer force of personality Hugh Trenchard had got his way, the Naval and Army air arms, RNAS and RFC respectively, had been merged to become the Royal Air Force, but jealousy and antagonism continued to be displayed by the older services. Whereas in the past, rivalry between the Navy and the Army was an on-going pastime, now the gentlemen in navy and khaki joined forces against the 'upstarts' in Air Force blue. The old-established services had the ear of a Parliament readily convinced that war-weary Britain should not fritter away its limited defence funds on aeroplanes—the lessons of World War 1 had not been learned.

Against this background, the immediate post-war years were a bad time for the aircraft manufacturers. Not only were they faced with the miserable task of making thousands of staff redundant, but civil aviation had barely started and orders for military aircraft were few. One by one, famous British aircraft firms such as Martinsyde, Airco and Nieuport went to the wall. Then on 10 September, 1920, all employees at Sopwith Aviation Co Ltd received the following strangely-worded note:

We must regret we find it impossible to reopen the works as the difficulties by restricted credit prevent the Company from finding sufficient working capital to carry on the business and it will therefore be wound up.

G. H. Mitchell
Works Manager

Next day the bombshell was dropped on the front pages of the newspapers: Sopwith Aviation, the firm that had captured the heart of the nation and provided the RFC with the fighters it needed to beat the Germans on the Western Front, had gone into voluntary liquidation. Until that moment, the Sopwith company had been ticking over, re-building old wartime aircraft for the Government and making a few prototypes. In an effort to preserve the old family spirit at the works, sports meetings, which Beatrix Sopwith helped to organize, were held every Saturday afternoon at Horsley Towers. Through the enterprise, good management and determination of its founder it might have been possible to keep Sopwith Aviation going on a hand-to-mouth basis until better times arrived, but the last straw was a massive claim from the Treasury for excess war profits. Sopwith offered to make full payment spread over a period of three years, but the Treasury refused this offer. It so happens that much of the claim would have been balanced by trading losses for the previous 12 months, but these could not be established in time to meet the Treasury's demand.

To safeguard the interests of all creditors, Sopwith felt bound to place the company into receivership. This surprised many, for had not Tommy Sopwith become a very wealthy man by the end of World War 1?

'Hard to say,' commented Sir Thomas many years later. 'There was a lot of money about certainly, but there were a hell of a lot of liabilities.'

Tommy Sopwith, still in his early thirties, went to Sir William Peat, a leading accountant in the City of London, and he arranged for one of his sons to wind-up Sopwith Aviation Ltd. In the event, liquidation took three years, so in the end the Treasury had to accept extended payment. However, in an effort to cut costs to a minimum, R. O. Cary, the Joint Managing Director, and H. P. Musgrave (Company Secretary) voluntarily resigned; their positions remained unfilled and the premises were mortgaged.

Although the accounts for Sopwith Aviation showed a balance of assets over liabilities of £279,120, so determined was its founder to ensure prompt payment of all creditors that he attempted to sell his much-loved Horsley Towers estate. These were drastic measures, but Sopwith could see the way that things were going; there were no orders for aircraft on the horizon and he was determined to cease trading while the company could pay its creditors in full. He had already sold the 'Duke of Wellington', a pub on his estate, and some of the land was disposed of in 1920. The remaining property was withdrawn from auction when bidding reached £99,500 and refused to go any higher. Eventually the estate was split into lots for disposal, while the Sopwiths continued to live in the mansion.

When Thomas Sopwith formed The Sopwith Aviation Co Ltd at Brooklands during 1913, he had put up most of the £26,000 capital himself. Due to a combination of building the right product and sound management its reserves had grown to £900,000 by the end of the war. Since its inception the company had produced 53 different aircraft designs and some 18,000 had been constructed by the company in conjunction with various sub-contractors. It was an act of Governmental folly at its worst that this outstanding concern, which had done so much to help the country in times of crisis, should have been destroyed by a Treasury that was not prepared to allow settlement of taxes over an extended period.

Sections of the Press attacked the Government for neglecting the defence of the realm and made the point that if only small orders for new aircraft had been forthcoming a great national asset, such as Sopwith Aviation Ltd, would not have to be forced to shut up shop. C. G. Grey, the hard-hitting editor of the *Aeroplane* magazine, ended one of his characteristic tirades with the words: 'Perhaps then some far-seeing capitalist will reassemble the staff which made Sopwith aeroplanes so famous in the past, and we shall once more be able to include them among the world's best aircraft'. He did not have to wait long, although the name Sopwith would never again appear on any new designs.

The Phoenix arises

The 'far-seeing capitalist' appealed to by C. G. Grey was none other than Thomas Octave Murdoch Sopwith himself, and on 15 November, 1920, his new company was registered in the name of H. G. Hawker Engineering Co Ltd. Capital was £20,000 in £1 shares and it was to:

. . . acquire from F. I. Bennett all the patents, rights etc. relating to the manufacture of motor bicycles, and to carry on the business of manufacturing of and dealing in cycles of all kinds, internal combustion and steam, motor cars, aircraft etc.

The directors were listed as:

F. I. Bennett, engineer	H. G. Hawker, aeroplane pilot
T. O. M. Sopwith, engineer	F. Sigrist, engineer
	V. W. Eyre, engineer

Tommy Sopwith discussed the possibility of financial help for the new company with his brother-in-law, Jack Joel, although Jack had no love of aeroplanes. As Jack's son, Jim Joel recalled almost seventy years later, Joel Senior was rather less than enthusiastic:

'He [Sopwith] was in a bad way. He went to my old man and wanted him to help with the Hawker business. And my old man said: "I don't know anything about my own bloody business; what is the good of my putting money into aeroplanes?"'

In the event, Sopwith, Sigrist, Hawker and Eyre each put up £5,000 to start the new company. V. W. Eyre had shared the schooner *Neva* with Sopwith in the pre-Great War days, and it was with some satisfaction that, supported by trusted friends, Tommy Sopwith was once more able to run his own business from the wartime factory and provide a few jobs for some of the old Sopwith staff. The revenue officers had dealt him a blow that was capable of destroying the will of the most determined man, but Tommy Sopwith had won through.

Arthur Woolgar had joined the Sopwith company, in 1920, at a time when ABC motorcycles were its main stock in trade. After the financial crash, when the new H. G. Hawker concern was employing not many more than a dozen men, Woolgar remembers Harry Hawker working on the bench along with the other fitters, borrowing tools to make parts for Hawker Motor Cycles which had replaced the previously built ABC machines. These he would then test-ride around the factory at Canbury Park Road.

Speaking of the H. G. Hawker Engineering Co Ltd during a talk to the Royal Aeronautical Society on 21 November, 1960, entitled *My First Ten Years in Aviation,* Sir Thomas said:

'Our object was to keep it small, to make aircraft when there was a need, and to keep the wheels turning by building motor cycles and a few other odd jobs. But things happen and look at the damned thing now.'

At the time of his talk the Hawker Siddeley Group was one of the largest industrial employers in Europe.

Company Secretary of the new H. G. Hawker Engineering Co was F. I. Bennett, and the Registered Office was Canbury Park Road, Kingston-on-Thames, while the old Sopwith factory at nearby Ham—which during the Great War had produced Camels and Snipes by the thousand—was taken over by Leyland Motors in 1920.

Because Sopwith Aviation was in the process of being wound up at the very time that the new firm was being established there was always a danger that, unless the name was changed, there might be some confusion among the suppliers and prospective customers. Also, Tommy Sopwith had always been of a retiring nature, preferring to lead from behind. On the other hand, the name Hawker had blazoned before the public on a number of occasions, not least as a result of the trans-Atlantic crossing attempt which so nearly succeeded. So when Sopwith Aviation was wound up and a name was required for the new company, it was felt that the famous one of Hawker might be to the advantage of the new enterprise.

Discussing the change of name with Tommy Sopwith many years later someone said that he felt it was rather sad that, from 1920 onwards, new aircraft had carried the name of Hawker whereas Sopwith Aviation fighters had played such a large part in gaining victory for the Allies during the Great War. Was it not due to Sopwith, himself, that the company carrying his name had become one of the largest aviation concerns in the world? Tommy Sopwith's response exemplified his modesty and generous spirit:

'I didn't mind. He [Hawker] was very largely responsible for its growth during the war, too.'

Although the business of making motor cycles and aluminium bodies for AC cars flourished, the work was regarded as a necessary chore in order to pay for the bread-and-butter. Sopwith never concealed the fact that he and his directors were primarily interested in aeroplanes. During this period such work consisted of re-building Sopwith Snipes and other makes to 'as new' condition. Then, gradually, this work began to replace the non-aviation interests. Also, spares were manufactured to keep the Sopwith Camels still in service flying.

Arthur Woolgar was once driven to Waddon Aerodrome, which used to be near Croydon until it was closed many years ago. There he was required to hacksaw the control sticks out of a row of Sopwith Snipes, which were ready for scrap, so that they could be used as spares for the re-building programme. There was not much elbow room in the cockpit of a Snipe and while settling into a suitable, if uncomfortable, position he broke his hacksaw blade. 'That's more than your job's worth', said his immediate boss; at the time, Woolgar was being paid the going rate of one shilling an hour.

At intervals, Fred Sigrist would visit the drawing office to tell everyone that their designs were '. . . bloody awful and couldn't be made'. A favourite technique of his was to ask what a particular part was to be made of. If the designer said steel, he would ask 'Why not duralumin?' and if it was duralumin, the question was 'Why not use steel?' The technique did not exactly endear Sigrist to his staff, but it had the merit of making people justify their decisions and question their own judgements. Although he remained with the Hawker concern, in later years Sigrist became a director of Reid and Sigrist, a firm that pioneered gyro-operated flight instruments.

Harry Hawker looked after motor cycle production at the factory and, from time to time, he and Sopwith took an active and successful part in various trials and competitions. During 1920 Hawker was racing a 350-hp Sunbeam and while practising at Brooklands the car took off from the banked track, went through a fence and jumped a ditch. Fortunately Hawker was not hurt and surprisingly little damage was done to the car. Following that incident his wife, Muriel, tried to persuade him not to race the big car—it was the only time she had ever discouraged him from dangerous activities and she regretted it thereafter. It so happens that on the day of the race Hawker stalled the engine at the starting line and was out of the event! At one stage of his working life he was designing a two-stroke racer, but a renewed interest in the air made him turn again to the aeroplane.

Hawker was killed on 12 July, 1921, while flying a Nieuport Goshawk which he was to race in the forthcoming Aerial Derby. There are various reports, most of them conflicting, as to what actually happened, but when the fire-engine got to the scene of the crash Hawker had been thrown some distance from the burning wreckage. He managed to say: 'Is the machine all right?' Then he died. He was only 32 years old.

During the inquest a doctor expressed the view that, before the accident, Hawker had only a few weeks to live because he had a tubercular spine which had been reduced to a shell. The doctor believed that a haemorrhage while flying the Goshawk would have paralysed his legs and caused the accident.

Many regarded Harry Hawker as the finest test pilot of his time; certainly his was a grievous loss to British aviation and it is often said there has never been another Harry Hawker. King George V said: 'The nation has lost one of its most distinguished airmen, who by his skill and daring has contributed much to the success of British aviation', while Lloyd George, the Prime Minister who led Britain during the Great War, wrote: 'The nation is the poorer for the loss of one who always displayed such splendid courage and determination. To such pioneers we owe our supremacy of the air during the war'. The magazine *Flight* commented: 'The name of Hawker deserves to live in the history of aviation . . .'. Events were to prove them right—Hawker is the only member of his profession to have had a large aircraft company named after him.

Harry's death was a shattering experience for Tommy Sopwith. Not only had he lost his best ever student pilot and closest colleague, but the original trio (Fred Sigrist, Harry Hawker and Thomas Sopwith—founders of the great Sopwith company) had been broken. Without that trio, the story of the Royal Flying Corps and the Royal Naval Air Service in the First World War would have been very different.

By 1922, it gradually dawned on an uncomprehending British Government that if no new aeroplane orders were placed the Royal Air Force would become ineffective, the country would lag behind other nations in aeronautical development and it would also lose most of its aircraft industry. It then became the policy for the Air Ministry to draw up specifications for new aircraft and offer these to a number of companies. Prototypes would be produced and a 'fly off' at some RAF establishment would follow. This was a good concept in as far as it generated competition and encouraged design talent, but unfortunately it had two inherent weaknesses—the specifications put out by the Air Ministry were, at best, below the capabilities of the aircraft industry and, at worst, totally unrealistic. Secondly, even when a design was adopted, the production order that followed was insufficient to meet the needs of the Royal Air Force. As far as the British aircraft industry was concerned, it was like offering crumbs to the starving.

By now, Fred Sigrist had become Managing Director of H. G. Hawker Engineering, Fred Raynham was Chief Test Pilot (the first pilot in the company to hold that title) and the directors had appointed Captain B. Thomson as Chief Designer. He embarked upon two new aircraft projects based on new Air Ministry specifications. One of them, called the Duiker, a parasol monoplane intended for reconnaissance, proved a disappointment. It was H. G. Hawker Engineering's first new aeroplane and not a good start for its re-born aviation activities. However, the other, a small night-fighter, named the Woodcock, attracted a development contract which ran during 1923. It soon became clear that Woodcock development was running into trouble and, early in 1924, Thomson was replaced as Chief Designer by W. G. Carter who made substantial design changes to the aircraft which became the Woodcock II. Carter's version was so improved that, the following year, it gained for Hawkers its first production contract for a new design. It was also the first purpose-built night-fighter to enter service with the RAF. Sixty-four Woodcock II's were built to replace Sopwith Snipes in some of the RAF squadrons, while another version, called the Danecock, was ordered by the Danish government. For the first time since 1918 Tommy Sopwith was in the aircraft business again.

In the early 1920s, with most aircraft firms being run on a shoestring, people were expected to perform a number of duties in addition to the main task. Thus, test-pilots were also required to act as demonstration salesmen and the Hawker company was fortunate in having a team of outstandingly talented and versatile people throughout the years of 'all-can-do'. Tommy Sopwith was no slave-driver, but he expected his key personnel to keep busy and this equally applied to the senior directors he had working for him when, in later years, the company had grown into a very large concern.

In 1923, on the recommendation of Chief Test Pilot, Fred Raynham,

Carter took on a 29-year-old draughtsman by the name of Sydney Camm who had been with the Martinsyde concern for a number of years. This was the same Sydney Camm who had founded the Windsor Model Aeroplane Club before World War 1 and who, as a youngster, had watched in admiration the day Tommy Sopwith landed his Howard Wright biplane in the grounds of Windsor Castle while visiting King George V. Sydney Camm's talents had become apparent while preparing a Martinsyde F3 which Raynham flew into second place during the first King's Cup race to be held.

In his masterly book *British Aviation, The Adventuring Years,* Harald Penrose describes Sydney J. Camm as a '. . . hard swearing, hook-nosed, tall 30-year-old'. In the years to come this explosive and demanding character was to design some of the finest military aircraft of all time. During a conversation with Penrose, Tommy Sopwith once said: 'I can't imagine why his men put up with him. He was a genius, but often quite impossible'. During a TV interview Sopwith also said of Camm: 'He was the finest designer of aircraft that there has ever been'.

At times Camm was regarded by some of his colleagues as too traditional in his design approach. While this may have been true during his early days of design responsibility, the criticism cannot be sustained when one studies his later masterpieces, the Hawker Harrier in particular. To this day it remains the only practical vertical take-off and landing (VTOL) aircraft in military service.

Once, Sir George Edwards (himself a great designer) asked Sydney Camm the secret of his ability to simplify the potentially complicated and Sydney answered: 'George, old boy, I have to design it simple or I can't understand it myself'.

For the 1924 Royal Aero Club Light Aeroplane Competition, the Hawker company entered an ultralight aircraft called the Cygnet. Carter, who probably regarded light planes as beneath his technical abilities, entrusted the design to Camm who lost no time in demonstrating his genius—the finished article had an empty weight of only 375 lb. Two examples were built and they won a number of aviation events. One of them can still be seen on display in the Sydney Camm Memorial Hall at the RAF Museum, Hendon. It was Camm's first design at Hawker's. By 1924 Hawker's had a number of new projects on paper and the future was looking good.

In 1925, when Carter left Hawker's to join the Gloucestershire Aircraft Co (later re-named Gloster Aircraft) Tommy Sopwith made the inspired decision of appointing Sydney Camm to the important position of Chief Designer, a position he held for 34 years until he became Chief Engineer in 1959. The appointment was a prime example of Sopwith's genius for picking the right people. He was never influenced by the conventional attitudes of the day—'Our Mr X has been doing the job longer than Y so he must be better'.

He had a sixth sense with people and a clear understanding that the relative newcomer may have the greater intellect and more talent than the old hand; in the complex industry of building aeroplanes intellect and talent are vital qualities in a designer. Eventually, Sydney Camm became Managing Director of Hawker's at Kingston.

It was during 1925 that Tommy Sopwith, in one of his astute, visionary moves, asked Camm and Sigrist to design aircraft in metal instead of wood. Thus was developed the famous Hawker metal construction method that was to form the basis of all Hawker aircraft up to and including the Hurricane. Metal fuselages were usually fabricated from welded steel tubes, but the Hawker method entailed rolling the tubes to a square section where a joint was to occur. The various vertical and diagonal tubes were rolled square at their ends and then joined to the long members by steel plates attached with tubular rivets. This system was cheaper than welding and easier to repair. Wing spars were of thin gauge steel strip, rolled to a complex shape for stiffness. In 1925 Thomas Sopwith was elected Chairman of the Society of British Aircraft Constructors, a position he held for two years.

A reduction in the demand for coal, followed by a warning from the pit owners that if mass redundancies were to be avoided wages must be cut, led to the miners going on strike on 3 May, 1926. Almost immediately the printers, transport workers and railwaymen joined them in sympathy, and so began the General Strike. The public at large regarded the strike as a kind of relief from the dullness of day-to-day life. Soon students, housewives and businessmen were maintaining public transport, even driving tube trains, while Winston Churchill kept the news-thirsty public informed with his *British Gazette,* a journal produced by him during the period when national newspapers ceased to appear. There was, of course, no television and, in most homes, 'wireless' consisted of no more than a simple crystal set, because those with valves were too expensive for the majority of people.

At most of the aircraft factories in the Home Counties little more than half of the employees attended but this was partly due to the lack of public transport: few shopfloor workers or junior design staff had their own cars in those days. Furthermore, there was not much sympathy for the miners' cause within the aircraft industry. Even in 1926 people were talking of converting from coal to oil. There were, however, some areas of discontent, and skilled metal-fitters with years of training behind them were quick to point out that on average they earned only £3 per week, whereas many folk in unskilled jobs were paid not much less.

Most trades and industries returned to work after nine days, but the miners held out for six months, losing wages and damaging their cause by adding to the unemployed. These were days of financial depression and there must have been times when Tommy Sopwith had cause to wonder if

Government contracts might be cancelled. Such a prospect would be very worrying because this would surely lead to the demise of his by no means lusty H. G. Hawker concern, which was, after all, only just getting into its stride.

During 1926 Camm designed the Hawker Horsley torpedo-bomber, named after Horsley Towers, the estate which Sopwith had sold when the Inland Revenue forced Sopwith Aviation into liquidation. This large biplane made the headlines when, in 1927, the RAF attempted a non-stop flight to India, a distance of approximately 4,500 miles. It was a project inspired by Lord Trenchard and Sopwith suggested that a suitably-modified Horsley fitted with long-range tanks might be able to make the long flight without having to land and re-fuel *en route*. Maximum take-off weight was increased from the normal 9,000 lb to 14,000 lb, and the standard 230-gallon fuel capacity became 1,100 gallons.

The aircraft, crewed by F/Lt Charles 'Roddy' Carr and F/Lt L. Gillman, departed from Cranwell South Field, narrowly missing a perimeter wall during the take-off! It was sighted over Wiesbaden, West Germany, then nothing more was heard for several days until, on 22 May, news arrived that Carr and Gillman had made a forced landing in the Persian Gulf as a result of a fuel blockage. At that stage of the flight the wing tanks were empty and the two crew members were able to spend a relatively secure night afloat in the Horsley. By then, they had covered 3,419 miles and established a world long-distance record. Unfortunately, for Carr and Gillman, their record was broken within a few hours when Lindbergh successfully crossed the Atlantic, having flown non-stop from New York to Paris, a distance of almost 3,600 miles. The Hawker Horsley remained in RAF service until 1935. During World War 2 Air Vice-Marshal 'Roddy' Carr became Air Officer Commanding No 4 Group, Bomber Command.

Only 16 years had elapsed since Thomas Octave Murdoch Sopwith had taught himself to fly and gone solo at Brooklands. In that time he had broken records on both sides of the Atlantic and built up the largest aircraft manufacturing business in Britain during the Great War. Too soon he was to see it destroyed by an Inland Revenue displaying more greed than intelligence. Harry Hawker, one of the original 'gang' was gone to an early grave and greatly missed. From the liquidation of Sopwith Aviation had grown a small engineering company, forced by circumstances to make things of little interest to Sopwith and his colleagues. Now there was a new light on the horizon and a few new aircraft were going through the shops. Compared with Sopwith Aviation, the new company was a tiny operation but at least the team was back in its chosen business. From that tentative re-entry to the world of aeronautics would grow an aviation giant of international proportion and importance.

CHAPTER
6

Changing Fortunes

DURING 1927 TOMMY Sopwith took his first steps towards transforming H. G. Hawker Engineering from little more than a series of workshops to a large aircraft manufacturing business. The seeds of expansion were planted when the Air Ministry issued Specification 12/36 calling for a day-bomber to replace older designs of Great War vintage. Sydney Camm went to work and, during the latter part of that year, construction began of the prototype of his Hawker Hart biplane. In June, 1928, it made its first flight at Brooklands in the hands of the Chief Test Pilot, 'George' Bulman. Following evaluation by the RAF, the Hart was chosen in competition with the Fairey Fox II and the Avro Antelope.

The Hart light bomber was a great advance on contemporary aircraft, being some 30 mph faster than the RAF fighters of the day. It remained in service until 1939, but its importance to Hawker's lies in the fact that it formed the basis of a whole range of specialized biplanes which sold to many countries.

It was at the time when the Hart first entered the scene that Tommy Sopwith's uncanny nose for success seemed to have deserted him. He and the team at Hawker's failed to recognize that, through their outstanding new biplanes, the company was on the threshold of a greatness rivalling that of the original Sopwith Aviation Co. Indeed, they chose this very time to lease the Ham factory to Leyland Motors for a period of 20 years, although, to be fair, the factory had stood idle for some time for lack of production orders. In the event, Tommy Sopwith and his Board were soon to regret parting with this valuable factory space when the demand for their new range of biplanes grew, and orders came in from the RAF and many foreign countries.

In 1928 the Hart airframe (that is, the aircraft without its engine and armament) cost £1,750. Production went apace and, in 1930, the Hawker company offered the Air Ministry a two-seat fighter version called the

Demon. The pilot had two Vickers machine-guns which fired through the propeller, and in the rear cockpit was a simple turret with a single Lewis gun for the air-gunner. In 1932 came the Audax, an army co-operation version. This was followed a year later by the Osprey Fleet Air Arm fighter/ reconnaissance development which had folding wings, and which could be fitted with floats. The Hawker Hardy, a general-purpose version intended for use in hot climates, actually saw operational service in Africa during World War 2 when it flew against the Italians to good effect. It was, however, outclassed by more modern fighters. The South African Air Force had its own model, named the Hartbees.

By 1935, when the British Government had at last come to terms with the fact that Germany was rearming fast with an eye to world domination, an improved Hart light bomber, called the Hind, was built in considerable numbers. Then the Audax was replaced by an up-dated army co-op version called the Hector.

Over a period of ten years, more than 2,800 Hart variants were built by H. G. Hawker Engineering and nine sub-contractors, two of them overseas. All of these outstanding military biplanes were the work of Sydney Camm. Tommy Sopwith's belief in the talents of his chief designer had proved to be well founded.

In 1930, at a time when the fortunes of his company were buoyant, personal tragedy struck Tommy Sopwith. He was on his yacht *Vita II* in Indian waters, taking a well-earned holiday from the business strains imposed by the rapid expansion of H. G. Hawker Engineering, when his wife, Beatrix, who had been suffering from cancer for some time, suddenly deteriorated and died at their home in England. Although she was much older than her husband, Beatrix had settled happily with Tommy Sopwith and it had been a successful marriage. He felt the loss deeply, particularly since he had been away in her time of crisis.

A year or two later he met Phyllis Brodie Leslie who, prior to her divorce, had been the wife of a Royal Air Force officer serving as ADC to the Viceroy of India. They married in January, 1932, and went to live at 32 Park Street, a prestigious address near Park Lane, London. The house had once been the Dutch Embassy before it was purchased by Queen Mary. Later the couple moved to nearby 46 Green Street. That year, on 15 November, his only child, Thomas Edward Brodie Sopwith, was born. Tommy Sopwith had become a father for the first time at the age of almost 45.

With so much going on within his fast-expanding company, did he ever have any time for his son? According to Thomas Edward:

'A certain amount, yes. To say that he was an obsessed father would be a monsterous exaggeration. But to say that he ignored me would be equally wrong. It was somewhere between the two. Put another way, I think I am getting an awful lot more fun out of my children than he got out of his. My loss was my mother's gain, in the sense that they were a unit of two, the whole way through their lives. My mother looked after him very well. As a marriage it was a very, very great success.'

Programme of expansion

While the various Hart biplanes were being manufactured H. G. Hawker Engineering Ltd, a growing but by no means large concern at the time, was actively developing a smaller biplane of similar concept. As early as 1925 Camm had, on paper, a two-gun monoplane fighter which he intended to be powered by a Bristol Jupiter engine. Despite Tommy Sopwith's lobbying, prejudice against monoplanes was to die hard in the RAF. Various biplane designs were considered over the next two years, but eventually a fighter emerged which the company named Hornet. This was renamed Fury by the RAF and became its first fighter to exceed 200 mph. There was also a Fleet Air Arm version called the Nimrod.

Because of Leyland Motors' 20-year lease on the Hawker factory at Ham, production of Hart variants and the new Fury fighter was confined to inadequate factory space at Canbury Park Road and Brooklands. As a result, the first order for Fury fighters had to be limited to 21 aircraft. It was, however, the start of a flood of orders because Hawker's embarked on a worldwide sales tour.

In the 1930s, it was the test pilots who acted as salesmen for Hawker's. There was no proper sales department and test pilots, 'George' Bulman, Philip Lucas, and Gerry Sayer, went around most of Europe demonstrating the Fury to good effect. It was not until 1932 that three Fury squadrons were fully operational in the RAF, but, in total, 336 Hawker Fury and Nimrod fighters were built.

During this period the normal procedure adopted by the Air Ministry, when ordering new military aircraft, was for the authorities to draw up a specification and offer it for tender to a number of aircraft manufacturers. This was a period when there were nine or ten separate firms capable of building military aircraft, and competition among them certainly encouraged some interesting designs. However, the weakness of this otherwise sound competitive tendering was that, too often, the specification drawn up by the Navy or the RAF fell short of the aircraft industry's capabilities.. Buoyed by the knowledge that he could rely on the support of his boss, Sydney Camm often felt that his experience of producing outstanding military aircraft gave him a unique advantage over the service policy makers. A situation gradually developed in which Camm would offer a design to the RAF, Sopwith would explain to the people who mattered the advantages offered by the aircraft, and the Air Ministry would then write its specification around Camm's ideas. It may have been a case of 'cart before the horse', but it led to some outstanding military aircraft.

By now, much to the delight of Tommy Sopwith and his colleagues, the need to make motor cycles and other non-aviation products had become less pressing. So a new mood of enthusiasm spread from Board level to workbench when H. G. Hawker Engineering became heavily committed to the manufacture of military aircraft. The years that followed were to see the most remarkable programme of expansion. In fact more than 80 per cent of the aircraft flying with the RAF were designed by the Hawker company during the early 1930s.

By 1933, Tommy Sopwith and his hand-picked team had brought the Hawker enterprise a long way down the road to prosperity. Its factories stood on the books at £168,613, jigs, tools, stock in trade and work in progress were valued at £329,027, there were investments of £287,195 and goodwill worth £100,000, while patents, current designs and various licences amounted to £272,000. Over the previous three years annual profits had averaged £137,773.

Business was expanding fast and Sopwith felt that the time had come to form a public company with a capital of two million pounds. Such figures may read like small-fry these days, but, in the 1930s, when a good Savile Row suit cost only £20 and a new Rover car could be bought for £300, they were very substantial sums of money indeed.

The new business empire

Business was booming for Tommy Sopwith and he was hard-pressed for production facilities. One of his many talents had always been an understanding of finance and in May, 1934, Hawker Engineering Ltd offered to purchase for £180,000 the Gloster Aircraft Company which owned some very large factories and an airfield just outside Gloucester. This firm had been going through a very bad period since 1932; its future looked bleak and the offer from Tommy Sopwith and his board came at an opportune moment. It was accepted and almost immediately Gloster started building Hawker Hardy biplanes at its Hucclecote factory.

It was at this point that the name of the newly-expanded Hawker concern was changed to Hawker Aircraft Ltd. Tommy Sopwith became Chairman and shared joint managing directorship with Fred Sigrist, each with an annual salary of £3,000 which was then considered to be very large. In the 1930s a man earning £1,000 per annum could live in an architect-designed house, run a car, have a full-time servant and send his child to boarding school.

From the early days of Sopwith Aviation Ltd, Tommy Sopwith had always recognized the importance of running a first-class apprentice scheme; certainly a Hawker-trained fitter or draughtsman was off to a good start within

The Sopwith School of Flying sheds at Brooklands. It was here that Hugh Trenchard, 'Father of the Royal Air Force', learned to fly.

Coventry Ordnance Works biplane entered for the 1912 Military Trials, the monstrosity that convinced Tommy Sopwith he could build better aeroplanes himself.

First of the Sopwith breed. The Hybrid contrived by Fred Sigrist which encouraged Tommy Sopwith to become an aircraft manufacturer in 1912. (*Via Mike Goodall.*)

The Sopwith Aviation Co in Canbury Park Road, Kingston-upon-Thames, south-west London. The building is one block away from the original skating rink where Tommy Sopwith built his early aircraft, and is now part of Kingston Polytechnic.

Harry Hawker and the Sopwith Three-seater of 1913.

Gustav Hamel with Oonie, Tommy Sopwith's wing-eating pet bear.

Tommy Sopwith and Harry Hawker standing by the Sopwith 'Tabloid' which Hawker took on his Australian tour.

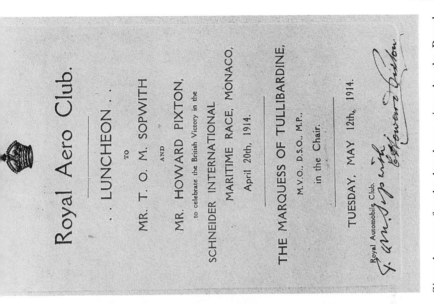

Royal Aero Club.

. . LUNCHEON . .

TO

MR. T. O. M. SOPWITH

AND

MR. HOWARD PIXTON,

to celebrate the British Victory in the

SCHNEIDER INTERNATIONAL

MARITIME RACE, MONACO,

April 20th, 1914.

THE MARQUESS OF TULLIBARDINE,

M.V.O., D.S.O., M.P.,

in the Chair.

TUESDAY, MAY 12th, 1914.

Royal Automobile Club.

Signed menu for the luncheon given by the Royal Aero Club in honour of Tommy Sopwith and Howard Pixton.

Howard Pixton winning the 1914 Schneider Trophy race in a seaplane version of the Sopwith 'Tabloid'. The building with the two towers is the famous Monte Carlo casino and to its left is the Hotel de Paris.

117

The Hon Beatrix Hore-Ruthven, Tommy Sopwith's first wife.

The Sopwith 1^1/$_2$ Strutter, a two-seat fighter of the Great War which was built in large numbers by Britain and France (picture shows the single-seat bomber version).

The Sopwith Pup was regarded by most pilots during the Great War as the light fighter with the very best handling.

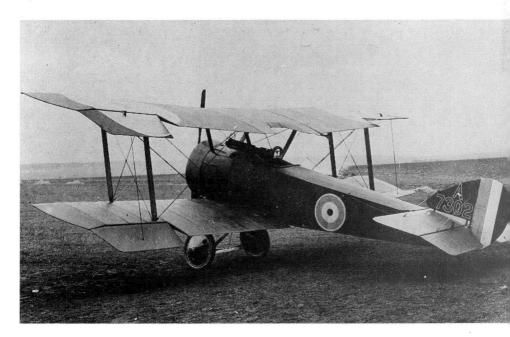

Demanding to fly and no respecter of fools, the Sopwith Camel was nevertheless a formidable fighter in the right hands. The example illustrated is the 2F 1 or 'Ship's Camel' with a Lewis gun mounted on the top wing and a single Vickers gun firing through the propeller arc.

Royal visit to the Sopwith factory at Kingston-upon-Thames, 19 April 1917. Fred Sigrist (*left*), The Maharajah of Bikanis, Tommy Sopwith, King George V, Queen Mary, R. O. Cary and believed to be Lt. Higginbotham RN. (*Copyright reserved. Reproduced by gracious permission of Her Majesty Queen Elizabeth II.*)

Mass production in 1918: an impressive picture of the Sopwith factory in the works now forming part of the British Aerospace plant at Richmond Road, Ham, near Kingston-upon-Thames.

Horsley Towers, the massive estate purchased by Tommy Sopwith at the end of the Great War.

Harry Hawker outside the Sopwith works at Richmond Road with the car he built in his own garage. It was based on a Mercedes chassis and powered by a Sunbeam aero engine.

The Sopwith Atlantic which almost succeeded in becoming the first aircraft to cross the ocean from west to east. The picture is signed by Harry Hawker and his navigator, Lt K. Mackenzie-Grieve.

A pensive Tommy Sopwith looks on while the engine of his Atlantic is given a power check.

Phyllis, second wife of Tommy Sopwith.

Tommy Sopwith with his only child, Thomas Edward Brodie.

The Hawker Hart light bomber of 1928, Sydney Camm's masterly creation which put the H.G. Hawker Engineering Company on the road to industrial might.

The Hawker Fury, first RAF aircraft capable of flying at more than 200 mph.

The Hawker Hurricane, first RAF aircraft to fly at more than 300 mph.

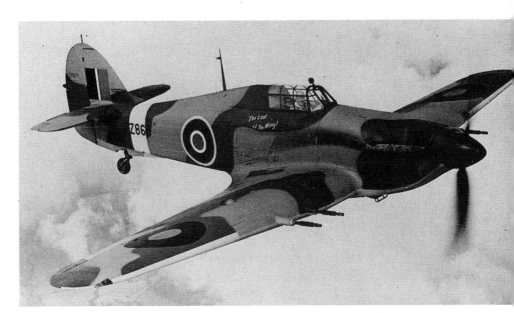

'The Skipper', Tommy Sopwith in his favourite yachting gear.

the aircraft industry. Sopwith was also a firm believer in trying to generate a family spirit although, as a firm grows larger, this becomes progressively more difficult to achieve. An example of this spirit occurred towards the end of 1933 when the entire staff, then numbering about 600 people, was taken out to dinner. It was an occasion for drinks-all-round on the boss, an act of generosity that impressed a young apprentice, named John F. Gale, who later became technical assistant to Philip Lucas, the famous Hawker test pilot. From time to time Sopwith would visit his test pilots to see for himself how the latest aircraft were progressing. Sometimes Lucas was in the air and John Gale had to entertain 'the boss'. This was a daunting task for a 25-year-old occupying a relatively junior position (eventually he became head of Product Support at Hawker's). The passing of almost half a century has not dimmed John Gale's recollection of how Tommy Sopwith would thank him for his time while waiting for Lucas to return. Sopwith's courtesy towards the most junior members of the staff earned him the loyalty of the shopfloor, and he could always rely upon its support when, for some reason, a crisis demanded pulling out all the stops and working around the clock.

Such was the demand for Hawker's elegant military biplanes that rival firms with shorter order books, such as Vickers, were glad to build them under licence. George Edwards (later Sir George Edwards OM, CBE, FRS, Chairman of the British Aircraft Corporation) gave an example of this when he recalled joining Vickers at Weybridge as a young man:

'The first day that I was there, the section leader I worked for, who was an old Vickers chap from the wilds of Dartford, said: "Lad, we had better take you round the factory so you don't get lost". And there were two things that stick in my mind even now. The first was the work's manager, stripped to the waist, breaking up a brand new civil aeroplane, the Viastra, because they couldn't sell it (and by gosh, that should have taught me a lesson, but it didn't). And the second one was the hangars full of aeroplanes that I knew weren't Vickers'. I expected to see Vildebeestes and Victorias [two Vickers' aircraft of the time] and all that sort of jazz spread about the place, but here was a long line of Hawker Harts. And I said: "But look! They are the others— they are not ours". And he said: "Cully [a popular term at the time used to signify one who is unworldly] don't talk such a lot of nonsense; they are what is going to pay your £5 at the end of the week". And that also taught me a lesson.'

The acquisition of the Gloster concern was as nought compared with the Tommy Sopwith master plan which followed only a year later. In July, 1935, the aircraft industry and city institutions were stunned by the news that Sopwith had set up a trust to buy the Armstrong Siddeley Development Company, a large organization formed originally in 1919 by J. D. Siddeley (Later Lord Kenilworth). It was engaged in the manufacture of motor cars, aero engines and aircraft. These activities embraced several companies which, in their own right, were large enterprises. It was another example of Sopwith's expertise in company finance and 'take-over' techniques.

The new empire consisted of Hawker Aircraft Ltd, Gloster Aircraft Ltd, Sir W. G. Armstrong Whitworth Aircraft Ltd, car manufacturers Armstrong-Siddeley Motors Ltd, the Armstrong Siddeley aero engine division, Air Service Training (a highly-regarded flying training establishment for professional aircrew based at Hamble, near Southampton), and the very large and old-established, Manchester-based concern of A. V. Roe & Co Ltd that produced Avro aircraft.

Thus was born the Hawker Siddeley Aircraft Company. Initially it employed 13,800 people and net profit for the year ending 31 July, 1936, was £700,000 before tax. It had a capital of six million pounds which, in those days, was a lot of money even by large company standards. Now that the original Hawker concern had become an industrial empire, it was only natural that the staff at Kingston saw less and less of Tommy Sopwith; there were other large companies in the group and much of his time was committed to chairing Board meetings, deciding future policy and administering company finance from his London headquarters.

At its peak in 1963 the Hawker Siddeley organization employed more than 127,000 people and of these 86,000 worked in the aviation division. During World War 2 it delivered some 40,000 aircraft ranging from single-seat fighters, through the mighty Lancaster bomber to the Meteor which was the first jet-fighter of the Allied air forces to fly operationally.

Some years ago, Sir Thomas, was asked during an interview: 'What was your most frightening moment?' Possibly the questioner was expecting one of those: 'There we were, upside down with nothing on the clock' answers that are the stock-in-trade of aviators. The response that followed must, therefore, have come as a shock, because the great man replied: 'The day I wrote a cheque in favour of Lord Kenilworth for two million quid—and I didn't have the money!'

Was Sopwith an easy man to deal with in the factory? From 1932 Frank Murdoch was in the design office on the staff of Sydney Camm and later had the responsibility of managing the production of Hawker Hurricane fighters. His reply is typical of those who worked for the company:

'Excellent; you would make a statement and he would say "Why?" It was no good coming up with something which was half-baked. It was OK if you said "I don't know but I'll find out". But he was very keen on always saying "Why?"'

The immortal Hawker Hurricane

While the remarkable success of the various Hawker biplanes was reverberating throughout the British aircraft industry, Camm was already planning a new-generation fighter. In fact, several years before Tommy Sopwith had transformed Hawker Aircraft Ltd into the Hawker Siddeley

Aircraft Co, Camm was already considering a replacement for his outstanding Hawker Fury biplane.

The Air Ministry had issued specification F.7/30 which called for an interceptor fighter, armed with four machine-guns. Most of the military aircraft manufacturers submitted designs and the contract eventually went to the Gloster Gladiator, which was the last biplane fighter to serve in the RAF. In many respects, the Gladiator was a wonderful fighter and, during the war, three of them, named *Faith, Hope* and *Charity,* held off repeated attacks on Malta by the Italian Air Force. However, Sopwith felt the time had come to replace biplanes, which had reached the end of their speed potential, and this was a view shared by Sydney Camm. In 1933 Camm offered the Air Ministry a new monoplane fighter based on Fury technology, but powered by a large steam-cooled engine known as the Rolls-Royce Goshawk. The original design had a fixed undercarriage and, at that stage, it was referred to as the Fury Monoplane. In 1934 the Rolls-Royce company was able to offer Sydney Camm a new engine developing more power than the Goshawk and as an added bonus, it was somewhat lighter. At the time it was known as the PV12, but very soon it was called the Merlin. When the fighting started but a few years hence, the world would come to recognize its distinctive sound and the enemy would fear its might.

Following exhaustive tests of a tenth-scale model at the National Physics Laboratory in nearby Teddington, Sydney Camm made a number of changes to the original design and the name Fury Monoplane was replaced by Interceptor Monoplane. A retractable undercarriage was introduced and, following representations by Squadron Leader Ralph Sorley of the Air Ministry Armament Research Establishment, the original four-gun specification was changed to eight wing-mounted guns firing outside the propeller arc. Even this version of the design was based closely on Fury biplane technology in as far as there was a steel tube fuselage and a fabric-covered airframe. But time was running out in Europe and Tommy Sopwith was realistic enough to understand the consequences for Britain if war broke out and the RAF had to fly biplane fighters against Hitler's Messerschmitts. If Sydney Camm's new fighter was to be available in time to defend the nation, speed of production was essential. Hawker's knew all there was to know about steel tube airframes. They were relatively quick to make and, although more modern forms of airframe construction were already being adopted by well-known manufacturers in the UK and various other countries, given the political situation at the time, the decision to remain with known technology was unquestionably wise. In any case, as a fighting machine Camm's new aircraft represented a giant step forward.

On 6 November, 1935, prototype K5083, which had been erected and ground-tested at Brooklands, flew for the first time in the hands of 'George'

Bulman. They called it the Hawker Hurricane and it was the first of more than 15,000 to be built.

Although Sopwith fully understood the technicalities of what was at the time an advanced fighter, he left the project to Sydney Camm, with just a quiet suggestion here and there. One important piece of advice was: 'Don't let the wing-loading get too high'. High wing-loadings generally result in fast landing speeds and, in some cases, unforgiving flying characteristics. Tommy Sopwith did not want Hawker to provide the RAF with a 'hot-rod', an aircraft so far removed from the previous generation of biplane fighters that pilots were in fear of it. In the event the Hurricane was a gentle machine to fly and its low wing-loading resulted in modest landing speeds, a viceless stall and the ability to make circles around most other aircraft, an important talent in the kind of air combat being fought with the machine-guns and cannon of the period.

Tommy Sopwith had good reason to be well pleased with Sydney Camm's new masterpiece and Sir Peter Masefield, a friend of both men for many years, described the Sopwith-Camm relationship thus:

'Sydney Camm had great respect for Tommy Sopwith and never interrupted when he was speaking. Sopwith was always the boss but Sydney was a curious chap, brilliant designer, autocratic in the design office but never to Tommy Sopwith. He realized Sopwith was the man that he owed everything to, and he spoke very respectfully to him. There were very few people he did speak respectfully to!'

In 1935 the moment of truth hit the British Government and it finally came to terms with the fact that, although Hitler was protesting 'All I want is peace', he was not saying which piece! Was it Poland, France or even Great Britain? So, an intensive expansion programme was put in hand for the Royal Navy, Army and Royal Air Force. Almost overnight, factories manufacturing guns, tanks and military aircraft were expected to make up for years of political neglect. Any junior fitter working on the bench could have told Parliament that one cannot step up the production of complex munitions of war simply by snapping the fingers. So it was that at Hawker Aircraft and the many other Hawker Siddeley factories, everyone from Tommy Sopwith down to the tea boy suddenly found himself working all the hours of the week.

Much as Tommy Sopwith enjoyed holidays relaxing on his yacht, by 1935 the pressures of expansion made this difficult, particularly when the time came to churn out Hurricane fighters to meet the needs of a war now lurking in the wings.

After members of staff had earned Sopwith's trust they were, in some cases, able to enjoy his friendship. One who made the grade with Tommy Sopwith was H. K. Jones. H.K. started as an office boy at Brooklands in 1912 and became one of Sopwith's most trusted confidantes. He was in many respects a marvellous man with a wonderful sense of humour. Management was not so compartmentalized then as it is today, and senior staff used to take on a multitude of tasks. Jones was a self-taught contracts man-cum-sales manager, and one of his many assets to the firm was that he seemed to know everyone everywhere in the aviation world. He was known throughout the British aircraft industry as 'Hawker Jones' and, as usual when Tommy Sopwith judged that there was real quality in a member of his staff, nothing was held back. He would show complete faith in the person, endow him with wide measures of authority, offer his full support and guide him in a gentle, kindly, courteous way. That is why the management at Hawker's so often achieved what many regarded as the impossible. Sopwith once said of Jones that he was: 'Very nice—I liked him a lot—and he did all Sprigg's work for him'. As the comment implies there were times when Sopwith's relationship with Frank Spriggs, who joined the company as office clerk and subsequently held a number of important directorships, wore thin!

Overseas sales

The importance of exports as a means of expanding the Hawker concern was not lost on Tommy Sopwith, but the cost of stationing full-time representatives in foreign countries could not, in those days, be justified. Months or even years of patient discussion involving meeting after meeting is entailed in the selling of aircraft, particularly when the buyer is a government. And, at the end of all this effort, the sale can fail to materialize because governments are often more interested in negotiating offset deals than buying the best aircraft (for example, 'We will give you 10,000 bottles of our best brandy for one of your fighters').

Rather than employ full-time staff away from home it was often the practice to commission a good agent with an intimate knowledge of local politics. To the present day, in some countries, this can be more important than the merits of what is on offer and it takes a skilled man with access to the right people to even start discussions, let alone clinch a deal. One such agent was Tom Mapplebeck. He was shot down in an FE8 during World War 1 and spent the rest of the war as a prisoner. When peace returned he took up a job in Belgrade and later bought a DH Metal Moth which he flew from Stag Lane Aerodrome, London, to Belgrade. He then folded the wings and exhibited the aeroplane in his motor showroom where he sold Morris cars. Eventually the Yugoslavian Air Force bought the aircraft from him and orders for more de Havilland aircraft followed. By then he was a trusted figure with the Yugoslavian Air Force and some of Yugoslavia's top civil servants.

It was through H. K. Jones, Sales Manager at Hawker, Kingston, that Tom Mapplebeck first came to know Tommy Sopwith. Whenever Mapplebeck was in England he and Sopwith would have long discussions.

Always with a shrewd eye to finding new business opportunities, Sopwith wanted to know what was going on politically in Yugoslavia and, being impressed with Mapplebeck's efforts to interest that country in the Hawker Fury, Sopwith arranged for his Chief Test Pilot, 'George' Bulman to fly out a two-seat Hart for inspection.

The Hart's aerodynamics were similar to the smaller Fury, but its extra seat enabled some of the Yugoslav Air Force officers to experience the superb handling of the Hawker breed at first hand. Faultless handling was something of a tradition at Hawker's, partly through Sydney Camm's brilliant skills as a designer but largely as a result of feedback from a succession of outstanding test pilots. Having been a test pilot himself from 1911-1913, Tommy Sopwith regarded his test pilots as key personnel; he recognized that good engineering alone does not make a successful aircraft.

An order for the Fury was hoped for and H. K. Jones arrived in Yugoslavia to look after the commercial details. With prospects for a major sale looking encouraging, Tom Mapplebeck laid on a party at his house which was built on the side of a hill. It was a good lunch and wine flowed unhindered into willing mouths. Consequently, when the party descended down some stone steps leading to the garden swimming pool there was some impromptu horseplay. Bulman, in trying to ride piggyback on an unprepared H. K. Jones, who promptly collapsed, crashed down the steps and broke his nose. Fortunately, the incident did not affect the success of the sale.

Many years later, when he was 94 years old, Tom Mapplebeck recalled his dealings with Tommy Sopwith over the sale of Hawker Furys to Yugoslavia:

'When we had to get some more performance out of the Fury, he [Sopwith] sent me up to Rolls-Royce in Derby and told me to tell them they had to give us another 100 horsepower. Then he sent me down to Cheltenham to an engineer named Dowty [founder of the famous firm of that name] who was developing an internally sprung wheel in place of all the usual nonsense. It was already on the Gloster Gladiator and I was to ask him if he could fix up the same arrangements on the Fury. With the Fury they [the Yugoslavian Air Force] won the race round the Alps [July, 1932] so that made me get on very well, of course, with Tommy Sopwith.'

Project Engineer, working under Camm on the Hurricane, was Stuart D. Davies. Although the new Hurricane fighter was the main priority at Kingston, the continuing overseas' sales of the Fury biplane were nevertheless commercially important. The Yugoslavian demand for more performance, however, came at an awkward time for Hawker. If the sale was to go through revised figures were needed in a hurry, but Camm was away. So the company turned to Stuart Davies who considered the problem and said: 'If we clean up this and that, alter the radiator a little, get Royce's to give us a little more power and move that to there we will get another five or six miles per hour'.

The revised performance figures were passed to the Yugoslavian Government and Hawker got its order. On his return, Sydney Camm was not at all pleased to hear that one of his staff had dared to improve his masterpiece and even given out a set of new figures before they had been checked by him. There were some choice words between the two men, for Camm's language could be 'picturesque' as could that of London-born Davies who was known in the works as 'Cock'. As a result, Davies resigned from Hawker Aircraft, although he and Sydney Camm were on good terms again in later years.

The talents of Davies had not gone unnoticed at Kingston and, because a number of people were anxious to retain him on the staff, a plan was hatched. When a new aircraft was designed by one of the manufacturers in those days it was the practice to send a brochure to the Air Ministry as a basis for discussion about a possible order. To be in time for the weekly meetings these had to be delivered to Whitehall by 10 a.m. on Tuesday mornings, but Tommy Sopwith always saw his company brochures first. He wanted to know all about his latest projects, so that the correct answers were at his fingertips when he was questioned by 'the right people'. The aircraft that eventually became the Hawker Typhoon was being offered to the Air Ministry and someone thought that 'Cock' Davies ought to visit Sopwith in his London office for the purpose of explaining the brochure to him. With his well-known charm, it was hoped that Sopwith might persuade him to stay.

In an effort to put Davies at his ease Sopwith offered him a cigarette. Most cigarettes in those days were cork-tipped and, since he had never seen one with a white filter before, Davies put the wrong end of the cigarette in his mouth, lit the filter and it burst into flames, much to the amusement of both men. Davies may not have known one end of a cigarette from another in 1936, but after World War 2 he designed the outstanding Avro Vulcan bomber which will go down in aviation history as one of the truly great military aircraft of all times.

Another war

By 1936 only the most committed optimists were refusing to believe that war was approaching. The British Government of the day had reluctantly come to terms with the fact; its policy of appeasement had failed to temper the ambitions of Adolf Hitler. Yet, although expansion of the three services had been instructed by the Government, Prime Minister Neville Chamberlain and his Cabinet seemed unable to comprehend the nature of air defence. The fact that Germany had fast monoplane fighters in great numbers, while the RAF was still flying the biplanes of another era should have encouraged the utmost urgency because, had the war started in 1936, Britain would have been unable to offer any resistance to the Luftwaffe. The Spitfire had only recently made its first flight on 6 March, and a great deal of development flying was required before it would be fit for operational duties; only then could its production be put in hand. But, although the Hawker Hurricane project had been started earlier and it was ready to be produced, no orders were forthcoming.

During this period Frank Murdoch, of the Hawker design office, was advising Sopwith on the design of his new motor yacht *Philante* then under construction at Camper & Nicholsons in Southampton. In February, 1936, Sopwith despatched Frank Murdoch to M.A.N., the German manufacturer which was supplying the diesel engines for *Philante*. While there, Murdoch was astonished at the number of U-boat engines in production at the works. One of the engineers arranged for Murdoch to visit the Heinkel aircraft factory. The extent of Germany's preparations for war was so obvious that Murdoch lost no time in giving an account of what he had seen to Sopwith. The far-reaching effects of what may, at the time, seem insignificant events can change the course of history and that was certainly true of this incident. Murdoch's report came at a time when Sydney Camm's wonderful Hurricane was ready for production and the Air Ministry was prevaricating over how many should be ordered for the RAF. For some time Tommy Sopwith had been concerned about the complacent attitude of key Government officials who seemed incapable of recognizing the scale of rearmament in Germany. It seems likely that Frank Murdoch's alarming report was the last straw for Tommy Sopwith. While the Air Ministry continued to dither over how many Hurricane fighters to order he called together his Board, the situation was discussed, agreement was reached and Sopwith put in hand tooling and jigs for 1,000 airframes. He did this without a single aircraft having been ordered. This was Sopwith leadership at its best and a decision that saved three months valuable production time. Three years later his courageous decision enabled the RAF to counter and badly maul the Luftwaffe during the Battle of Britain. It was the first time the all-powerful German Air Force had been given a bloody nose and the Sopwith Camel story had been re-enacted 23 years after the Great War. Without that decision, one taken at considerable financial risk to Hawker Siddeley, the outcome of the decisive Battle of Britain may well have been very different, for by 1940 Spitfire production was only just getting into its stride. It was not until 3 June, 1936, that an order was received from the Air Ministry for 600 Hurricanes. By then detail drawings had been issued to the workshops. Frank Murdoch, who had advised Sopwith during the America's Cup Races, (see Chapter 7) was charged with the awesome responsibility of mass-producing the aircraft.

At intervals Tommy Sopwith would gather together his co-directors Bennett and Spriggs, H. K. Jones the Commercial Manager at Hawkers, and Frank Murdoch from the Hurricane production line. Everyone was under intense pressure at the factory and, mindful of the need for a little relaxation,

Sopwith would take them to the Richmond Golf Club for lunch. 'You might as well eat what you like, lads, otherwise it will all go in excess profit tax', he would tell them, doubtless remembering the events of post-World War 1, when Inland Revenue demands caused the demise of Sopwith Aviation.

With such large orders for the Hurricane to complete, Hawker's existing facilities were inadequate and by the end of 1938 a new plant, complete with airfield, was established at Langley, just a few miles from today's Heathrow Airport. Production of Hurricane fighters started at a rate of one a day and reached 35 a week by 1942.

With shadows of World War 2 lengthening it seems strange that the Hawker concern should have been allowed to continue exporting fighters in the last months of peace. One Hurricane actually arrived in Poland not long before the German troops invaded the country in September, 1939, while others were delivered to Belgium, Turkey, Yugoslavia and Rumania. Of greater significance were the examples sent to Canada. As a result of this, the Canadian Car and Foundry Corporation set up a production line that started to deliver Hurricanes early in 1940. That year 180 Hurricanes reached Britain by sea although 20 were lost through U-Boat action.

In 1939 the Hawker element of Hawker Siddeley employed some 4,000 people in the Brooklands, Kingston and Langley factories, and by the time Britain went to war 500 or so Hurricanes had been delivered to the Royal Air Force. Of the 52 operational squadrons available for action during the Battle of Britain, 32 flew Hurricanes.

It was mentioned previously that, in designing his 'Sopwith Camel of the 1940s', Sydney Camm decided to remain faithful to well-known technology and, in many respects, the Hurricane airframe was similar in concept to the Fury/Hart biplanes. Conversely Reginald Mitchell's outstanding Spitfire was of more modern, stressed skin construction. In aeronautics nothing is gained without cost and the high performance of Mitchell's legendary fighter had to be paid for in terms of structural complexity; only 10,000 man-hours went into the manufacture of a Hurricane, whereas the Spitfire required 15,000 hours.

While Hawker's workshops hummed with activity, other companies within the Hawker Siddeley empire were also engaged on their own projects. At its Coventry works Armstrong Whitworth were turning out the twin-engine Whitley bomber, a project that was already under way when Tommy Sopwith took over the Armstrong Siddeley Development Co in 1935. It was also building a small number of AW27 Ensign four-engine airliners for Imperial Airways. Even by present-day standards these were large aircraft, although only 33-to-40 passengers could be carried. Meanwhile the Gloster Aircraft Company was heavily engaged in extending its factory and building the Hawker Hurricane. At its peak, which occurred in 1941, the Hucclecote factory near Gloucester delivered 1,359 of them during a 12-month period.

It even produced jigs and tools for the rival Vickers concern.

In the Manchester area the A. V. Roe division of Hawker Siddeley was building the twin-engine Avro Anson, first as a light civil passenger aircraft but later in its main role as a trainer for pilots, navigators and wireless operators. Some were even fitted with a gun turret and, early in the war, they flew operationally with RAF Coastal Command. The Anson enjoyed a long life and a modernized version continued in production until 1952. By this time an astonishing 11,020 of the various Anson models had been made over a period of 17 years. On a less happy note, plans were under way for the ill-fated Manchester bomber although, in the years ahead, it did manage to convert itself from 'Ugly Duckling' to 'Prince Charming' in the form of the outstanding Avro Lancaster.

Reviewing the situation as it existed up to the start of World War 2, the genius of the man behind the success of Hawker Siddeley Aviation shines through, but aviation was by no means Tommy Sopwith's only interest and the time has now come to look at his marine activities.

CHAPTER
7

Sopwith the Sailor

TO APPRECIATE THE extent of Tommy Sopwith's outstanding prowess at sea it is necessary to put back the clock some 40 or more years, prior to World War 2. School holidays spent on the Isle of Lismore (six miles north of Oban, Scotland) with his mother and seven sisters afforded him opportunities for sailing in relatively sheltered waters, and the yacht captured his imagination long before the balloon or the internal combustion engine. In one form or another balloons had been around for almost 120 years by the time Tommy was old enough to be let loose in a sailing dinghy. But whereas his ballooning activities were confined to a 12-month period, boats in general, and yachting in particular, remained an abiding love throughout his long and active life.

In 1904 he had been refused permission to go ballooning on his own because, at the age of 16, he was considered too young. As previously mentioned, two years later he shared ownership of a rather untidy-looking balloon with Philip Paddon which they called the *Padsop*. However, that was in 1906, and his sailing had started some years previously when he was a child.

The first boat Tommy Sopwith actually owned is believed to have been a fishing cutter, the *Margery Daw,* for which he paid £100 in 1907. This was followed by a small yacht called *Gleaner* which also had a little steam engine. However, by 1909 Tommy had teamed up with his friend Bill Eyre to purchase the 166-ton schooner, *Neva,* which had been built in 1867. By then *Neva* was 42 years old and in poor shape. It was the ambition to fit a new-fangled internal combustion engine to *Neva* that led Tommy to meet Fred Sigrist in 1910.

Tommy's marine interests were not confined to sail. He was also a powerboat addict and in September 1912 he won the British International Trophy in the racing boat *Maple Leaf IV,* which was built by Saunders and owned by the Canadian, Sir Mackie Edgar. By 1912 the 24-year-old Sopwith had been flying for two years and was about to set up the Sopwith Aviation Co. Starting a new business, however small, is a time-consuming exercise, yet this did not prevent Sopwith repeating his powerboat triumph the following year at a speed of 48 knots (55 mph). In 1913 that was a world record; indeed, few cars were capable of 55 mph at the time. During these important races he managed to beat off challenges from France and the USA.

After the Great War and as the Hawker enterprise began to prosper, Tommy Sopwith graduated from one diesel yacht to another, each one larger than the previous. In 1925 there was the 170-ton *Osprey,* followed by the 340-ton *Vita* in 1927. Two years later he bought *Vita II* (502 tons), and then the 752-ton *Vita III.* For a short while he owned the 471-ton *Aaola,* but soon there would be *Philante,* a magnificent private liner, which is described later in this chapter.

For a number of years Tommy Sopwith was widely regarded within the yachting fraternity as the world's leading Twelve Metre Class helmsman. It was a type of racing that appealed to him greatly and his first yacht of this category was the *Doris* which he raced with some success in 1926. However, a few years later Camper & Nicholsons built for him another of the breed called *Mouette,* and with this yacht he was 12-Metre champion during the 1928, 1929 and 1930 racing seasons. His 108 trophies, which include 75 first prizes, bear witness to that, and in 1930, because of his standing in the sport, he was elected a member of the Royal Yacht Squadron.

J Class yachts

During the 1930s Tommy Sopwith became interested in the J Class yachts. By then his aviation interests had made him a very wealthy man, an essential qualification if one aspired to sailing these very large vessels with their masts towering 150 feet or so above the water. The J Class yachts which took part in the America's Cup races before the war, are not to be confused with those being sailed today. These are less than half the length and a fraction of the weight. A single mainsail on one of the J Class yachts could weigh a ton. It was a totally new kind of racing for Tommy Sopwith but, fortunately, he was able to turn for advice to Frank Murdoch, someone he had raced against several years previously and who now worked in the design office under Sydney Camm at Hawker's Kingston factory.

Although his father was British and Frank Murdoch's school had been in England, he was born in Antwerp, Belgium, where his grandfather had set up a shipyard in 1867. It was a sizeable firm employing some 1,500 staff. All members of the Murdoch family were keen sailors and Frank had been an enthusiast of the marine world long before his involvement in aeronautics. His interest in aeroplanes was first stimulated when, in the late 1920s, he saw the Hawker Fury and the Fairey Firefly competing for an order from the Belgian Air Force. Since the family shipbuilding concern was likely to go to his older brother, he decided to become an aeronautical engineer.

In 1930, while studying in England for an engineering degree, Frank Murdoch devoted his leisure time to sailing and it was the sail-and-the-sea that brought him into contact with the man who was to have such a profound influence on his future. A race had been arranged from Ramsgate to Ostend in which Murdoch was entered to captain a Belgian-owned 12-metre yacht. The weather was very bad and everyone dropped out except Frank Murdoch and one other competitor—Tommy Sopwith in his all-conquering yacht *Mouette*. It was a race under particularly rough conditions and Sopwith managed to win by five minutes. Following the two competing boats was Sopwith's motor yacht, *Vita II,* carrying, among others, his first wife Beatrix. Fifty-eight years later, when Frank Murdoch was invited to have lunch with Sir Thomas who was nearing his 101st birthday, the old sportsman recalled the race to Ostend and said:

'Do you know, I was seasick 10 minutes before the finish and that's the first time I ever was.'

In 1932 Frank Murdoch joined Sydney Camm's design department at Hawker's, Kingston factory, so when the following year Tommy Sopwith decided to mount a challenge for the America's Cup it was to his former Ramsgate-Ostend adversary that he turned for advice. Camper & Nicholsons, the old established boat builders, were retained for Tommy Sopwith's challenger and the J Class racing yacht, *Endeavour,* designed by Charles E. Nicholson, was without doubt a thing of great beauty. However, in those days yachts were largely designed by eye. Very little science was involved and, mindful of how early aeroplane designers had been forced to progress from rough sketches on the back of a cigarette box to state-of-the-art techniques and proper methods of stressing, Sopwith decided that aeronautical practice had something to offer his new racing yacht. So it was that Frank Murdoch found himself called upon to design the mast and rigging. Fortunately, Charles Nicholson agreed because Murdoch was soon to find how little was known about the various loads that were imposed on, for example, the mast of a yacht under sail. It was a case of 'We broke this five-eighths wire before, but this time we used three-quarters and that's held'. He was unable to adopt professional engineering principles for want of technical information.

J Class racing was a totally different kind of sailing, certainly another dimension after being used to 'Twelve Metre' events, and to gain experience Tommy Sopwith bought the yacht *Shamrock V.* It had been built for Sir Thomas Lipton's last America's Cup challenge and, during the 1933 season, *Shamrock V* was raced while Frank Murdoch went around the deck measuring loads at strategic points in the rigging. He was then in a position to design the very advanced winches and the welded steel mast fitted to *Endeavour.* The yacht embodied a number of features that were years ahead of their time. For example, a wind vane on top of the mast transmitted its readings to an indicator positioned in front of the helmsman, and a lot of use was made of materials that had been developed for the aircraft industry. Contract price for the yacht, complete but without sails, was £24,000 and that included the 83 tons of lead in the keel. Total weight of *Endeavour* was 143 tons.

For the 1934 America's Cup race, Sopwith's yacht, *Endeavour,* had various fittings made at the Hawker factory and A. Benns, who later designed jigs and tools for Hurricane fighter production, can remember Thomas Sopwith standing on the stairs leading to the drawing office at Canbury Park Road and thanking his staff in the assembly shop below for their help. *Endeavour* was the first racing yacht to incorporate a quadrilateral jib, an advantage that was soon copied by the Americans.

Unfortunately, just before leaving England his professional crew went on strike for higher pay. The walk-out deeply wounded Tommy Sopwith and it was something he talked of to the end of his days whenever the America's Cup was mentioned. Likewise, the incident is a part of folklore on the East Coast of England where most of the crew lived. The majority of them were professional fishermen, times were hard and to supplement their earnings outside the fishing season they crewed the big racing yachts. When Tommy Sopwith sacked them for letting him down at the last moment it came as a shock to many of the families who expected their demands to be met. There was ill-feeling on both sides with Sopwith believing he had done his best to help the fishermen only to be held to ransom at the last moment. In the event he was forced to enter the race with a mixed bag of nine professionals and a number of amateurs.

In the first race Sopwith beat the Americans by more than two minutes. He also won the second race by more than 50 seconds. In the third race *Endeavour* had a six-minute lead but the wind dropped and, by clever helmsmanship, the American skipper of the defending *Rainbow* forced the British challenger into still lighter winds and won the race. Incidentally, *Rainbow* was crewed by Scandinavian professionals. The American defenders were so shaken by Tommy Sopwith's two wins that the rival camps of Boston and New York joined forces. Frank Paine, designer of *Yankee,* the yacht owned by the Boston Syndicate, loaned what was regarded to be the finest spinnaker in America to *Rainbow,* its ballast was changed and, when the next race started, it was a different yacht and a different crew with Harold Vanderbilt at the helm.

During the fourth race the American boat persisted on a collision course and Sopwith was forced to turn away even though unquestionably *Endeavour* had right of way. Ignoring Sopwith's luff was a deliberate act on the part of the Americans that could have seriously damaged both yachts and possibly led to injury or death, yet the New York Yacht Club committee refused to accept a protest on technical grounds. Thus was born the famous saying: 'Britannia rules the waves, but America waives the rules'.

Among the *Endeavour* crew was Frank Murdoch and he recalls that, afterwards, Sopwith behaved in his usual gentlemanly manner. There was no fuss, but he was deeply upset by the New York Yacht Club's refusal to investigate the incident, so much so that, for a time, he seriously considered withdrawing from the contest and returning home. Frank Murdoch formed the opinion that after the near-collision, and the way his complaint was handled, Tommy Sopwith lost interest in the other races. In modern times, the ruthlessness of the Americans taking part in the America's Cup races has become well-known, and it existed even then. Often as much effort seems to be devoted to interpreting the rules to US advantage as to designing, building and sailing a fair race. It could be argued that if the Americans are too competitive, the British are not aggressive enough. But the American determination to be way out in front, by whatever means, is regarded by some as an unattractive characteristic in an otherwise generous-natured people.

It was during the race that Tommy Sopwith met for the first time his old wartime adversary, the Dutch aircraft manufacturer Anthony Fokker, who had supplied the Germans with some of their finest fighters during the Great War. One of the races in the series had just ended and Sopwith was being towed back through literally thousands of vessels of all shapes and sizes:

'. . . I forget whether the race was won or lost—and I was very tired. And a motor launch came up alongside with a party of four or five people on board and a dog. And the fellow at the helm looked up at me and he said: "You Sopwith?" I said yes. He said: "I'm Fokker". I said "Christ! Come on board and have a drink".'

On board the liner taking him home, Tommy Sopwith was interviewed by the Press as it neared Southampton. Naturally the journalists asked him to comment on the behaviour of the New York Yacht Club. This was his reply:

'We are very glad to be back again. In spite of not being able to see eye-to-eye with the New York Yacht Club over the interpretation of some of their rules I hope that we shall be able to reach agreement within the near future.'

It was a restrained statement by a gentleman who was too polite to tell the world what he really thought of his treatment. Instead he went on to say:

'We have had a series of the most wonderfully close races and I find the greatest difficulty in expressing my gratitude to our crew, amateur and professional, for the wonderful work they have done—they have all worked like slaves. May I say that we are not downhearted.'

The beautifully streamlined light alloy engine cowlings on Sydney Camm's biplanes then under production were all fabricated by hand but the imperfections of panel-beating made it difficult to ensure interchangeability if ever a damaged cowling had to be replaced at the squadrons. So, after the races were over, Sopwith arranged for Frank Murdoch to visit some of the large aircraft factories in the USA where they had developed an economical method of producing large dies for use in conjunction with a drop hammer. It was quick, less labour-intensive and if the need arose to fit, say, a new top cowling, one could be sure it would mate with the existing side and other panels. The technique was adopted at Hawker's.

The last race between the big J Class yachts was held in 1937 and Sopwith entered a new challenger, *Endeavour II*. The American defender was *Ranger,* a massive yacht more than 135-feet long with a steel hull and a mast 165-ft high. The sails were enormous and it is said that the spinnaker, the largest ever made, covered more than two-fifths of an acre. Not that *Endeavour II* was exactly small, in fact she weighed 160 tons. Like the earlier *Endeavour,* the 1937 yacht had its steel hull painted an attractive blue with a white waterline and red anti-fouling paint underneath. Considering his aeronautical engineering experience it is surprising that Tommy Sopwith's *Endeavour II* did not enjoy the advantage of tank-testing at the design stage. Furthermore, Charles Nicholson, the designer of the original *Endeavour,* which, with a professional crew may well have beaten the defending *Rainbow,* quite astonishingly made details of its hull design available to the Americans who were quick to test models of it in a tank. There must have been suspicions in the American camp that the British were feeding them false information because it is very hard to understand why Charles Nicholson should want to present a competing team with such an advantage. The Americans most certainly did not send details of their yacht to the Sopwith team—they rightly regarded these as a closely guarded secret.

Charles Nicholson was, perhaps, the last of the great artist designers, but times had changed and science had overtaken art. Frank Murdoch is of the opinion that the 1934 yacht should have won, and indeed would have won, but for the near collision and the way Sopwith's protest was handled by the New York Yacht Club. In the 1937 race, however, *Endeavour II* was outclassed and beaten fairly by the technically-superior American defender.

After the 1937 America's Cup races, the Tommy Sopwith—Harold Vanderbilt yachting contests continued on a smaller scale. For the 1939 racing season the American entered his 12-Metre yacht *Vim,* and to meet the challenge Camper & Nicholsons was asked to design a new boat for Sopwith which was named *Tomahawk.* It managed to beat all the other boats in its class except Vanderbilt's.

Tommy Sopwith's love of competitive sailing did not inhibit his passion for motor yachts. From 1910 until he gave up ownership of such vessels, Lloyds Register lists a succession of ever-changing marine hardware in his name. At one period he was swapping motor yachts as freely as most people trade in cars. Studying the varied list of boats owned by him, it seems clear that Camper & Nicholsons enjoyed the major share of these Sopwith orders which ranged from 12-Metre sailing yachts to the enormous J Class racers *(Endeavour* and *Endeavour II)* as well as the various motor yachts which became bigger and better every few years.

John White was a youngster in the drawing office when one day the Sopwiths visited Camper & Nicholsons. The Works Manager, who happened to be his father, sent for him and said: 'Jump on your motorbike and deliver this package for Mrs Sopwith to this address'. On his return, Phyllis Sopwith opened her handbag, looked inside, closed it, then, turning to her husband, said: 'Tommy have you got a fiver? I want to pay the boy for his petrol'. Sopwith looked at his wife and said: 'A fiver! You're paying for his bloody bike!' Today £5 does not last very long and can be spent on a few quite trivial articles. In the 1930s a man could buy a made-to-measure suit for that.

Not long after the fiver incident, Tommy Sopwith wanted some alterations made to the interior of his current motor yacht which was called *Vita III.* Drawings were prepared by Camper & Nicholsons for three alternative schemes and the ever-willing John White was sent on his motor cycle to show them to Tommy Sopwith in his office at Hawker's. 'I think I like scheme "A" ', the valued customer said, whereupon young White said a polite good afternoon and assured him that his father would send an estimate that evening. 'Never mind the estimate,' replied Sopwith in jovial mood, 'tell him to get on with the bloody job'. Fred Sigrist happened to be in the room at the time and, as White was leaving, with a pained look on his face he turned to Sopwith and said: 'Tommy, you've forgotten to give him your cheque book with all the cheques signed'. After the war John White became Managing Director of Camper & Nicholsons.

A private liner

In 1937 Camper & Nicholsons built for Tommy Sopwith the diesel yacht, *Philante,* a name derived from those of his wife, Phyllis and Thomas Edward, his son. It was very much the small liner and one of the finest private yachts afloat. *Philante* was 263 ft long with a beam of 38 ft and a gross tonnage of 1,628 tons. The hull featured a double bottom with six watertight bulkheads and, although the weather decks (that is those exposed to the elements) had the usual camber to carry away water from heavy rain or sea spray, interior decks were flat to provide hotel standards of comfort. The latest radio such as it existed in 1937 was fitted and there was a Sperry gyro-compass which controlled a number of repeater dials and also provided heading information to the automatic helmsman. Whereas air pilots used to refer to their autopilots as 'George', the sailing fraternity used the name 'Iron Mike' for its marine versions.

Two 8-cylinder M.A.N. diesel engines, each developing 1,500 hp at 285 rpm turned 7 ft diameter, four-blade propellers and these gave *Philante* a cruising speed of 14 knots over a range of 7,000 nautical miles for which 200 tons of fuel oil were carried. There was also tankage for 15 tons of lubricating oil and, although no doubt other forms of refreshment were provided, up to 127 tons of fresh water could be carried on long journeys. In the bow area was accommodation for 24 crew followed by cabins for 18 junior officers and stewards. There were cabins for three maids in addition to the 42 crew needed to operate the yacht. Moving back along the hull, there was a sick bay, a carpenter's shop, a store room, a linen room and a 1,220 cubic ft cold storage. Midships was the 50-ft long engine room. Catering was enacted in a 23-ft by 15-ft galley provided with a choice of oil, electric or solid fuel cookers. A well-equipped workshop had a lathe, an electric drill and a milling machine. There was a steel-lined store for the sails and tackle belonging to Sopwith's J Class and 12-Metre yachts.

Accommodation consisted of eight state rooms, eight bathrooms and eight clothes rooms (in place of the usual wardrobes). The owner's 'cabin', if it can be so called, measured 30 ft by 26 ft and its furnishings included a massive four-poster bed. These were the days before stabilizers were in common use on ships and, in a heavy sea, it would have been unsafe to risk sleeping in a domestic-type bed, consequently, a small staircase led from the master state room down to a smaller sea cabin below decks. There, one could wedge into bunks when the ship was rolling.

There was a 25-ft by 13ft living-room with a proper fireplace and a ceiling domed at each corner. This led through an arch to a 12-ft by 21ft sitting room. From here, double doors opened on to the aft deck. A magnificent Adam-style dining-room, 30-ft long and 22-ft wide, featured french windows at each end. There was also a smoking room, an office and a fitted gymnasium. Décor throughout was to a very high standard, fire-resistant paint was used and a Lux CO_2 fire-fighting installation was installed. Central heating was via 80 concealed radiators, a master clock displayed the time on 37 dials throughout the yacht, a radiogram played music through 13 extension speakers and there was a grand piano.

Philante was the stuff that dreams are made of and it was probably the largest private diesel yacht ever to be built in Britain, although two slightly larger steam yachts had been launched some years previously. It seems hard to credit that, in 1937, the contract price for this magnificent private liner was little more than £100,000 excluding furnishings. In 1989, for example, such a ship would cost more than £30 million. In conjunction with Camper & Nicholsons, Tommy Sopwith took an active part in the design of *Philante* and Phyllis Sopwith worked closely with the interior designer. When *Philante* was sold, much of the furniture was used in the Sopwith's Hampshire home.

Tommy Sopwith used to hold some big parties on board *Philante.* Although he never spoke unless there was something of importance to say, he used to enjoy taking in the conversation of others. On one such occasion, some well-informed people were commenting on a number of new Government appointments that had just been announced in the Press. 'I see (so-and-so) has been made Minister of Agriculture,' said one of the guests to which another protested: 'Yes but he doesn't know anything about it'. 'And a very good thing too,' boomed the deep voice of their host.

For the 1937 America's Cup races it was originally intended that *Endeavour II* would be towed across the Atlantic by *Philante,* but the motor yacht was not ready in time. Having been towed across by an ocean-going tug the new J Class yacht joined the Sopwith contingent later. It was quite a gathering. By then the 1934 boat, *Endeavour,* had been sold to Herman Andreae, founder of Kleinwort Benson, the merchant bankers, but Fred Sigrist chartered it for use as a pacemaker while practising for the big races. So, in the Sopwith party were the original *Endeavour, Endeavour II,* the motor yacht *Philante* and Sigrist's 500-ton diesel yacht *Viva.* All told there were 104 people on the payroll—all of it privately funded because no syndicates were involved. Most of *Philante's* crew came from the Scottish Western Isles and it was almost impossible to find anyone whose name did not start with Mc or Mac. The Captain was Donald McKillop and the rest of the crew abounded with such names as McLeod. However, Sopwith's racing crews on the *Endeavour* yachts were from the east coast of England.

The return to England after the 1937 America's Cup races brought tragedy to the Sopwith team. *Philante* was towing *Endeavour II* across the Atlantic when, two days out from America, a hurricane struck and conditions at sea became very bad. Then Captain Williams, Master on board *Endeavour II,* suffered a burst ulcer. There was a medical officer on board *Philante,* but sea and wind conditions made it impossible for him to be transferred from one vessel to the other. The doctor was able to give advice over the ship-to-ship radio, but the situation was becoming critical. The White Star liner *Georgic* altered course and made for the scene of the crisis, but unfortunately Captain Williams died before he could be brought to the ship's hospital. After the races Sopwith had flown back to England and they radioed the news, so that permission could be obtained to bury Captain Williams at sea.

To add to the troubles, the original *Endeavour's* tow rope parted in the storm and a week passed without news while everyone feared the worst. Then news came that she was limping home under her own sail. She was first spotted by Mr Barnet Saidman, chief photographer of the now no longer published *News Chronicle,* who had been sent in a chartered aeroplane to locate the yacht.

Fun and games

Among his many interests Tommy Sopwith was a keen naturalist and on two occasions he sailed *Philante* to the Galapagos Islands which abound in unusual wildlife. Among the guests was his niece from America, the daughter of his eldest sister Violet. Her name was also Violet, although she is known as 'Toots' among the Sopwith family. More than 50 years later she remembered the wonderful party spirit on board. Tommy Sopwith was in great form and they brought back eight iguanas and twelve penguins for the London Zoo. To assist in identifying their unusual passengers, letters 'A', 'B', 'C', 'D' and so on were painted on the iguanas. The penguins rapidly became used to humans and one can picture Sopwith and his sophisticated guests playing with these endearing creatures while sailing on one of the finest private yachts in the world.

While at anchor, small purpose-designed harnesses were fitted to the birds, a fishing-line was attached and, to give them exercise, they were dumped over the side to splash around in the sea. When time came to shout: 'Come in number 25, your time is up', the lines would be wound in and the penguins came back aboard to waddle to their pen. A penguin's great charm and friendly nature is apparently accompanied by a total lack of intelligence. If, on the way back to their pen, someone's feet were in the way they would never consider avoiding them. With some difficulty first one would hop over and, having set an example, all the others would do the same. These antics were a source of endless enjoyment to the Sopwith's and their guests.

During the second visit, while still some distance from the islands, the crew of *Philante* picked up a distress signal from the diesel yacht *Sans Peur III* which had struck uncharted rocks off the coast of Mexico. On board was the Duke of Sutherland, a friend of Sopwith's and a fellow member of the Royal Yacht Squadron. Fortunately, they managed to beach *Sans Peur III* before offering the shipwrecked party a comfortable, safe passage on board *Philante*.

Someone once asked how many crew were required to run *Philante* and Tommy Sopwith replied: 'We made do with 42'. 'And how many guests did you carry on these long trips?' was the next question, which brought the response: 'Never more than eight—and by the time we got to the Needles they were all arguing among each other'.

As a youngster, Thomas Edward Sopwith's special treat for Sunday lunch on board *Philante* was ginger beer and a baked potato. On one Sunday he vividly remembers going through the Kiel Canal and passing one of the German Pocket Battleships steaming in the opposite direction. One wonders who was the more impressed—those on board *Philante* at the sight of Hitler's pride-and-joy, or the German sailors contemplating Tommy Sopwith's private liner, one of the largest diesel yachts in the world.

Change of ownerships

During World War 2 Commodore (later Vice-Admiral) Sir Gilbert 'Puggy' Stephenson was ordered to set up and run some anti U-boat patrols in Norwegian waters. Needing a headquarters he asked the Admiralty for a suitable ship in which to base himself and they told him to go out and get one, much as one might tell the gardener to buy a new lawnmower. Enquiries among the London club fraternity revealed that *Philante,* by then impressed into the Royal Navy, was being somewhat underemployed in the Portsmouth area, picking up practice-torpedoes out of the sea, and she became his HQ soon afterwards.

During the war *Philante* returned to Camper & Nicholsons for a re-fit and, learning of this, the Sopwiths motored to see their beautiful yacht in the shipyard and had drinks with the captain on the bridge. John White arrived to see the Sopwiths' Rolls-Royce parked on the quayside and, recognizing the chauffeur, he enquired: 'Hallo, Duncan, how are they?' Back came the reply: 'She is the same as ever and he, as ever, would sooner spend ten-thousand quid than ten bob'.

Donald McKillop, the captain employed by Tommy Sopwith before the war, had remained skipper of *Philante*, but admiring it in the hands of others must have felt rather like being invited to visit the home that had been taken away from you. Frank Murdoch accompanied the Sopwiths during the visit to Camper & Nicholsons and he remembers how sad they were after seeing their once beautiful ocean-going yacht in its stark, wartime condition.

The Admiralty actually paid for *Philante* and, after the war, she was bought back by Tommy Sopwith. However, with memories of post-war conditions following the 1914-18 conflict, he readily accepted an offer for her from the Association of Norwegian Ship Owners. In 1947 *Philante* was bought by the association, re-named *Norge* and presented to King Haakon VII on the occasion of his seventy-fifth birthday, for use as the Royal Yacht, a duty she performs to this day. Since then, there have been a number of changes to the superstructure and the interior has been completely re-fitted to suit the needs of various members of the royal family and staff. It so happens that, some years previously, while 12-Metre yacht racing in Scandinavia, Tommy Sopwith had come to know the King of Norway who, in turn, admired *Philante*. So, if Tommy Sopwith felt it necessary to dispose of his beautiful yacht, at least he knew she was going to a good home.

The sale of *Philante* to the King of Norway had an amusing sequel because, in 1954, Tommy Sopwith noticed that a horse named, *Philante,* was running in one of the races. He decided to place a small bet on behalf of himself and the King. Although the horse failed to win, it was placed and, on 7 June 1954, Tommy wrote the following letter to the King's Private Secretary:

I am glad that His Majesty's sporting instinct allowed him to take an interest in our little wager, which has shown a small profit, as we backed Philante "both ways", and the net result is that I owe His Majesty £10, made up as follows:

> *£5 invested to win at 50-1*
> *£5 invested for a place at 5-1*
> *producing £25 for place*
> *less   £ 5 loss for stake to win*
> *   £20*
> *Half cash £10*

Now I am in trouble. How can I send you £10 without breaking our laws? [In 1954 there were restrictions on sending money out of Britain.].

If you agree I will leave it with your ambassador who will, I am sure, know how to deal with it.

Will you please thank His Majesty for his kind message. Alas we could never hope to derive as much pleasure from this Philante as the original, but I would like to wish His Majesty many years happy cruising in Norge.

Tommy Sopwith decided to deliver the King's share of the winnings personally to the ambassador, but, for some reason, he entered the Soviet Embassy believing it to be Norwegian. There he was held in an outer office and treated with some suspicion while some officials 'checked him out'. The cash eventually reached the King of Norway through his embassy in London.

The subsequent story of Tommy Sopwith's first J Class yacht, *Endeavour,* which came near to winning the 1934 America's Cup races, is remarkable. Many years after the war it was found derelict on a mudbank, plates rusted through and the sea pouring in and out with the tide. The Maritime Trust bought the wreck and wanted to restore it, so an approach was made to Tommy Sopwith who made it clear that he was more interested in looking forward than trying to re-create the past. While refusing to help finance the project, he sent a £10,000 donation to the Trust.

Some time later *Endeavour* was bought by Mr John Amos, an enthusiast of limited means, who bravely tried to rebuild the 130-ft hull. More than 60 quarter-inch thick steel plates measuring 14 ft × 3 ft 6 in had to be rolled to the correct shape before they could be replaced and they were costing him £200 each. The quotation for a new keel was £60,000, a replacement 160-ft mast would have been another £30,000 and some of the main sails were expected to cost about £25,000 each.

It was a brave attempt, but the money ran out and Amos was forced to sell the partly-repaired hull to Miss Elizabeth Ernst Meyer, a keen American yachtswoman who is a member of the *Washington Post* family. During the late 1980s *Endeavour* was restored to its former glory at a shipyard at Vollenhove, Holland, and, because of his intimate knowledge of the yacht, Frank Murdoch was retained as consultant. In 1989 he was a remarkably youthful and active 85-year-old, making regular trips to Holland and the USA during the restoration of this historic yacht.

Usually, whenever Frank Murdoch or the owner visited Holland the wind blew and it poured with rain, but for the recommissioning ceremony, held on 20 May, 1989, a blue sky smiled down on perfect weather. Some 600 people attended the party which started with a speech by the Mayor of Vollenhove, followed by appropriate words from the owner of the shipyard, the naval architect and the new owner, Miss Elizabeth Ernst Meyer. Then Frank Murdoch was called upon to give a potted history of *Endeavour*. During the barbecue that followed there was music, dancing and champagne flowed. The party ended with Elizabeth Ernst Meyer being hoisted to the top of the mast which is more than 160 feet above the water. The height of her ascent was exceeded by the magnitude of the final account—the cost of restoring *Endeavour* has been quoted as approaching eight million dollars.

The fate of Tommy Sopwith's other J Class yacht, *Endeavour II,* was less happy. In 1947 he sold her for a mere £7,000 to a firm which promptly removed the 87 tons of lead from the keel and then put the hull on sale. Sadly, this magnificent yacht was reduced to scrap. However, the events just described have taken us many years ahead of the story which must now return to pre-war days when racing 12-Metre yachts and the big J Class boats was of such appeal to the sportsman in Tommy Sopwith. This was an outlet for his competitive spirit, but his great pride was the magnificent ocean-going motor yacht *Philante.*

Sadly he was only able to enjoy owning *Philante,* one of the finest private vessels in the world, for little more than two years before Hitler set events into motion that resulted in Europe being ablaze for the second time in 25 years. Then the delights of luxury sailing and competitive yachting had to make way for the challenges of building aeroplanes on the grand scale. They had to be good. And they had to be manufactured quickly, because they were desperately needed for the defence of Britain and the defeat of Nazi Germany.

CHAPTER
8

The Challenges
of World War 2

WHEN LATE IN 1939 conflict erupted in Europe and rapidly became global, Tommy Sopwith found himself, for the second time in his life, running a large aircraft manufacturing concern in times of war. To visualize this period of his career it is first necessary to set the scene and recount the events leading up to World War 2.

During the 1920s and early 1930s a succession of pacificatory British governments allowed the defences of the nation to languish as a matter of deliberate policy. The Army seemed more interested in horses than tanks (a policy that was to cost it dearly when war broke out a few years later), the Royal Navy continued to regard the aeroplane as some kind of toy (it learned better when the Japanese Air Force destroyed its mighty battleships in the Far East) while the Royal Air Force had to make do with biplanes long after the rest of the world had consigned these to the museum.

The policy of unilateral pacifism and appeasement knew no political boundaries; it was pursued by Tory Prime Minister Stanley Baldwin, furthered by the Labour Prime Minister Ramsay MacDonald, and continued with tenacity by his Conservative replacement, Neville Chamberlain. A sincerely-held belief in pacifism is, of course, not to be ridiculed but, in the face of all the signs emanating from a truculent Germany under Adolf Hitler, it could be argued that to pin one's faith in appealing to the man's better nature was an act of folly. And when pacifism is extended to denying the nation its means of defence, those responsible must surely be accused of, at the very least, wilfully neglecting one of their prime duties, safeguarding the security of the state.

By 1935 the constant warnings of Winston Churchill, at times a lone voice in a hostile and unreceptive House of Commons, had proved to be true. Despite Hitler's constant plea that all he wanted was peace, Germany was rearming fast, the Luftwaffe had a range of modern aircraft at its disposal, most of them battle-tested during the Spanish Civil War which broke out in 1936. U-boats abounded, and German tanks were the finest in the world; at no period in the war could any Allied tank match the German's.

Both within and outside the Hawker Siddeley company new, and in some cases, excellent military aircraft were on paper or at the prototype stage. Unfortunately, politicians have difficulty in grasping that paper aeroplanes cannot defend nations or win wars. Prototypes have to be built, tested, modified in the light of experience, and only then put into production, *provided* the design is up to expectations. Some aeroplanes never reach that stage; they fall by the wayside because of serious design flaws. The problem with this procedure is that it requires that most valuable of commodities in periods of crisis—time. And in the mid-to-late 1930s, with Germany annexing Czechoslovakia, followed by Austria and greedy eyes turned on Poland, time was something that Britain and its ally, France, did not have.

Poland was the moment of truth for Britain and France. Both countries had signed agreements promising aid to the Poles if Germany invaded their country but by then the damage was done. Neville Chamberlain had sold out Czechoslovakia because, in his opinion, it was a far-away country, unknown to the British people and not of sufficient consequence to merit thoughts of war. Many well-informed people believe that this was a prime misjudgement because the Czechs had a long engineering tradition and their powerful, well-equipped armed forces, combined with those of France and Britain, could have called Hitler's bluff or even defeated the German army and air forces as they existed at the time. In the event, Chamberlain and his Cabinet chose instead to make their final stand behind a Poland whose army was even more ill-equipped than the British ground forces, and whose air force was hopelessly outclassed.

It is perhaps natural that having seen Britain and France stand by while he marched into neighbouring countries, Hitler felt secure in the belief that his entry into Poland would provoke nothing more serious than verbal rebukes. This was hardly surprising; German audacity had paid off on several previous occasions, each time strengthening Hitler's position *vis-à-vis* his more cautious high command, each time building up confidence at a converse rate to his respect for the Allies. A strong body of opinion now believes that Hitler was misled into the Polish invasion by the previous inaction on the part of Britain and France. Be that as it may, march into Poland he did and on 3 September Britain and France were at war with an expansionist Germany for the second time in living memory.

What happened next is well-documented history; German tanks were pitted against Polish horses and, understandably, Poland collapsed in a matter of weeks. The bankruptcy of Chamberlain's policy of disarmament and appeasement had been dramatically confirmed and so had Tommy Sopwith's fear that, because of that policy, war with Germany was inevitable.

After a false period of inactivity while Germany reorganized its military machine and the French deployed its troops underground within the Maginot Line, the Allies were surprised when Hitler's magnificent army burst through Belgium, outflanked the Maginot Line and a demoralized French army found itself hopelessly outclassed. Britain's small expeditionary force fought a rearguard action to Dunkerque on the coast and, in the face of heavy German land, sea and air attacks, a high proportion of the men were brought back to England, albeit without their equipment. Now the United Kingdom faced the might of Germany alone and preparations were put in hand to counter an expected invasion.

In 1940, Britain's situation was very serious. Its exhausted army was, in the main, without equipment, modern or otherwise, and pathetic measures were being taken to arm the Home Guard (a home-security, part-time army consisting mainly of Great War veterans) with crude petrol bombs and pikes made from broomsticks fitted with welded steel points. Tiger Moth trainers were fitted with light bomb racks and, at an Elementary Flying Training School operated at Desford by Major George Reid (who had earlier set up a business with Fred Sigrist making aircraft instruments), a Tiger Moth was fitted experimentally with a small hand-scythe on the end of a ten-foot steel tube. When, as was now expected, the German paratroops arrived, scores of Tiger Moths were supposed to lower their scythes and fly among the parachutes, cutting their canopies. Thus, the 'weapon' was called the 'Paraslasher'. Only one was made and fortunately, thanks in the main to Tommy Sopwith's Hurricane and smaller numbers of Spitfires, it never had to be used.

Minister of Aircraft Production during the early part of the war was the dynamic and at times theatrical Lord Beaverbrook who did much to stimulate the rate at which aircraft were being turned out at the factories although there were times when his methods, while often effective, were more than a little dramatic. One of his less praiseworthy acts was to announce that it was the duty of every garage mechanic to apply for a job at the nearest aircraft factory. At the Hawker plant in Canbury Park Road 3,000 people formed a queue and wanted to get in. The firm was swamped and unable to deal with such an influx of new labour on this scale. The staff department had no idea who was on the payroll (and, even worse, who was not) and the situation became chaotic. It so happened that John Lidbury had just arrived at Hawker's as Assistant Company Secretary. Turmoil was rampant and his first task was to bring order to the chaos. Lidbury had known Tommy Sopwith and Frank Spriggs in 1938 when he was with the Royal Exchange Insurance Company. At their invitation, he joined Hawker's at Kingston in 1940, at first to look after company insurance then, as time went by he became more involved in aircraft.

Eventually, he reached Managing Director level and gained a knighthood—another example of Tommy Sopwith picking the right person for the job.

Fred Sigrist

Fred Sigrist, one of Tommy Sopwith's original 'gang', was regarded as ruthless with his staff, very ambitious and passionately fond of money which he preferred to keep rather than spend. Certainly he was good at managing his assets and, as previously mentioned, when H. G. Hawker Engineering was formed in 1920 he had an equal shareholding with Sopwith. Many years later Sir John Lidbury, by then Managing Director of Hawker Siddeley Aircraft, asked his Chairman how it was that Sigrist, a man with little education and without formal engineering training, had become so wealthy within a relatively few years. Tommy Sopwith replied:

'Didn't you know? When we got going at the rink [the original works in Kingston] in 1912, I said to him: "Fred I'll give you 50 quid for every aeroplane we produce". We had an order for two, then we built four the next year; then the war happened and we built thousands of aircraft and I had to cough up.'

In fairness to Fred Sigrist, when during the Great War aircraft started pouring out of the Sopwith factory at an undreamed of rate, he suggested a smaller bonus per aircraft. Needless to say, Tommy Sopwith insisted on keeping his end of the bargain and so the garage mechanic from Southampton became a millionaire. He was fortunate to have been born at the right time with exceptional engineering talents. And he was even more fortunate to have become involved with Tommy Sopwith who steered his talents in the right direction.

Some of those who knew Sigrist well felt that his ruthlessness was a reaction to what he imagined to be his social inequality. If that were so it was a pity because the man had genius and had made his mark in the aviation world. His disposition towards those junior to himself became worse towards the end of his active life with the company. He suffered from asthma, ulcers and a decline in general health, but Sopwith always claimed that behind his tough exterior was a kind heart. If ever Sigrist sacked anyone (which was not an unusual occurrence) he would always ensure that there was no financial hardship while another job was being found. But his attraction to making money was a byword among the workforce and on one occasion, when they held a staff party, someone produced a monologue entitled *A day in the life of Hawker Aircraft,* part of which went something like this:

8:00	Work Starts.
11:00	Sigrist arrives.
11:05	Sigrist in touch with stockbroker.

12:00	Sigrist still talking to stockbroker.
12:45	Sigrist goes to lunch. Stockbroker buys new Rolls-Royce.
13:00	Lunch at Station Hotel. Spriggs offers cigars. Sopwith smokes his own.

Sopwith liked a good cigar but Spriggs had a habit of buying the cheapest in the land, although he too could have afforded the best.

At the start of the war Fred Sigrist was in such poor health that he was sent by his doctor to the Bahamas where it was hoped that the climate would do him good. By then he was a multi-millionaire and he increased his wealth several fold by investing in property. By 1940 he had recovered sufficiently to join the British Air Commission as a 'trouble shooter' dealing with US manufacturers on the west coast of America which were supplying the RAF with aircraft during the early part of World War 2. His daughter 'Bobo' was something of a socialite on the island and rarely out of the newspapers for one reason or another. When Sigrist left Britain, Tommy Sopwith bought from him Warfield Hall, his beautiful mansion near Bracknell, and the Sopwiths lived there until Compton Manor, with its 2,200 acres of countryside, was purchased at the end of the war in 1945.

*   *   *

When World War 2 started in September 1939 Tommy Sopwith's son, Thomas Edward, was a boy of seven. Being the only child of a man with an industrial empire, it is natural that his father should have considered the consequences if Hitler's armies had invaded Britain. In the opinion of Thomas Edward Sopwith, however:

'I think he made the wrong decision for totally the right reasons; I was evacuated to America. If I had been in his position I would have done exactly the same thing. But what it meant was there was a three-and-a-half year period of my life when I literally didn't see him at all. But then lots of other people didn't see their parents during the war because they were away fighting.'

In this respect, Thomas Edward Sopwith, son of a wealthy father, was no different to many hundreds of other children who were also evacuated to such countries as Canada and the USA. At the time, not only was there an invasion risk but the Luftwaffe bombs were falling, great areas of Britain's larger cities were being destroyed and their populations were dying in the thousands. It was a war policy that the Germans would live to regret when RAF Bomber Command grew in strength and paid return visits with bombers carrying five times the war-load of the best aircraft available to the Luftwaffe.

Many of the RAF bombers that took the war into Germany were Avro Lancasters built at Hawker Siddeley's Manchester factory and elsewhere.

However, young Thomas Edward was packed off across the Atlantic, initially to stay in a hotel near his 'Uncle' Fred Sigrist who was already in the Bahamas. Sigrist, incidentally, was Thomas Edward's godfather. With him was his beloved Aunt May who had been his father's faithful supporter during his pioneer flying days. They remained in Nassau with the Sigrist family for a year before going on to the USA. A rough diamond and ruthless with his staff Fred Sigrist may have been, but Thomas Edward was very fond of a man whom he regards to this day as absolutely genuine and 'the salt of the earth'.

Air power

In 1940 no country recognized the importance of air power more clearly than Germany although, paradoxically, Britain was later to prove more adept in its application. However, before Hitler could bring his victorious armies across the English Channel in the face of the Royal Navy, he had first to destroy the Royal Air Force which was known to have a small but modern force of fighters. It was what the Germans did not know that had such a profound influence on the events to come. As early as 1940, Britain had a series of radar station at a high state of readiness and these allowed Fighter Command to position its limited aircraft to best advantage and at short notice. Usually the RAF fighters were up there waiting for the Luftwaffe as it swarmed in across the English Channel; this gave the impression that Britain had a much larger fighter force than was envisaged by German intelligence.

The Battle of Britain, which was fought between July and November, 1940, has assumed such importance because, for the first time, Hitler's 'invincible' Luftwaffe had been stopped and defeated by a smaller and less experienced air force. Of the 55 RAF squadrons available to defend Britain, no fewer than 26 of them flew Hurricanes, while 20 had Spitfires, 2 flew the Boulton Paul Defiant, and 7 operated the obsolete twin-engine Bristol Blenheim. On 6 July, that year, the RAF mustered only 871 fighters against which the Luftwaffe was able to launch more than 3,300 aircraft of all types. By the end of the battle Germany had lost 1,733 aircraft and another 643 had been damaged, a total of 2,376 compared with a not very exaggerated figure of 2,692 claimed to be 'destroyed' by RAF pilots in the heat of battle.

By the end of the Battle of Britain, the RAF actually had 200 more fighters at operational readiness than when the action started. At that stage Reichmarschall Goring decided to stop sending his aircraft over Britain in daylight before he no longer had a Luftwaffe. The invasion of Britain was off. Tommy Sopwith's decision to put in hand 1,000 Hurricanes without waiting for the Government order was probably the most important single factor in the outcome of that historic battle.

During the period 1 June to 2 November, 1940, Hawker Siddeley manufactured 1,423 Hurricanes while Vickers Supermarine built 765 Spitfires over the same period. Being a more modern design the Spitfire was some 40 mph faster and it had a slightly better rate of climb. The Hurricane, however, was a very effective fighting machine, quick to build, immensely strong and easy to repair; most of the enemy bullets simply went through the fabric covers, leaving holes that could easily be patched. What Tommy Sopwith had achieved with his Camel during the Great War was repeated during 1940 by Sydney Camm's steel-tube-and-fabric masterpiece. Compared with the Sopwith Camel of the First World War the Hawker Hurricane was more than five-and-a-half times the weight, eight times the power, almost three times as fast, and it carried eight guns instead of just two. Yet it was far less demanding to fly than the old biplane.

The 12 May, 1942, issue of the *News Chronicle* featured an interview with Sydney Camm. He told the reporter that he had never seen one of his Hurricane fighters fire its guns in anger and said: 'I never imagined it would be used against the Germans'. This is surprising because events in Europe had for a number of years been rolling towards the edge of disaster, yet until the last two weeks of August, 1939, Camm refused to believe that there was going to be a war. Tommy Sopwith, on the other hand, had no illusions.

Stuart 'Cock' Davies, who was actively connected with the design of the Hurricane, was once asked after the war why the Spitfire seemed to have captured the public's imagination and he replied: 'We don't mind who gets the credit so long as we don't get the blame'. Although, later in the war, the Hurricane was outclassed as an interceptor fighter it continued to give a good account of itself as a ground-attack aircraft. It was the first Allied fighter during World War 2 to be equipped with rockets, while another version sported two massive 40mm-guns which caused havoc among German vehicles and their smaller coastal ships.

By early 1943 more than 12,500 people were employed by Hawker's and production of Hurricanes had reached its peak at 279 per month. Its production continued until July, 1944. By then 15,195 had been built (3,000 of them for Russia) and the final example, named *The Last of the Many,* was repurchased by Hawker Siddeley and is now flown in pristine condition by the RAF Battle of Britain Flight.

It would be unreasonable to expect all aircraft from Sopwith's remarkable Hawker Siddeley concern to be winners. An example of one that failed to make the grade was the Hawker Henley which was originally intended to be a light bomber, one of those unrealistic ideas that emanated from time to time from the pre-war Air Ministry. During the war it soon became the practice to carry bombs on fighters and the Henley was relegated to the task of target-towing, a hazardous occupation for the pilot who was required to trail a sleeve at the end of a long cable while others practised air-to-air gunnery with live ammunition. Some would argue that it was the Air Ministry's concept which was wrong, not Sydney Camm's design, which was some 50 mph faster than the Fairey Battle that was eventually awarded the contract for the RAF, and which suffered badly at the hands of the Luftwaffe when the fighting started.

Another Hawker Siddeley aeroplane that did not make the grade was the Albemarle built by Armstrong Whitworth Aircraft Ltd, of Baginton, Coventry. Because it was intended to be an insurance against a possible shortage of light alloys should U-boat activities deny the supply of aluminium ore to Britain, the Albemarle was constructed of wood and steel. Although it was originally intended to be a bomber, payload of the production examples was so disappointing that the Albemarle was relegated to towing gliders. In fairness to the Armstrong Whitworth team, the design originated from the Bristol Aeroplane Co as its type No 155. It was not, however, one of that company's better efforts.

The Avro Lancaster bomber

When people write about Tommy Sopwith there is a tendency to confine his aviation activities entirely to Hawker. This, of course, is understandable because the company named after his prodigy, Harry Hawker, represented the re-birth of Sopwith Aviation. But he was also very involved with the Armstrong Whitworth Whitley twin-engine bomber which performed an important, if limited, role early in the war; the Avro Manchester, which failed because its Rolls-Royce Vulture engines could not be developed to give reliable service in the time available during World War 2; and the aircraft that later replaced the Manchester, the four-engine Avro Lancaster. However Sopwith's involvement with these aeroplanes was largely confined to the boardroom. Although the serious problems being caused at A. V. Roe through the failure of the Rolls-Royce Vulture engine were naturally discussed by the main Board directors, the task of discontinuing the Manchester design and concentrating on the outstanding Lancaster would have been left to the local Managing Director and his Chief Designer.

The old established company of A. V. Roe operated from two large plants in the Manchester area, one at Chadderton and the other from the firm's own airfield at Woodford. The scale of Tommy Sopwith's wartime aircraft industry may be understood when it is realized that, in 1941, when money values were very different from those of today, the wages bill at A. V. Roe alone was in excess of one million pounds per month. Chief Designer during the war period was the brilliant Roy Chadwick and the Managing Director was Roy Dobson (later Sir Roy), a tough character greatly admired by Tommy Sopwith, although the two men were of totally different temperament.

While the uninspired but dependable Whitley (a product of the

Armstrong Whitworth division of Hawker Siddeley) mounted the early bombing raids over Germany in company with the excellent Vickers Wellington, work was pressing ahead within the UK aircraft industry on two four-engine heavy bombers. First to enter RAF service was the Short Stirling, a massive, square-cut flying battleship with a rather ungainly double-jointed undercarriage. It could carry about 14,000 lb of bombs, more than three times the load of the twin-engine Wellington, but then its maximum operating altitude was little more than 12,000 ft where it was well within reach of Germany's accurate anti-aircraft guns.

Next heavy bomber to appear was the Halifax, a product of the Handley Page company and a rather smaller aircraft than the Stirling, although it could carry a similar bomb load both faster and higher. After it seemed clear that the Rolls-Royce Vulture engine would have to be scrapped, Roy Chadwick was pressed to concentrate on a version fitted with four of the tried-and-true Merlins. Thus was born the Avro Lancaster, which Air Chief-Marshall Sir Arthur Harris (AOC in C Bomber Command during the war) later claimed was the greatest single factor in winning World War 2. While Tommy Sopwith was not involved in the detailed design of this superb aircraft its emergence and production was yet another of his overall responsibilities. The Lancaster was, far and away, the best heavy bomber flown by any air force at the time, on either side in the war. It carried a bomb load of up to 22,000 lb—three times that of the B17 Flying Fortress. Because it flew faster than the other heavy bombers, and considerably higher than either the Stirling or the Halifax, statistically a Lancaster crew had a higher life expectancy than its opposite numbers flying other types of heavy bomber. The Lancaster was strong, reliable, loved by its crews and a monument to its outstanding designer, Roy Chadwick. Nearly seven thousand of the big bombers were built in Britain and another 430 came from Canada.

Naturally, the various divisions within Hawker Siddeley had their own management teams but if things went wrong the buck ultimately stopped at one desk—that of Tommy Sopwith. When World War 2 started in September, 1939, Sopwith was almost 52 years old. From small beginnings he had built up two very large aircraft industries over a period of 30 years and although he had known good times he most certainly had an intimate knowledge of the bad. He never forgot the tragic loss of his father, his first wife had died while he was away and there had been the forced liquidation of his greatly-admired Sopwith Aviation. However, when meeting the man face-to-face there were no outward signs of strain, and the ups-and-downs of life seemed not to have left a mark.

What was Sopwith like to work with in the 1940s? John Lidbury (later Sir John, Managing Director of Hawker Aircraft and Deputy MD of the Hawker Siddeley Group) remembers that Tommy Sopwith never had any

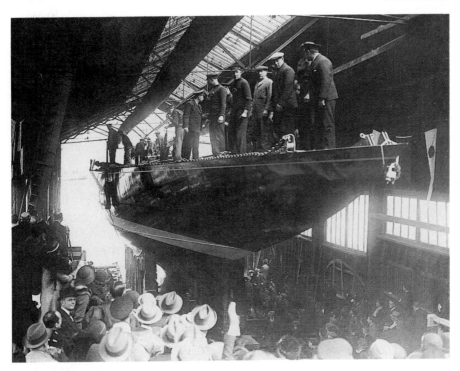

The launch of *Endeavour*, Sopwith's first challenge for the America's Cup.

Endeavour (near camera) under trial.

A study in concentration: Tommy Sopwith at the helm of *Endeavour* while Phyllis Sopwith looks on.

Endeavour II under sail.

Relaxing on deck. Tommy Sopwith sits on a capstan while *Endeavour II* makes its way. To the right of Phyllis Sopwith (foreground) is her sister, Kay Strickland.

A private ocean liner, the magnificent 1,600 ton *Philante* diesel yacht built for Tommy Sopwith by Camper and Nicholsons and launched in 1937.

Philante's main vestibule.

Tommy Sopwith's study on board *Philante*.

A corner of *Philante*'s smoke room.

The owner's stateroom on board *Philante*.

The *Philante*'s dining room.

The grand piano in the right-hand corner gives scale to this picture of *Philante*'s lounge.

Part of *Philante*'s engine room.

Tommy Sopwith and his penguin passengers on board *Philante* during a visit to the Galapagos Isles.

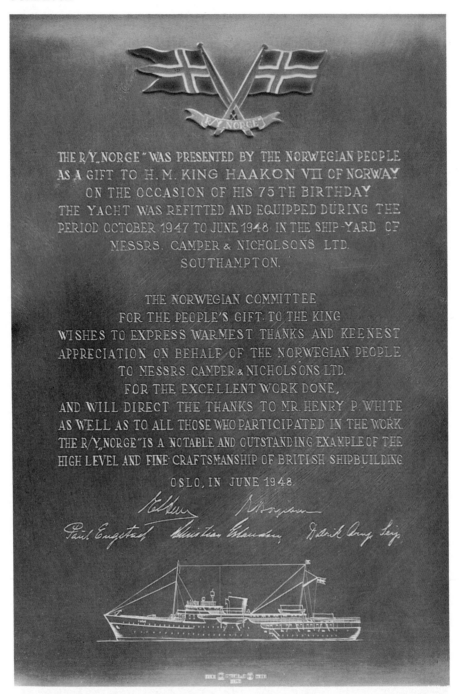

THE R/Y. NORGE "WAS PRESENTED BY THE NORWEGIAN PEOPLE
AS A GIFT TO H. M. KING HAAKON VII OF NORWAY
ON THE OCCASION OF HIS 75TH BIRTHDAY
THE YACHT WAS REFITTED AND EQUIPPED DURING THE
PERIOD OCTOBER 1947 TO JUNE 1948 IN THE SHIP-YARD OF
MESSRS. CAMPER & NICHOLSONS LTD.
SOUTHAMPTON.

THE NORWEGIAN COMMITTEE
FOR THE PEOPLE'S GIFT TO THE KING
WISHES TO EXPRESS WARMEST THANKS AND KEENEST
APPRECIATION ON BEHALF OF THE NORWEGIAN PEOPLE
TO MESSRS. CAMPER & NICHOLSONS LTD.
FOR THE EXCELLENT WORK DONE,
AND WILL DIRECT THE THANKS TO MR. HENRY P. WHITE
AS WELL AS TO ALL THOSE WHO PARTICIPATED IN THE WORK
THE R/Y. NORGE" IS A NOTABLE AND OUTSTANDING EXAMPLE OF THE
HIGH LEVEL AND FINE CRAFTSMANSHIP OF BRITISH SHIPBUILDING

OSLO, IN JUNE 1948.

Paul Engstad   Christian Brandsum   Fredrik Anny Leip

Plaque of appreciation, commissioned by the Norwegian Committee for the People's Gift of the Royal Yacht *Norge* (ex *Philante*) to the King of Norway on his 75th birthday.

Warfield Hall, the country mansion Tommy Sopwith purchased from Fred Sigrist when he retired to the Bahamas in 1940.

Hawker Hurricane fighters in the final assembly shop at Langley, one of several production lines that churned out more than 15,000 of these immortal aircraft.

A formation of Hawker Typhoon fighters of No 56 Squadron. This formidable aircraft was built to replace the long-serving Hurricane.

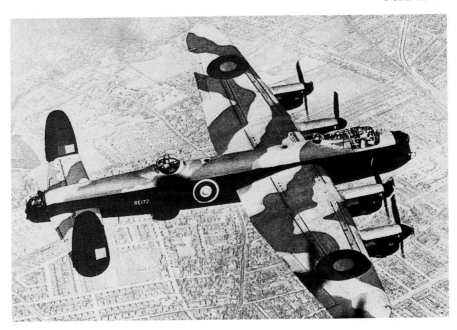

The Avro Lancaster, finest heavy bomber to serve in the European theatre during World War 2.

Roy Chadwick, gifted designer of the Lancaster and other successful aircraft.

Avro Anson Mk 20, a post-war development of the original design which emerged in 1935. It was built in great numbers, initially for coastal patrol duties although later its main role was as a pilot and aircrew trainer.

Hawker's Langley factory which was opened in 1939, shortly before the Second World War, to deal with mass production of Hurricane fighters.

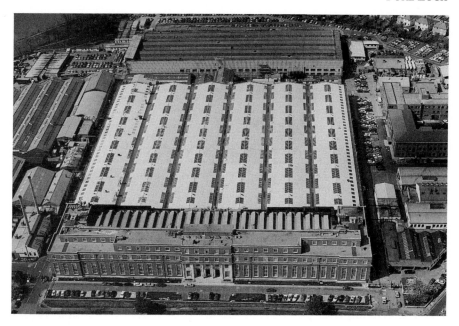

For many years headquarters of the Hawker company, the administrative and drawing offices fronting Richmond Road, Kingston-upon-Thames, were rebuilt under the direction of Sir John Lidbury, but not without some opposition from his colleagues.

The Avro factory at Chadderton, Manchester.

Avro's other works and company airfield at Woodford, Manchester.

The Second World War shadow factory at Squires Gate, Blackpool, in the north of England, where Hawker Hunter jet fighters were later produced in the 1950s.

small talk; if he had nothing to say his lips were sealed. At Board meetings he would sit there taking in what was being said, polishing the bowl of his pipe against the side of his nose, and making no comment unless there was a need. But he always knew what was going on and his fellow directors were never in any doubt about that. Among many of the top brass at Hawker Siddeley, he was known as 'The Skipper', a title that originated from his yachting exploits. Others referred to him as 'Mr Sopwith', until he was knighted; then most people called him 'Sir Thomas'.

The Typhoon and Tempest

Just as during the Great War aircraft manufacturers on opposing sides were constantly striving for more and more performance in an effort to beat their respective enemies, so it was between 1939 and 1945. Initially the Messerschmitt Bf109 could match the level speed of early Supermarine Spitfires, and it was faster than the Hawker Hurricane. However it was dreadfully noisy, difficult to see out of and unforgiving when mishandled. As a consequence, it was unable to match either of the British aeroplanes as a fighting machine, although it could outdive both. As a bewildering succession of new models appeared the Spitfire rapidly increased its performance lead. Then the remarkable Focke Wolf 190 arrived on the scene; the Luftwaffe had produced the proverbial rabbit out of a hat and the 190 could out-perform the contemporary Spitfire V. However, it was not long before the Supermarine company found the answer in still further improved models and, from the Spitfire Mk IX onwards, the Germans were never able to match the RAF's piston engine fighters.

In contrast to the Spitfire, which was built in more than 20 different models, Hawker's Hurricane was confined to only six. It should not be thought, however, that this reflected any lack of energy on the part of Tommy Sopwith and his Board. Aircraft designers have to be several jumps ahead; what enters production this week is last week's news—today has brought a new challenge. The key to better performance rests largely on the availability of suitable engines and this applies equally to civil or military aircraft. Step by step with advancements being made by the airframe manufacturers, aero engine designers strive for more power, lower fuel consumption, lighter weight and better reliability. So it was that by the mid-1930s, several of the leading British engine manufacturers were proposing to build motors delivering more than twice-the-power of the original Rolls-Royce Merlin.

The Bristol concern was developing its 18-cylinder Centaurus, Napier had the 24-cylinder Sabre in the pipeline, and at Rolls-Royce work was in progress on the ill-fated Vulture, which proved to be one of the few unsuccessful engines to emerge from that great company. Under more normal circumstances the Vulture might have been developed into a reliable power unit, but time was pressing during World War 2, the Rolls-Royce Merlin was in constant demand and continually being developed to provide more power, so the Vulture engine was dropped.

The Hurricane had barely reached the production stage before Tommy Sopwith and his Board were taking note of these new engines and the opportunities that they presented for a new generation of fighters. Work on a new project, capable of exploiting these high-powered engines, was put in hand and Sydney Camm designed a big, tough-looking fighter, very much heavier than either the Hurricane or the Spitfire. Originally it was to be armed with no fewer than 12 machine-guns, while an alternative version would have had six 20-mm cannon, but there were delays in the delivery of these heavy machine-guns.

Sopwith and his Board sanctioned design studies for versions using each of the three new engines. The one fitted with a Rolls-Royce Vulture was called the Hawker Tornado. However, continuing engine problems led to the cancellation of the aircraft. Another design with more or less the same airframe as the Tornado but powered by Napier's massive Sabre engine, which eventually delivered 2,260 hp, was called the Typhoon and made its first flight on 24 February, 1940. The Sabre engine was far from trouble free. It was a sleeve valve design and, possibly because Napier lacked experience with this type of engine, it was plagued with failures. In fact, the fate of the Typhoon hung in the balance until the late Air Commodore 'Rod' Banks, at the time Director General of Engine Production (later Director of Engine Research and Development), insisted on the Bristol Aero Engine company supplying its well-proved sleeves for the Napier engine. Although it was outclassed at height, the Typhoon developed into a formidable and highly successful ground-attack aircraft.

History had yet again repeated itself; the old Hawker Fury biplane of 1929 was the first RAF fighter capable of 200 mph and it was followed not many years later by the Hurricane, the first 300-mph fighter to enter RAF service. Now the RAF was taking delivery of its first 400-mph fighter, the Hawker Typhoon, and once again it was one of Tommy Sopwith's companies that had made the breakthrough. However, proud as he must have been with Hawker's 'Hat Trick', the Typhoon was to cause him more than a little anguish because the problems were not confined to its engine. During one of the early test-flights the rear fuselage split. With great courage and airmanship (for which he was awarded a George Medal), Philip Lucas, the test pilot, managed to make a landing and the fault was traced to engine vibration setting up a destructive resonance within the structure. Little was known about the problem of resonance at the time but, following modifications it was cured. Soon afterwards a number of test pilots were killed in the aircraft, among them

Gerry Sayer, the veteran test pilot who had joined H. G. Hawker Engineering in 1929. This time the cause was traced to an elevator trim tab and a simple remedy was put in hand. As always, Sopwith's designers were pushing out the frontiers of knowledge and, when war conditions demand rapid advances, risks are bound to be taken. Unfortunately such risks often bring with them loss of life. In this respect, it was the development of the Typhoon that led us to the threshold of what was, at the time, a little understood phenomenon, the so-called 'sound barrier'. Compressibility, to use the correct term, occurs when a body (aircraft, rocket or rifle bullet) moves at a speed approaching that of sound or faster than sound. If an aircraft designed for subsonic flight is made to approach supersonic speeds, and Sydney Camm's Typhoon could easily do that in a dive, the airflow converts into shockwaves that affect both the supporting lift and the flying controls. Instead of flowing smoothly the air builds up along the wing leading edge like snow in front of a plough.

In 1940 the 'sound barrier' presented a very serious challenge to designers on both sides of the war and a more refined design, based on the Typhoon but using a sophisticated wing of eliptical planform that was 5 in thinner than the original, appeared in 1941. This elegant fighter was called the Hawker Tempest and it had a maximum speed of 438 mph. It entered RAF service in the closing stages of World War 2 when its high performance made the Tempest particularly successful against Hitler's V1 'Flying Bombs'. In fact more than 600 of them were destroyed by one Tempest Wing alone (a Wing usually numbered 60 aircraft). Nevertheless, of the almost 6,700 V1s launched by Germany and aimed at London, nearly 3,000 got through killing 5,500 people, and destroying 23,000 houses in the process.

The Tempest was also fast enough to take on and shoot down the German Messerschmitt Me 262 jet fighter. After the war Sydney Camm developed another version for the Fleet Air Arm, the Sea Fury, which was fitted with the Bristol Centaurus engine. It had a maximum speed of 460 mph and was one of the fastest piston-engine fighters of all times. Versions of the Hawker Sea Fury monoplane were still being built by Hawker's for foreign governments as late as 1960.

Sydney Camm

For many years Sydney Camm had served his company well. He was, after all, designer of the Hart/Fury biplane family which had turned Hawker into a big concern. Then, in time for the war, came the Hurricane, Typhoon and Tempest. Tommy Sopwith, being the kind of man he was, wanted to show his appreciation. So at a Board meeting, he turned to the Group Treasurer and said: 'I think we ought to recognize what Sydney's done and give him a couple of thousand pounds bonus'.

Sydney Camm was highly delighted. At that time the value of money was such that you could buy a very beautiful house for £2,000, the type of property that would cost about £400,000 in 1989. As soon as the meeting was over Sir Frank Spriggs, the Group Managing Director, sent for Camm and said he would arrange to pay half the bonus immediately and let him have the rest at a later date. It was a strange quirk of this otherwise capable man that he hated others to enjoy money. Normally Camm was more than a little afraid of Spriggs, but on this occasion he stood his ground and threatened to see 'Mr Sopwith' if part of his bonus was withheld. The money was paid forthwith.

For good reason, Tommy Sopwith regarded Sydney Camm as one of his greatest assets. Sydney knew better than the Air Ministry what the RAF should be flying and he had a loathing for bad design. His favourite expression, on being confronted by something that did not reach his very high standards, was: 'It looks as though mother done it!' Yet this great designer disliked flying. Although he could be hard with his staff—it was not unknown for him to rip up a drawing that had been worked on for several weeks and make the unfortunate draughtsman start again—Camm was not without a sense of humour and could be quick with the apt remark. Like the time when a young John W. R. Taylor (later to become editor of the famous aviation directory *Jane's All the World's Aircraft*) joined the drawing office at Kingston. It was 1941 and all the staff were in smart, city suits, something young John could not afford at the time. He was wearing green corduroy trousers, a red shirt and an amber sash denoting that he was a member of the Home Guard when Sydney Camm walked in, did a double take and said: 'What are you supposed to be—a ruddy traffic light!'

*   *   *

Tommy Sopwith could be very generous over important matters but, as with so many wealthy people, he watched the pennies like a hawk. When he and some of his directors went out for lunch he would often say: 'I'll leave my hat and umbrella in your office because it costs a lot of money in their cloakroom'. Although he kept a straight face, his colleagues suspected he was pulling their legs, because that same man would entertain like a king whether you were a retired draughtsman or a senior director. In fact, Tommy Sopwith disliked meanness and, in near disbelief, he used to tell of his days with the Hon Charles Rolls, founder with Henry Royce of Rolls-Royce, who used to go ballooning with him. After one balloon flight the two young men went into a Lyons Tea Shop for some refreshments. The bill came to about one shilling each (5p) and Sopwith left a tip of three old pence (a little more than 1p which would have been considered about right in 1908). Sopwith was embarrassed when Rolls left the waitress only one penny. 'What's wrong with that?' said the wealthy man-about-town. 'It's about ten percent, isn't it?'

Another of Tommy Sopwith's quirks was the wealthy man's habit of often not carrying any money in his pockets. As one of his senior staff used to say: 'For Gawd sake never walk out of the Ritz behind the Skipper, you will end up paying for the taxi'.

The stresses of war

During the war aircraft production was not allowed to go unchallenged by the Germans and there were determined attempts by the Luftwaffe to bomb vital factories. In 1940, with security in mind, the Hawker Design Office was banished by Tommy Sopwith to Claremont House at Cobham in the country, where it was away from the areas that were being bombed by the German air force. It was a sensible precaution because a near-miss during that year, which destroyed the First Aid Centre at Hawker's Canbury Park Road premises, very nearly set back work on several important projects, including the Typhoon which was scheduled to replace the Hurricane. On 4 September, 1940, there was a bad raid on Brooklands and, although staff at the adjacent Vickers works were killed, the Hawker factory actually managed to increase Hurricane fighter deliveries by a useful 10 percent that month.

Aircraft factories were among the prime targets for the Luftwaffe because Hitler recognized that during the early years of the war Britain's only means of hitting back at Germany itself was through its Royal Air Force. The Luftwaffe had lost the Battle of Britain and, to make matters worse for the Third Reich, the RAF was growing in strength all the time.

As an insurance against Hawker Aircraft losing everything in a bombing raid, vital components were dispersed into various premises commandeered under emergency powers for the purpose. Somewhat appropriately ex-insurance man, John Lidbury, who had recently moved from the company's insurance department to the Hawker factory at Kingston, was given the task of safeguarding the supply of components in the event of a serious air raid. It was a sensible plan based on not having all the eggs in one basket. One of the premises requisitioned was Benaters, a large garage at Surbiton, not far from the Kingston factory, where, at one time, several thousand Hawker Hurricane undercarriages were stored.

In 1940 petrol for motor vehicles was strictly rationed and it could only be obtained for essential transport. So, when during a routine visit to Benaters Garage, John Lidbury saw Tommy Sopwith's enormous pre-war Rolls-Royce parked by the pumps, while 22 petrol cans were being filled in full view of the street, alarm bells began to ring. Lidbury went up to the man doing the filling and said 'What the hell are you doing?' Back came the reply: 'Filling up Mr Sopwith's car, sir. He always collects it here, sir.' While all this was going on the chauffeur was out of sight, having a cup of tea, but John Lidbury got him to take the car back, and then made an urgent appointment to see Tommy Sopwith. In the conversation that followed Lidbury explained his concern and it became clear that Sopwith was totally unaware of the regulations. 'My God!' he said 'What have you done?' 'I told him to stop it,' replied Lidbury. 'Quite right, too. I'll get rid of the car,' said his boss and he laid up his Rolls-Royce Phantom III for the rest of the war.

To discourage the Luftwaffe from attempting accurate, low-level attacks there was a balloon barrage surrounding Brooklands during the war. The balloons were tethered to the ground by steel cables which were capable of inflicting serious damage to any aircraft flying into them. During 1941 one of the balloons was sent down in flames by an RAF Tiger Moth trainer. It appears that at nearby Fairoaks Aerodrome, where pilot training was in progress, disenchanted flying instructors with ambitions of joining an operational squadron had devised a form of entertainment to relieve their frustration. This entailed waiting until low cloud obscured the Brooklands' balloons from the ground, leaving them to bask like sleeping whales in the sun above. The idea was to climb through the cloud then run the wheels of the Tiger along the top of the balloon. Flight Lieutenant Bernard Barton accidentally managed to burst one, the Tiger's exhaust set fire to the escaping gas, the balloon emerged in flames through the clouds over Brooklands and a shaken Barton arrived back at Fairoaks without his eyebrows. Much of the fabric was burned off the right-hand side of his Tiger Moth and how he escaped a Court Martial remains one of the mysteries of World War 2.

Tommy Sopwith already had a long history of aviation 'firsts' to his credit and the tradition continued when the Gloster division of Hawker Siddeley produced the first Allied jet aircraft, the E.28/39. The aircraft was designed by W. G. Carter and powered by Frank Whittle's first 'airworthy' turbojet, the W.1. Sopwith had shown an early interest in Whittle's gas turbine experiments and, when Hawker Siddeley tendered for the prototype contract, Carter was entrusted with the task of designing it. Carter was well known to the boss of Hawker Siddeley because many years previously he had run the design office at Sopwith Aviation. The E.28/39 was really a testbed for what was then a revolutionary form of propulsion, untried in any other country except Germany where the jet-powered Heinkel He 178 had briefly flown on 27 August, 1939.

The Gloster E.28/39 was taken to RAF Cranwell which offered particularly long runways and had the advantage of being away from the public eye. Gerry Sayer, at the time Gloster's Chief Test Pilot, made the first flight at 7.45 p.m. on 15 May, 1941. Unlike the test in Germany two years previously, when the undercarriage refused to retract and the jet engine failed, Sayer's flight was uneventful. From the E.28/39 was developed the Gloster Meteor which made its first flight on 5 March, 1943. This too was designed by George

Carter who had left Hawker's to join Gloster Aircraft in the mid 1920s, only to find himself one of Tommy Sopwith's senior staff again when the Hucclecote factory was bought by the Kingston company in 1934.

To what extent was Tommy Sopwith involved in the decision to proceed with or terminate a new design? According to Sir Peter Masefield, who knew the Hawker concern in the 1930s and had dealings with many of its key figures while a journalist with the *Aeroplane* magazine:

'Oh I think he had the final say and this was particularly so in the case of the two aeroplanes on which the fortunes of Hawker and then Hawker Siddeley were founded, first of all the Hart and then the Fury. I think there is no doubt that, when Sydney Camm had done the first layout and then took it to Tommy Sopwith, he would make some comments. I believe it was certainly true that of the aeroplanes that led up to the Hart and Fury he said "Well, you know, I don't think much of this—you must do better". And so finally, in 1928, after Sydney had tried his hand at quite a few things like the Hawfinch, the designs gradually got refined until by 1928-29, the Hart was designed, which was the great take-off of Hawker's.

'And George Bulman, of course, had a good deal to say. He was the first scientific test pilot—another hand-picked by Tommy Sopwith. George Bulman was at Martlesham [the RAF unit where new military aircraft were tested] in those days and when new Hawker aeroplanes were sent there for test, George Bulman would express an opinion on them. Tommy Sopwith got to know that he was the man who was commenting and offered him a job. Bulman retired from the RAF early to come to Hawker's.'

The stresses of war, with aircraft pouring out of all the factories under his control and new designs either on the drawing board or at the prototype stage, might have induced many a man in Tommy Sopwith's position to live on the job, burn himself out and go to an early grave. But this was not his style; he never believed in employing good people and then trying to do their jobs for them. To their cost, many employers find it hard to delegate and, as a result, talented staff become discontented, the boss is over-worked, team spirit sinks to the lowest possible levels and the firm is on the road to disaster. At Hawker Siddeley key personnel were expected to make decisions and see them through. The 'Skipper' was always in the background for advice; he was usually in a good mood, always calm, never rude and it was more or less unknown for him to be wrong.

Pressures there most certainly were, but for Tommy Sopwith these were relieved from time to time by engaging in one of his relaxing country activities. For example, although his sister Olive had died on 17 December, 1937, Tommy Sopwith and her stepson, Jim Joel, maintained contact through common friends and a mutual interest in shooting. Among Jim Joel's beautifully-bound shooting diaries is a record that on 23 and 24 of August, 1943, Tommy Sopwith shot at Dallowgill, a moor owned by Joel in Yorkshire. The party included Mr O. Oppenheimer (an old friend and business rival of the Joel family). On another occasion Sopwith took part in a shoot at Childwick Bury, Jim Joel's Hertfordshire estate, in the company of Lord Marchwood, O. Oppenheimer and The Hon Harold Balfour, a veteran pilot who flew Sopwith aircraft during the Great War. He later became Lord Balfour of Inchrye, Under Secretary of State for Air, a position he held during the crucial Battle of Britain.

With factories located at Kingston, Coventry, Manchester and Gloucester, it was necessary for Hawker Siddeley to maintain a small fleet of communications aircraft so that key personnel could visit the various plants quickly and at short notice. One of these, registered G-AEUJ, was a two-seat Miles Whitney Straight light aircraft which in 1989 was still flying 53 years after it left the Miles factory. On 5 April, 1945, Tommy Sopwith was flown in the Whitney Straight from Langley to Hucclecote, the Gloster Aircraft Company's airfield, by a young Squadron Leader named Neville Duke. Squadron Leader Duke, who was on rest after a period of operational flying in Italy, had been seconded to Hawker's as a temporary test pilot. He remembers that flight well:

'T.O.M. [Sopwith] navigated a devious route to Hucclecote, directing me via "so and so's" country house. Scenic navigation seemed to be the way he got around and we meandered to Gloucestershire in a most interesting and educational manner.'

Neville Duke, who later broke the World's Air Speed record in a Hawker Hunter, recalls that: 'After a successful salmon-fishing exercise it was Sopwith's wont to deliver the biggest and best of the catch to deserving friends'.

The end of the war

By 1945, with the Russian armies advancing west while British, American, Canadian and other Allied forces pushed back the still cohesive German army from west to east, the writing was on the wall for Hitler's so-called 'Thousand-Year Reich'. By 2 April, 1945, the Ruhr and its 325,000 defending troops were encircled and, on 2 May, a delegation headed by Admiral Friedeburg surrendered all German forces in North-West Germany, Denmark, Scleswig-Holstein and Holland to General Bernard Montgomery. Total surrender to the Allied Supreme Commander soon followed, coming into effect at midnight on 8 May.

It was the end of the war; millions of men and women on both sides of the conflict discarded their uniforms and went home to an uncertain future. For the second time in his life Tommy Sopwith would have to face the traumas of running down his factories and concern himself with the daunting task of keeping the Hawker Siddeley empire intact.

In varying degrees the British aircraft industry had served the nation well. Shorts had produced the magnificent Sunderland flying boat and the Stirling heavy bomber. Handley Page had built the Hampden and the Halifax. Vickers were responsible for the Wellington, mainstay of Bomber Command until the four-engine 'heavies' came along, and their Supermarine division had produced the wonderful Spitfire fighter in its many versions. Fairey's contribution had been the Swordfish, Britain's only successful naval aircraft during the war, while de Havilland had built Tiger Moth trainers by the thousands and the peerless Mosquito fighter/bomber. Bristol's most significant contribution to victory had been its excellent engines and the sturdy twin-engine Beaufighter. Other firms—Airspeed, Miles, Blackburn, Rolls-Royce and so on—had all taken a vital role. But Tommy Sopwith's Hawker Siddeley Group had been responsible for Anson trainers, Hurricane, Typhoon and Tempest fighters, Albemarle glider tugs, Whitley medium bombers, the phenomenal Lancaster heavy bomber, the York four-engine transport and the Meteor—first of the Allies' jet fighters.

After the end of the Great War aeroplanes were unwanted, but this time it was different. The jet engine had arrived and it promised to revolutionize aviation, civil and military. Such a challenge was irresistible to Tommy Sopwith.

CHAPTER
9

Into the Jet Age

BY 1945 TOMMY Sopwith, for a man of 57, was both youthful and very active. His only child, Thomas Edward, was a lad of 13 and he had returned to England, after three years of evacuation in the USA, in an aircraft carrier no less. When Thomas Edward was born his parents had entered him for Eton but possibly due to the pressures of war they had forgotten to confirm his place by the due time, so he went to Summerfields, Oxford, then Stowe. After public school the decision facing him was whether to continue his education at Oxford (where he had gained a place at New College) or join his father's firm, Hawker Siddeley. The attractions of things mechanical, something he had inherited from Tommy Sopwith, was the deciding factor and university gave way to a six months apprenticeship with AST (at the time one of the Hawker Siddeley companies) at Hamble. National Service in the Army completed, he embarked on a second apprenticeship, this time with the Armstrong Siddeley car division at Coventry, and was eventually put in charge of its research department.

Having built up one of the largest engineering concerns in the world it would have been natural for Tommy Sopwith to want his son in the business, yet he never tried to influence Thomas Edward in any way. The decision to join Armstrong Siddeley Cars instead of going to Oxford, Thomas Edward now feels might have been a mistake, particularly since after a while it seemed that the car division was the poor relation of a poor relation. After World War 2 the Armstrong Siddeley division, of which Armstrong Siddeley Motors formed a part, was perhaps less successful as a creative enterprise than other parts of the Hawker Siddeley empire. So Thomas Edward left Hawker Siddeley to run his own business and manage the family finances through Endeavour Holdings Ltd.

Was Sir Thomas disappointed not to have his son in his industrial creation? As Thomas Edward said:

'Half of him thought it would be jolly nice if I followed in his footsteps, which was very unlikely with a modern public company, the way that it is. The other half probably thought it was quite a good idea that I had got the gumption to go out and do my own thing anyway. And I suspect the latter half won.

'I think that the old man was instinctively reluctant to interfere in my life; I might or might not have regarded it as help. The thing that he was not good at was helping me if I had a problem with my mother and I was right—and I am prepared to admit that I wasn't always right. Because he took the view that he lived 365 days a year with her and I saw her on an occasional weekend.'

Thomas Edward Sopwith has been a powerboat enthusiast and racing motorist in his day, although, following such incidents as loosing a wheel at speed during one of the events, his parents insisted on their only son finding a less lethal outlet for his sporting talents. He flies his own helicopter with considerable skill and uses this as others might drive their cars for business. Sadly, it was in a helicopter accident that his first wife April was killed. In 1977 he married Gina Hathorn, an Olympic-class skier, and they have two daughters, Samantha and Candida.

Mixed fortunes

In 1945 Tommy Sopwith bought Compton Manor, a beautiful estate at King's Somborne in Hampshire. Almost six and a half miles of the River Test flow through the 2,200 acres which offer splendid fishing and excellent pheasant shooting. The estate includes 25 cottages and four farms and the elegant house has fine rooms for entertaining, 14 bedrooms and nine bathrooms. It stands on a hill and the views to the west are magnificent. Until 1910 the estate was owned by the Hennessy brandy company, then it was left to a Mrs Milburn who eventually sold it to Tommy Sopwith.

The early post-war period brought mixed fortunes for Tommy Sopwith. There were the human problems of cutting back a workforce swollen by the needs of war, although many of the staff were women who, as happened after the Great War of 1914-1918, quickly left their jobs and went home to look after husbands returning from overseas and children who, in many cases, had never seen or were unable to remember their fathers. There were other problems too, some of a serious nature, and to explain these it is necessary to digress from the central character of this book.

The performance of member firms within the Hawker Siddeley Group during the immediate post-war years was by no means uniformly successful. For example, in 1949 the Armstrong Whitworth team at Coventry made a brave attempt to enter the civil market with the Apollo, a four-engine turboprop carrying 31 passengers in a pressurized cabin. But Vickers had a rival aircraft, the famous Viscount, which was a better design and it prevailed to capture a large worldwide market while the Apollo faded away.

Immediately after the war the A. V. Roe factories were building an improved version of the wartime Avro Anson. There was also a civil version of the Lancaster heavy bomber called the Lancastrian, and a passenger aircraft, the Avro York, based on Lancaster wings and tail surfaces. Both aircraft were being used by several airlines when civil air transport resumed operations after the war. The Tudor, Avro's attempts at building a modern four-engine airliner with transatlantic capabilities, failed partly through the technical shortcomings of its systems. Its cabin heating could be made to work only rarely, and its four engines were called upon to deliver more power than was good for their reliability. According to Sir John Lidbury, Sopwith's involvement in these projects was minimal:

'He had no room for civil aviation. He used to say "You are going to lose your money in those"—and they all did. He was absolutely right. You couldn't get him enthusiastic about it.'

Another contributing factor in the demise of the Tudor was the unrealistic environment in which the British airline industry had to operate during the immediate post-war years. These were the days when Prime Minister Attlee and his socialist government had embarked on a policy of taking State ownership to its zenith. Three nationalized airlines were set up, British Overseas Airways Corporation (BOAC), British South American Airways Corporation (BSAAC) and British European Airways (BEA). In an arrangement that was breathtaking in its naïvety, aircraft for these airlines were purchased by a committee of civil servants which then instructed the State airlines to operate them.

The Tudor had been ordered by the civil servants for BOAC, but when early examples emerged and their performance had been assessed the airline categorically refused to accept it. However, the managing director of British South American Airways, Air Vice-Marshal Donald Bennett (founder and AOC of the Pathfinder force during World War 2), regarded its designer, Roy Chadwick, as the finest in the world. He was, after all, responsible for the Avro Lancaster and Bennett had good reason to be well satisfied with that aircraft which had played a major role in Pathfinder operations. So, with his support the Tudor went into service on the South Atlantic routes. Two of them repaid his trust by disappearing over the sea, events which led to Bennett being removed from the managing directorship of British South American Airways and the airline being amalgamated with BOAC soon afterwards.

The lamentable saga of the Avro Tudor did not end there because Roy Chadwick, Avro's Chief Designer, and S. A. Thorn, test pilot, were both killed when G-AGSU crashed while taking off on 23 August, 1947, due to incorrectly-connected aileron controls. The truth was that while Britain had built large numbers of very successful fighters and bombers during the war, some of them the best of their kind on either side of the conflict, its resources had not allowed for parallel development of transport aircraft. The Americans excelled in the field of civil airliners and, after the war, the UK was at least five years behind them, possibly even more. Equally, it cannot be denied that, almost without exception, the Hawker Siddeley Group had up to the 1960s devoted all its energies to designing and producing military aircraft. Civil airliners were a totally different line of country.

When a company invests time and effort in a new airliner a lot of money is involved. Today, computer-aided design (CAD) has, to a considerable extent, removed some of the unknowns of devising new aircraft. But during the immediate post-war years the electronic computer had yet to arrive—CAD was unknown—and the future of a new airliner could represent a make or break situation unless the company was very large. Even to a big manufacturer, like Hawker Siddeley, the demise of the Avro Tudor was a serious matter. It was typical of Tommy Sopwith's character, however, for him to exhibit no signs of stress. His attitude was: 'If worrying will help, then worry'.

Mention was made in the previous chapter of the first Allied jet to fly during World War 2, the Gloster E.28/39 and the Gloster Meteor that followed. The first named was never intended to be other than a flying testbed for the new turbojet engine then being developed by Flight Lieutenant Frank Whittle in the face of strong opposition from those who should have known better. The Meteor, on the other hand, entered RAF service in the closing stages of the war and gave a good account of itself destroying the German V1 flying bombs over open country before they could reach London.

Simple as the Meteor might appear when compared with a modern jet fighter, it was light years ahead of the Sopwith Pups and Camels of 1916-1918. Yet, in addition to chairing Board meetings, advising his group Managing Directors and watching Hawker Siddeley's finances, Tommy Sopwith had to move with the times. His role in the designing of Britain's first jet fighter may not have been so intimate as it was with the Sopwith aircraft of 1913 to 1920, but his chief designers at the various plants were expected to discuss their projects with 'The Skipper'. He kept abreast of fast-moving developments in aeronautics and, at a practical level, his opinions carried a lot of weight.

First jet engines

It is worth digressing at this point to explain the background to Britain's first jet engines because this has a bearing on the Sopwith story.

Since his earliest days in the RAF, Frank Whittle had believed in the gas turbine, and while the Germans were first to fly a jet aircraft they were unable to produce engines offering more than a few hours reliable running time. Whittle, on the other hand, based his turbojets on the well understood

technology of the day, and it was Whittle-type engines that made the Gloster
Meteor a more reliable jet fighter than the technically more advanced aircraft
being supplied to the Luftwaffe. Frank Whittle (later Sir Frank) had joined
the RAF as a boy apprentice in 1923, but his talents were soon recognized.
He was given a commission and then sent to the RAF College at Cranwell.
There he wrote a paper on gas turbine engines which so impressed the Royal
Air Force that he was released from duty to obtain a degree at Cambridge.
Naturally most of the other students had entered university straight from
school and Frank Whittle found himself being regarded as the old man of the
lecture halls. There he met a brilliant young student named Arnold Hall, who
was later to figure prominently in the life of Tommy Sopwith.

Even in those days Whittle had a deep understanding of supersonic
airflow and thermodynamics, and he left Cambridge fully convinced that a
turbojet engine could be made to work. Unfortunately, governments tend to
appoint establishment figures as advisers and the establishment figures of the
day advised their masters that Whittle's engine had no future. Some even
announced with the utmost conviction that, in their view, a gas turbine would
not run at all. As a result, Whittle had the greatest difficulty in financing the
first engine. This was eventually made to his design by the British Thomson
Houston Co, based at Rugby. Fortunately, and to its credit, this great company
made the engine very cheaply for him. This was essential because little money
was available from the Government's Department of Scientific Research,
which funded the project during its early stages.

As a friend and supporter who believed in the project, Arnold Hall
remained in contact with Frank Whittle. Consequently, he was invited to be
present during the exciting occasion when the engine ran for the first time and
accelerated to such incredible RPM that it threatened to blow up.

Some months later, when the engine was running more or less under
control, Tommy Sopwith paid a visit to the unprepossessing group of huts at
Lutterworth where Whittle was developing the engine that would, in the not
very distant future, revolutionize air travel and military aviation. Clearly the
new form of propulsion offered exciting possibilities and these were not lost
on Sopwith. He went away suitably impressed, so much so that a few years
later he tendered for and was awarded a contract for the first flying testbed
which, as previously recorded, was built by his Gloster division to the design
of George Carter.

Compared with the modern workshops and the test facilities enjoyed by
the Germans, the Whittle operation was being run like an ill-equipped village
garage and a small one to boot. Yet despite the impoverished conditions
suffered by the Whittle team, Britain managed to produce reliable jet engines
in time for the closing stages of World War 2, whereas the Germans, for all
their technical resources, never did.

To satisfy the war effort, established British aero engine manufacturers were committed to producing such piston units as the Merlin, Hercules, Sabre and so on, so it was decided to hand over development and production of the Whittle turbojet to the Rover car company. This was a foolish decision because Rover was in unfamiliar country with compressors and turbines. The project stalled and eventually Rolls-Royce swapped development of a new tank engine with Rover in exchange for the jet engine.

By 1945 Britain had several reliable, if fuel-thirsty jet engines flying, and the Russians lost no time in asking if they could buy some of them. Air Commodore 'Rod' Banks (at the time in charge of engine production and development) was asked for his views and he warned that if Britain agreed it would be selling its birthright. Sir Stafford Cripps, Labour President of the Board of Trade and a great admirer of Russia, stepped in and on his insistence the engines went East against the advice of the experts. Not many years later, copies of these early jet engines were powering MiG 15 fighters that were being flown in combat against British and American pilots during the Korean War.

While German jet engines were not as reliable as those in RAF service, their high-speed airframe design was in advance of ours. Although Carter's Meteor gave many years of good service in the RAF and a number of other air forces, it was nevertheless dated from the moment it flew. The Meteor really belonged to the piston engine era, much as the Hawker Hurricane had been based on Hart-Fury biplane technology. Tommy Sopwith had always counselled the wisdom of backing known technology until more advanced ideas had been proved experimentally and, on 7 November, 1945, Gp Capt H. J. Wilson broke the world airspeed record in a Meteor F.4 at a speed of 606 mph. Then, on 7 September the following year, Gp Capt E. M. Donaldson broke it yet again at 616 mph. Dated in many respects it may have been, but Sopwith had good reason to be pleased with George Carter's Meteor. It remained in production until 1954. By then, 3,215 had been made in Britain, 330 in Holland and 30 sets of components were assembled in Belgium. Tommy Sopwith had another winner on his hands.

*   *   *

The Gloster Aircraft Co was one of Tommy Sopwith's brighter stars during the 1940s and 1950s. The firm did well with the Meteor which, apart from equipping the Royal Air Force, was bought in significant numbers by various foreign air forces all over the world. Later the company brought out a massive and formidable all-weather fighter, named the Javelin, which first flew in 1950. This weighed considerably more than some of the airliners flying at the time and one version climbed to 40,000 feet in only 6.6 minutes. In its day this big, delta wing jet was among the most advanced military aircraft flying.

By 1946 Hawker Aircraft was producing aircraft at Canbury Park Road, Kingston, and Richmond Road, Kingston (the premises previously leased by Leyland Motors) as well as the airfield at Langley where the factory had been enlarged. However, nearby Heathrow Airport was also expanding, so in 1958 the Langley test facility was moved to Dunsfold Aerodrome, near Guildford, Surrey. By then several jet fighter designs were being developed, most important being the magnificent Hawker Hunter which proved to be another Sydney Camm masterpiece. A Sopwith company had repeated history yet again by producing Britain's leading fighter and, over the next decade, more than 2,000 Hunters were built for the RAF in addition to a number of foreign air forces. The prototype flew on 20 July, 1951, in the hands of Neville Duke. Two years later, on 7 September, 1953, he broke the World's Absolute Speed Record in a Hunter by flying at 727.6 mph.

Demand for the Hawker Hunters was such that it was beyond the resources of the Kingston factory, in terms of manpower and floorspace. So, Sopwith instructed John Lidbury to look around the wartime 'shadow' factories and let him have his recommendations on which would be most suitable. Lidbury selected the one located on the edge of Squires Gate Airport, Blackpool, Lancashire, a building of around a two-and-a-quarter million square feet area, which was completely empty. Lidbury remembers being so overwhelmed by the sheer size of the place that he remained in his taxi to be driven around inside the building.

Like all towns, Blackpool was anxious to attract any enterprise that could provide employment for its population. During the war the factory at Squires Gate had produced Vickers Wellington bombers, so there was a pool of unemployed skilled and semi-skilled aircraft engineers available. Blackpool Town Council knew that the Hawker Siddeley board was looking around the country for additional production facilities so after John Lidbury's visit Tommy Sopwith and a few of the directors were invited to visit the town so that they might be given 'the treatment'. One of the pilots who ferried the directors to meetings in those days was Frank Murphy, an ex-RAF officer from New Zealand who flew during the war and was awarded a DFC. Later he was seconded to Hawker Aircraft where he eventually became Chief Production Test Pilot at their Dunsfold base. Murphy remembers the Blackpool visit particularly well, and in his own words:

'The Blackpool civil authorities were very keen that Hawker should take over the factory and had arranged a programme with an official reception in the Mayor's parlour and an official lunch, tour around the coast and factory and an evening tour of the entertainment facilities of Blackpool.'

To those who have never visited Blackpool it is a resort on the grand scale with miles of good beach, no fewer than three piers (North, Central and South), the famous Blackpool Tower which is a smaller version of the Eiffel

Tower in Paris, a very large fairground, countless private boarding houses and 'private hotels' (with landladies who have created a mythology of their own) and some of the largest ballrooms in Britain. Blackpool is different things to different people. In years gone by it was Paradise on Earth to the industrial workers of the North although others might describe it as eight miles of gleaming concrete on three levels. Certainly it was a totally new experience for the country-loving Sopwith and, as Frank Murphy recalls, it came as a cultural shock to the yachting, shooting and fishing man:

'Sir Tom always insisted that pilots who flew the directors on these trips were accommodated in the same hotel and, where possible, integrated in the entertainment side. On the evening of our arrival after dinner I had happened to mention to Sir Tom that I knew Blackpool slightly as I had spent some war time leaves from my Air Force squadron with an aunt in the area. As usual he asked that we should all keep our eyes and ears open and he had asked me to stick close by as the only person with some knowledge of the area, however limited. Blackpool was completely alien to Sir Tom by way of his life and upbringing. The highly organized mass entertainment reflected by the Pleasure Beach, Tower Ballroom and Winter Gardens as shown to us on our evening tour really surprised him.

'In the Winter Gardens Sir Tom and myself had fallen a little behind as we looked into bars etc. and as we came into sight of the vast floor covered with dancing people he came to a halt, absolutely fascinated. It was the only time I had ever seen him astonished and surprised and he was quite silent for a minute or so. I made some comment to the effect that every afternoon and night there must be probably over a thousand people in the complex, all spending on drinking and dancing. His mind was well ahead of me as he come out with some sums based on the product of numbers 'X' and he said "it's absolutely fantastic—BIG BUSINESS Frank". If some entertainment entrepreneur had been on hand and in need of a little capital I am sure Sir Tom might have diversified into mass entertainment and we should have had computerized theme parks alternating on the production line'.

John Lidbury's choice of Squires Gate received the backing of Tommy Sopwith and his board. Blackpool was once again playing host to the aircraft industry, staff was gradually built up to 5,500 and, at the end of 18 months, the factory was turning out Hunters at a steady rate.

A belated knighthood

In 1953, Thomas Octave Murdoch Sopwith received a knighthood for his services to aviation and so did his prodigy, Sydney Camm. It is natural to ask why Frank Spriggs, someone Tommy Sopwith had employed as a clerk in 1913, gained a knighthood in 1941 and a KBE in 1948, whereas his boss of long standing had to wait another 12 years. There are no clear answers and, as is the way in these matters, little if anything is on record. One can only look at the facts and make an inspired guess at the answer. Being in charge of the day-to-day affairs of the great company, Frank Spriggs was more in the eye of the civil servants than Tommy Sopwith, a modest man who tended to keep in the background. Then, in those days, broken marriages carried a stigma that hardly exists today and the fact that his second wife was a divorcée may have weighed against him. These are matters of conjecture but, whatever the reason, Sopwith's knighthood when it arrived was long overdue—particularly having regard to his contribution to the security of the nation through the development and construction of aircraft that were superior to those of Britain's enemies. Many people feel strongly that he should also have received the OM.

Although he had done very little competing in his younger days, the racing driver in Tommy Sopwith was never entirely displaced by the aeroplane, and this was illustrated by an incident soon after Britain's first motorway, the M1, was opened. Sopwith expressed a wish to see this new marvel of road engineering, and as Armstrong Siddeley's motor division was building a large and powerful car called the Sapphire, one was produced complete with Hawker's senior chauffeur and in got Sopwith, along with another Director who was of a rather nervous disposition. They went up the M1 in sedate fashion and after a while turned off at a junction for the return journey. At this stage Sopwith said to the driver: 'You get in the back—I'm driving'. There was no speed limit then and, as the M1 was so new, there was little traffic on the road. Sopwith must have been about 70 years old at the time and he drove flat out, well in excess of 100 mph, all the way back to London. His co-director was a nervous wreck, so was the chauffeur, and the car was never the same again!

The design and production of even quite small aircraft is a complex business, but the creation and mass-production of a heavy bomber such as the Avro Lancaster demands organizing skills to match the engineering talents responsible for such an outstanding design. Obviously the task of designing, stressing, drawing and setting up production is shared by several teams working under the chief designer, but the decision to further a design and secure orders rests with the company directors. The Hawker Siddeley board had good reason to respect the views of its chief, Tommy Sopwith; he had been proved right too often for his judgement to be questioned. And by any standards, the Lancaster and, to a lesser extent, the slightly larger Avro Lincoln that followed, must surely be regarded as one of Hawker Siddeley's great achievements during Sopwith's wartime chairmanship of the company. But now the jet engine had arrived and the Air Staff wanted jet bombers for the post-war RAF. These became known as 'V' bombers and three designs were ordered, each from a different company.

First to enter RAF service was the rather conventional four-jet Vickers Valiant. Of more advanced concept was the Handley Page Victor, but the one that enjoyed the longest active service was Hawker Siddeley's offering, the mighty Avro Vulcan designed by 'Cock' Davies, a very large delta-wing design which proved a worthy successor to the great Lancaster. It first flew on 30 August, 1952, and, in developed form, it could carry a 21,000-lb bomb load at 620 mph.

Another successful project undertaken at A. V. Roe while Tommy Sopwith was Chairman of Hawker Siddeley was a 50-passenger turboprop called the Avro 748, and almost 350 of these were sold to airlines around the world.

At Hawker's Kingston factory Sir Sydney Camm, always several jumps ahead of events, barely awaited the early flights of his new Hunter jet fighter before plans were being drawn for a supersonic version. Unfortunately, the project was turned down by the Government and Britain was to pay dearly for its lack of resolve. By not continuing with high-speed research several other countries were able to forge ahead of the UK in the development of supersonic flight, and the nation that had introduced the first reliable jet engines to the world was, in consequence, left behind.

The remarkable Hawker Harrier

The mid 1950s were a bad time for the British aircraft industry. Projects, some of them very promising, were being cancelled by Government on both sides of the political spectrum. This had the double-edged effect of damaging the country's defences and discouraging the great pool of UK inventive talent from developing new ideas. During this period many gifted engineers left the UK to work in other countries. There was nothing to choose between the two main political parties but, even when viewed against a background of the aeronautical ignorance which seems to be something of a tradition among many British politicians, the Duncan Sandys decree, which suggested that the days of manned service aircraft were over (even if this was not said in so many words), was unique in its lack of reality. Of it, Sir Thomas Sopwith said:

'We knew this was stupid and dangerous, so we ignored it and manoeuvred behind the scenes to get the decision scrapped. It didn't take long. The manned aeroplane is still with us and will be for a long time yet.'

Then there was the case of the TSR2, a very advanced military aircraft that had reached the development stage. It had been designed by the British Aircraft Corporation, a rival concern to Hawker Siddeley. In Parliament the Socialists were going through their 'Little Britain' phase, and the TSR2 was constantly being thrown in the face of the Conservative Government as an illusion of grandeur, a project that it should not be attempting on its own. One of the first acts of the Harold Wilson Government when it came into power was to cancel the project. This was another instance when the British nation was to pay dearly over many years for an act of political vindictiveness.

Against this background of 'cancel British and buy American'—and both Conservatives and Labour were equally guilty—it is hardly surprising that, when Stanley Hooker (later Sir Stanley) of the Bristol Engine Company got together with Sydney Camm and devised a fighter capable of taking-off and landing vertically, the project was met with a coolness born of stupidity. No doubt many will regard these as harsh words, but regrettably they are true.

The background to what is now widely known as the Harrier 'jump jet' (although it does not, in fact, 'jump' at all) is fascinating. In 1984, when Raymond Baxter interviewed the then 96-year-old Sir Thomas for BBC Television, he asked which of the many Sopwith and Hawker Group aircraft was his favourite:

'I find that a very difficult question to answer. It's rather like asking the father of a large family to pick out his favourite daughter. I think the Harrier is the greatest stride in the development of all our aircraft'.

To his credit, Sydney Camm had always made a practice of encouraging his project office to think up new ideas. However, the idea of a vertical take-off and landing project really surfaced in 1957 when a self-employed French engineer, named Michel Wibault, suggested that one of the Bristol jet engines, then in production, be fitted with four nozzles, two on each side, which could be rotated through 90° or so. In effect, the usual jet pipe at the rear of the engine would be replaced by four smaller jets capable of being vectored to discharge straight down for vertical lift, then gradually rotated back to create forward thrust. The idea was brilliant, and it later proved to be one of the greatest breakthroughs in aeronautical design since the advent of the jet engine. Sadly, Michel Wibault never lived to enjoy the success of his idea.

Initially, the revolutionary concept appeared to be suffering from lack of support, even from the aircraft manufacturers, and at Hawker Aircraft Sydney Camm was casting a sceptical eye on Hooker's activities. By now, all British aero engine manufacturers had been amalgamated under the banner of Rolls-Royce, and the company was well aware of Camm's lack of confidence in the vectored thrust concept. It was therefore with some surprise that Hooker received a letter from Camm which said:

> Dear Hooker,
> What are you doing about vertical take-off engines?
> Yours,
> Sydney.

By then Rolls-Royce had named its revolutionary engine Pegasus. A brochure had been produced and one was duly sent to Camm. A few weeks later an explosive Camm was on the telephone to Hooker—'When the devil are you coming to see me?' he demanded, to which Hooker replied whenever is convenient but '. . . what is the subject?' To Hooker's astonishment Camm replied that he had an outline design for a vertical take-off aircraft. And so he had, the Hawker P. 1127, which paved the way to another version known as the Kestrel which, in turn, was eventually developed into the world-renowned Harrier.

Up to the year 1990 only the Hawker team, led by Sydney Camm, had managed to produce a practical, operationally-successful vertical take-off and landing aircraft. During the Falkland campaign it proved itself more than the equal of supersonic fighters by shooting them down; it could virtually stop in the air, skip sideways and do all manner of unnatural things. The version used in the Falklands campaign was the Sea Harrier (that is, modified for operating from ships) and although two were shot down by fire from the ground none was destroyed from the air. The following Argentine military aircraft were confirmed as having been destroyed by the two Sea Harrier squadrons that operated from the aircraft carriers HMS *Hermes* and *Invincible:* 19 Mirage, 5 A4, 3 Helo, 2 Puccara, 1 Canberra, 1 C-130 Hercules. In all, a total of 31.

Although for many years there was no proper sales department at Hawker Aircraft Ltd, the company set up a marketing office after the war with a Technical Sales Manager by the name of John Crampton. During the war he had flown as an RAF bomber pilot and remained in the service for a few years after the return of peace. It was while applying for a job at Hawker's that he came face to face with Sydney Camm for the first time. During the interview Camm never looked at John Crampton or spoke a single word to him. Everything was directed through Camm's assistant, Roy Chaplin, and the conversation went like this:

Camm to Chaplin: 'Well, what does he do?'
Chaplin to Camm: 'He flew aeroplanes with the RAF.'
Camm to Chaplin: 'Any bloody fool can do that!'

Nevertheless, John Crampton was taken on and for years afterwards, whenever they passed in the corridor, Sydney Camm would look at him and say: 'You all right?' as though he had only just joined the company!

*　　*　　*

One day, in 1963, Sir Thomas Sopwith and Sir Roy Dobson visited the Kingston factory to inspect the Harrier production line. John Crampton and Bill Bedford (who was Chief Test Pilot at the time and who had made the first flight of the prototype on 7 July, 1961), were detailed to show the 75-year-old Chairman of the Hawker Siddeley empire and his Group Managing Director, the latest Hawker product.

History had repeated itself with the Harrier because, like the Hurricane of 30 years earlier, Sopwith and the Hawker Board decided to go ahead with the project even though no orders had been received from the British authorities. Naturally Sir Thomas was well pleased with the work of his talented design team and first-class engineers. It was the first time John Crampton had met Tommy Sopwith and he was particularly impressed with the way the great man gave his full attention when something was being explained. Like everyone who had dealings with the 'Skipper' John Crampton became an instant fan. At the end of the presentation Sir Thomas turned to Crampton and Bedford and, with great courtesy, quietly thanked them for devoting so much time to him, ending with the words: '. .. my chauffeur has a little present for you both in the boot of the car' (It was a brace of pheasants.) Sir Thomas always gave presents to members of his staff who did something for him personally.

Talking about the Harrier with Mike Ramsden, one-time editor of *Flight* magazine, Sir Thomas once said:

'I still don't believe the Harrier. Think of the millions spent on VTOL [vertical take-off-and-landing] in America and Russia, and yet the only successful one is the Harrier. When I saw it hovering and flying backwards under control, I reckoned I'd seen everything. And it is not difficult to fly.'

It is sad to report that the outstanding success of the Harrier owes little to the support of successive British governments. But for the fact that the necessary research for the revolutionary vectored thrust engine was funded by the Americans through a Mutual Weapons Defence grant, the western world would most probably still be waiting for a vertical take-off-and-landing fighter. Tommy Sopwith was always mindful that American money had made it possible for Rolls-Royce to develop the Pegasus engine which is, of course, the very heart of his favourite aircraft.

There is always a demand for speakers who can talk about historic events and one day a letter arrived on the local Managing Director's desk at Hawker Aircraft, Kingston. It was from the Institute of Mechanical Engineers requesting a talk on the history of Sopwith Aviation and the various Hawker companies at Kingston-upon-Thames. John Crampton returned from his summer holiday to find a copy of the reply which, in essence, said that he would be pleased to undertake the task. This came as a shock for John Crampton because his knowledge of Sopwith Aviation, H.G. Hawker Engineering, Hawker Aircraft and so on, was very limited—and public speaking was not on his list of accomplishments. 'I cannot possibly do this,' he told his director, 'because I know little of the company's history.' This brought the response: 'Just the man we want.' Naturally, wishing to seek advice from the best possible source, John Crampton asked if it would be possible to see Sir Thomas Sopwith who was still Chairman of Hawker Siddeley. Back came a typical reply from Sir Thomas: 'You had better come for lunch.' It was the first of many such occasions that John Crampton would enjoy in the future. He had been warned to come prepared with a list of questions and he rapidly found that, if Sir Thomas could see that you had done your homework and the interview was being conducted in a professional manner, he would open up and talk freely in that beautiful English of his about momentous past events.

At a later date, Sir Thomas sent for John Crampton, handed him two chapters of a book that was being written about Sopwith aircraft and asked if he would check the entire manuscript on his behalf. Crampton went back to his Managing Director at Hawker's and said: 'What am I to do? I am not really qualified to represent the old boy in this regard'. Back came the reply: 'John, whatever Sir Thomas Sopwith asks Kingston to do, Kingston does'. It was another way of saying that Tommy Sopwith's courteous request was really an order. But then all of his orders were in the form of courteous requests. At the time Sir Thomas was 81 and becoming concerned at the various delays in publishing the book. 'You had better get on to them and say I would like to see the book before it is too late', he told Crampton, little realizing that he had another 20 years ahead of him!

A face-lift for Hawker

Although the Hawker Siddeley concern was one of the world's leading manufacturers of military aircraft, important foreign visitors were usually taken aback when they saw the company's headquarters for the first time. They found it hard to believe that this could possibly be the corporate headquarters of the great Hawker Aircraft Ltd. Sydney Camm, for example, used to refer to his drawing office as 'That inverted lavatory block', and the entire set-up was a typical example of British eccentricity. John Lidbury, by then Managing Director, felt that time was long overdue for re-building the Richmond Road administrative offices, drawing office and corporate headquarters. It is perhaps not widely known that the Hawker element of Hawker Siddeley was almost unique in the world of aviation because it had never traded at a loss, yet in some respects it looked like the poor relation. This was the time when Roy Dobson, Managing Director of A. V. Roe, Manchester, was pouring millions of pounds into Canada, while setting up an Avro company in that country. Lidbury acknowledges that Dobson was doing an excellent job because the expansion into Canada was showing great potential at the time but, as fast as he made money at Hawker's, it was being syphoned by Head Office into Dobson's Canadian venture. Naturally, Lidbury felt entitled to plough back a fair proportion of his earnings into the Hawker operation, and he was not alone in considering that the existing headquarter's building was long overdue for replacement.

The first architects consulted by Lidbury had grand ideas for an ultra-modern glass building with a tower and all the usual trimmings that one expects of a shopping precinct. Eventually he got someone to design a headquarters of more classic proportions. When the project was presented to the Hawker Siddeley Board, its normally united members were in some disarray as to whether or not the re-building should proceed, while Tommy Sopwith, who was then nearing his sixty-ninth birthday, gave the impression he could not care less either way. For once, there was indecision among the directors so John Lidbury gave himself a casting vote and got on with the job. In 1956 money, the new building was a large one and it was going to cost one million pounds.

News came back to Lidbury that Roy Dobson was complaining to anyone who would listen about the money being spent on the new Hawker building and, sure enough, one afternoon he received a telephone call from Sir Frank Spriggs who, at the time, was Group Managing Director:

'Lidbury!' Spriggs said, 'Are you going on with that building?' 'Yes, Sir Frank, I am going on with that building,' Lidbury replied.

'Well, you are to stop it at once, you understand me—stop it at once,' said Sir Frank.

'I am very sorry, Sir Frank,' said Lidbury. 'I must come and see you,' which brought the response:

'I've given you my instructions; you are to stop it at once.'

By that time contracts had long since been signed, the old building was demolished and work had already started on the new one, so John Lidbury telephoned Frank Spriggs' secretary for an appointment. Half an hour later Spriggs rang back and said:

'John, it's all right, only "Dobbie" was with me kicking up a dust about the money you were spending. I thought I had better tell you to stop it; you can't can you?' When Lidbury answered 'No', Spriggs replied: 'Good job, too!'

Although Dobson was the cause of so much anguish to John Lidbury he is quick to tell you: ' "Dobbie" was a great man; don't make any mistake about that'. However, it seems hard to credit that such pantomimes went on among senior Directors. It is possible, however, that by then Tommy Sopwith had reached the stage where he was for the quiet life, although he could still put his foot down when the need arose. There was, for example, the occasion when a number of the Directors voted for the introduction of a staff bonus scheme. For some reason Frank Spriggs and another Director were not present when the decision was taken. At the next Board meeting angry voices demanded that the matter should be reconsidered, but Sopwith politely and firmly said: 'That item was discussed and decided upon at the last meeting. Next business please'. And next business it was.

*   *   *

When the new Hawker headquarters building was nearing completion, John Lidbury got wind of some disturbing news through various colleagues on the board. Apparently, Sir Frank Spriggs had told another of the Directors: 'I hope that bugger, Lidbury, hasn't gone in for any marble 'alls, because we're not having any of that'. Now this was bad news for John Lidbury because it so happened that the main entrance hall was beautifully faced in marble. To make matters worse, it was announced that the top brass, Sir Thomas Sopwith, Sir Frank Spriggs and Sir Roy Dobson, would be coming to have a look at the new building before the official opening. In near panic Lidbury telephoned his architect to say he was in the hot seat and to ask if he could suggest anything that might get him out of trouble. He said: 'They don't want any marble halls—and you know what we've got!' 'Easy,' the architect replied. 'Tell them it's travertine.'

The three knighted gentlemen walked into the new building with an apprehensive John Lidbury in tow. They looked around this palace of aeronautics and one could have heard a pin drop. In as firm a voice as he could muster, Lidbury announced: 'This is all travertine, you know.' 'Is it?' said Sir Frank Spriggs in astonishment. ' "Dobbie", what do you think of this? It's travertine!' With amazement written across his face, Sir Roy Dobson replied: 'Oh, is it? Marvellous what they can do with plastics these days.' Sir Thomas Sopwith is reported to have hooted with laughter, although he did not say a word. Alone among the three knighted directors present, *he* knew that travertine originated from *travertino,* the very finest-quality Italian marble.

Speaking to people who worked at all levels for Sopwith the words 'courteous', 'considerate' and 'gentleman' are constantly mentioned. And part of his success, in all walks of life, was a determination to find the reason for events, good or bad. He would never accept a situation at face-value and his method of finding the truth could seem like an inquisition to those on the other side of the desk. Such occasions are clear in Sir John Lidbury's memory:

'Although he was a man of few words, if you went to him with a proposition or he asked a question as to what was going on in the company and you gave him the answers, he could be a very difficult man to talk to. If something had happened, and he wanted to know what had happened, and you said: "This, that and the other", he would look you straight in the eye and say: "Why?". Then you would say, "Well, because of so-and-so and so-and-so"—again "Why?". After about five "whys", you didn't know what to say. It was very disconcerting—but he got to the nub of the point.'

People always knew when Tommy Sopwith was on the shop floor by the whiff of cigar smoke that announced his approach and, although he was a man of few words, he would always stop and have a chat with people on the staff who he recognized as having been with his firm for a long time. Sometimes the newest apprentice would also receive the same treatment.

Whereas Sir Roy Dobson was a hustler who wanted the most complicated of matters explained in a few words, Tommy Sopwith was a patient listener. Sir John Lidbury remembers an occasion when Stuart Davies had an idea he wanted to put forward. An appointment was arranged and the Cockney Davies was marched in to see his Lancashire boss. Dobson had the highest regard for 'Cock' Davies, but that did not stop him from glaring at the man and growling: 'What's up with you?' in his ripe Lancashire accent. 'Oh, there's nothing wrong with me,' replied the Cockney with conviction. 'Well, get on with it then,' said Dobson, whereupon Davies started to explain that if they did this-and-that to the wing, and removed that from here and added it there, he would be able to guarantee an improvement of 'X'. At intervals Dobson would urge him along with explosive interjections of: 'Yes! Yes-yes!' Davies continued at some length until he had finished what he had come to say.

'Well, come on man,' roared Dobson, 'get on with it!'
'I've dun,' replied Davies in a sort of mock Lancashire.

Lidbury was present during the conversation and, for a moment, he thought Dobson was going to hit 'Cock' Davies.

Giant leaps forward

A large addition to the Hawker Siddeley Group was made during December, 1959, when the internationally-respected de Havilland Aircraft Company came into the Sopwith orbit. Aircraft from this Hatfield-based concern had for many years captured the imagination of the world. There was the Mosquito, a high performance, all-wooden design that flew in the role of night-fighter, high-speed camera aircraft and light bomber. As a bomber it was capable of flying a 4,000-lb bomb to Berlin, something the much larger Boeing B17 Flying Fortress was unable to do. The de Havilland concern had built the Vampire, (the second jet fighter to enter RAF service) and its Tiger Moths, almost 9,000 of which had been built, were used in the initial training of most Commonwealth pilots who flew during World War 2.

After the war the de Havilland company produced the world's first jet-powered airliner, the graceful Comet. It was a giant leap forward in aeronautical technology, offering smooth flight and levels of quietness that had never been experienced before, not to mention a great increase in speed over contemporary piston-engine airliners.

On 10 January, 1954, BOAC Comet G-ALYP crashed into the sea near the Italian island of Elba killing all passengers and crew on board. Then on 18 April, that year, Comet G-ALYY plunged into the sea near Naples, again with the loss of all on board. All Comets were grounded while much of the aircraft was salvaged and sent to the Government-run Royal Aircraft Establishment at Farnborough. At the time, Director of the RAE was the same Arnold Hall who had befriended Frank Whittle at Cambridge many years earlier, and his brilliant investigations revealed that the two crashes had been caused by fatigue failures which had started at the edge of one or more of the windows in the pressurized passenger cabin.

A combination of lost orders and the cost of re-designing the Comet, which, in revised form, went on to give excellent service for many years afterwards, placed the de Havilland Aircraft Company in a serious financial position. At its peak in 1944 it had employed more than 38,000 people at home and abroad. Now the priority was to save the company. The saviour was Tommy Sopwith and his Hawker Siddeley Group. It seems hard to credit that on 17 December, 1959, the entire de Havilland organization was purchased for only £15 million.

A few years after the de Havilland concern joined the Hawker Siddeley orbit, Tommy Sopwith sent Sydney Camm over to Hatfield on a courtesy visit. Although Camm was acknowledged to be a fighter designer *par excellence* he had little, if any, experience in the civil field. Nevertheless, the Hatfield design office showed him the DH125 business jet then being developed. It has remained in production ever since and, by 1990, the total number sold worldwide was fast approaching 780 aircraft. On his return to Kingston, Camm let it be known that he had told '. . . that de Havilland lot that the fuselage wanted another yard in it—not another foot or ten inches; a whole yard!'

Another Sopwith acquisition was Folland Aircraft Ltd of Hamble, a firm that had been founded by Henry Folland who, during the Great War, had designed the Royal Aircraft Factory's SE5s. This was the only British fighter of the period to rival the Sopwith Camel. Folland's company had made a very small jet, called the Midge, and this was developed into the Gnat, a little hot-rod of a jet fighter that was made famous by the RAF Red Arrows aerobatic team. The company was purchased for £814,000. Turnover of the Hawker Siddeley Group in 1960 was £324 million, a staggering figure at the time, and net profit was not far short of £21 million.

It is interesting to compare the cost of Hawker military aircraft and their engines over the 40-year period from 1928 to 1968, although it should be remembered that the figures relating to the chosen examples are distorted by the fall in money values due to world inflation:

Year	Aircraft	Total Price	Engine Type	Engine Price
1928	Hart	£2,200	R-R Kestrel	£300
1935	Hurricane	£7,500	R-R Merlin	£2,000
1951	Hunter	£120,000	R-R Avon	£20,000
1967	Harrier	£11.3M	R-R Pegasus	£1.1M

Between 1928 and 1935 there was little if any inflation, so the difference in price between a Hart and a Hurricane is comparable on a straight figure basis. Inflation has plagued most countries since the war, but even allowing for this, much of the difference in price between the Hawker Hunter and a Harrier (quoted above at its 1988 price) is, to a considerable extent, a reflection of the growing complexity of modern fighter aircraft. It illustrates the problems that Tommy Sopwith had to face while keeping abreast of fast-changing aeronautical technology during his long chairmanship of Hawker Siddeley. Remember he had been involved in building aircraft from the days of stick-and-wire and remained to see his company design and produce the only operational vertical take-off and landing aircraft in the world.

*   *   *

Sir Sydney Camm never had the satisfaction of seeing his Harrier enter operational service. On 12 March, 1966, at the age of 72, he died while playing golf and Britain lost the most gifted military aircraft designer of all time. He had come from humble beginnings, one of 11 children raised in a small house. But under the guiding hand of Tommy Sopwith he had been encouraged to extend his talents and the fruits of his genius turned H. G. Hawker into a massive concern of international importance. Camm could be a fire-eater and at times he was very hard on his staff; but it was all in the quest for perfection. If ever a pilot was hurt or, worse still, killed in an aircraft of his design, he was so overcome with grief that one felt he was blaming himself for events that could not have been forseen. Such accidents during test flying are usually the price of progress. Camm's aircraft played a vital role in the defence of the free world, and his efforts earned him a well-deserved knighthood in 1953.

The Hawker Siddeley Group had weathered the years of change since the end of World War 2. It had prevailed, while other companies had been forced into mergers or take-overs as an alternative to going into liquidation, and its strong position was the product of wise leadership by Tommy Sopwith and his talented Board. The stage was set for still greater achievements because the leading players were all professionals—creative designers, first-class engineers, prudent businessmen and good managers. But amateurs, inspired by political dogma and an urge to interfere in a business they did not understand, were soon to destroy Tommy Sopwith's work of a lifetime.

CHAPTER
10

The Soaring
Eagle Falls

BY THE MID 1950s radical changes were taking place in most manufacturing industries, not just those engaged in building aeroplanes; and the Hawker Siddeley Group was faced with policy decisions that would have taxed a much younger man than Tommy Sopwith. Some of these changes were the result of technical advancement, others came about because of an American-inspired belief that 'big is beautiful'. UK companies latched onto this idea and merged to form large combines, much as Sopwith had done as long ago as 1936. Another factor was the influence of politicians, sometimes good, often not, and sometimes motivated by irrational political doctrines.

The history of the Hawker Siddeley Group over the 20 or so years starting from 1955 is interesting because it provided opportunities for Tommy Sopwith to exercise his many outstanding qualities, particularly his talent for selecting the right people for his team. At this stage, it is opportune to introduce one such talented person who eventually became Chairman of Hawker Siddeley and who, in many respects, carried on from where Sir Thomas left off. He is the previously-mentioned Arnold Hall and, in recounting the story it is necessary to go back over some of the events mentioned in previous chapters.

As a friend and supporter from Cambridge days, Arnold Hall accompanied Frank Whittle in 1935 when he managed to persuade Whitehall Securities to advance him £5,000 towards the first jet engine. It was the first investment made in this historic aeronautical development. In 1937, not long after the first jet engine had run, Hall recalls that:

'Sopwith turned up to see this engine, surrounded by a lot of chaps. He had come over from Coventry because all this was happening at Rugby. He looked, asked a lot of questions, and was his usual enthusiastic self. He said little about his impressions, but then you wouldn't expect him to. It was a totally new thing to him and the Whittle invention was, at that time, surrounded by controversy because so many people said that it wouldn't work. One of the standard things that was said before it ran, was that it wouldn't run!

Sopwith struck me as young, vigorous, interesting—I suppose this was round about the time when he was doing a lot of yachting. I knew little about him except that he was the Chairman of the Hawker Siddeley Group and that he was the great yachtsman.'

Arnold Hall has often wondererd what happened after that visit because, initially at any rate, Hawker Siddeley appeared to take little interest in the jet engine.

Although there was so much apathy about the turbojet, more imaginative minds had switched on to the opportunities that might follow if such an engine were to succeed. In a rare flash of official astuteness a 600-mph wind-tunnel was built at Farnborough at a time when the fastest aircraft had managed to achieve little more than 400 mph. It was to prove a sound investment over the next few years. The main problem facing designers trying to achieve higher speeds was the inability of very large piston engines to cool themselves because of the enormous power required. Whittle's engine discharged the surplus heat out of its tailpipe in the form of thrust, and this was one of the turbojet's prime advantages. Hall worked on the high-speed tunnel from its inception and he was, therefore, closely involved with the early development of the jet engine.

Interest in jet propulsion was now growing at the Air Ministry, and, as a result, it was decided to build an experimental aeroplane to prove the Whittle engine. As previously recorded, the Gloster Aircraft Co was selected for this important project and Arnold Hall became involved in what was then regarded as high-speed aerodynamics. It was his first real contact with the Hawker Siddeley Group on a working basis. He feels that Tommy Sopwith must have remembered his visit to the Whittle testbeds of a few years previously and that, as a result, he would have encouraged Gloster Aircraft to bid for the contract.

Arnold Hall had spent the war years at the Royal Aircraft Establishment at Farnborough and then left to resume his chosen career in the academic world. After the war he was appointed Professor of Aeronautics at Imperial College, London, where he held the chair endowed in 1915 by Baron Zaharoff. As he once modestly said: 'There, I was, doing no harm to anybody—not that I would claim I was doing very much good'. In 1951 the director of the Royal Aircraft Establishment died suddenly. His death was totally unexpected and, in consequence, no plans had been made for his replacement. Arnold Hall was approached by the Churchill Government of the day and asked if he would be prepared to go back as Director of that important establishment. The Korean war had started, it was developing into a conflict of major proportions and, with fears of it becoming World War 3, pressure was mounting for intensive scientific investigation into, among other subjects, high-speed aerodynamics.

Hall agreed to take on the appointment for five years but no longer—he had no wish to become a permanent civil servant. This he regards as a brave decision because, in those days, they were unable to remove you from a university professorship except for 'sins you didn't know how to commit.' Furthermore, he had no idea what he might do at the end of his period as Director. It was common knowledge throughout the aircraft industry and the Civil Service that he would be leaving Farnborough at the end of five years and he was shown in the official lists as a 'temporary'.

When he was nearing the end of his directorship at the RAE, a number of people offered him senior appointments, including the Civil Service which wanted him to stay. By now Arnold Hall had received a knighthood. However, probably at the instigation of Sir Roy Dobson who was then director in charge of A. V. Roe, Tommy Sopwith telephoned Arnold Hall and said he would like to be shown over the RAE. After an extensive tour of the establishment, Sopwith floated the idea of Arnold Hall joining Hawker Siddeley. He felt such a move would be mutually beneficial. In his own words, he said: 'I think it would be right for both of us', although he immediately qualified this with: 'I can't guarantee you anything at all'. Sopwith must have regarded the occasion as one of great importance because, notwithstanding his many commitments, he spent the whole day at the RAE. In the event, Arnold Hall agreed to join Hawker Siddeley, more because he had formed an instant regard for Tommy Sopwith than through any particular ambition to be involved in the aircraft industry. As Hall said:

'This was Sopwith's mysterious quality with people—people did have a regard for him almost instantly. He had a curious mixture of sense, humour, attractiveness—"no side" as people used to say. Modesty and yet attainment made an appealing man of him, and that was part of his mystique throughout his life.'

As a result of that meeting in 1955, Arnold Hall became Technical Director for the Hawker Siddeley Group. At that time almost the entire work of the company was on aircraft, most of them military, although it had started making missiles. His appointment could have caused serious staff problems because, throughout the organization, there were a number of Chief Designers, older men than himself, most of them talented and some with strong personalities.

Arnold Hall was well aware that his entry to the Hawker Siddeley Group at director level was causing 'a bit of a flurry', and he had no intention of telling the likes of Sydney Camm how to design his aeroplanes. Sopwith's idea was to have someone on the main Board who could take a broad view of what was going on throughout the company as a whole, although Sir Arnold feels certain that the title 'Technical Director' was invented so that a home could be found for him within the organization. It was a first step towards rationalizing a company that had grown enormous, but remained a collection of separate entities.

Sydney Camm, by then a long-standing servant of the company with a list of highly-successful aircraft behind him, was not on the Board but, fortunately, Camm and Arnold Hall were old friends. Camm would appear most Friday afternoons in Hall's office at the RAE and say: 'Can you test . . . for me in one of your wind tunnels?' Contrary to the belief held in some quarters, Sydney Camm was not distrustful of the scientific approach, quite the reverse, but surprisingly he never had a wind-tunnel at Hawker's. The staff at Farnborough, however, admired him sufficiently to work on his various projects at weekends if necessary. The lack of a suitable wind-tunnel would eventually have its repercussions because, when Sydney Camm died, Hawker Aircraft were to see the centre of fighter development shift from Kingston to other parts of the Hawker Siddeley Group where better facilities were available. Discussing this many years later Sir Arnold Hall said: 'It was one of my very great pleasures to put Sydney Camm on the Board when I became Chairman.' Like so many others in a position to express such opinions, he regarded Camm as the best fighter designer the world has ever seen.

Arnold Hall was based at the Hawker Siddeley headquarters in St James's Square, London (where it remains to this day) and there Tommy Sopwith's attitude towards his newly-appointed Technical Director was one of: 'Don't ask me what I want doing, but do what your imagination leads you to'. Thus it was that Sir Arnold Hall went around the Group and discussed design projects at each factory, so that he could report back to the Board of Directors and press for money when he thought a particular project should be supported.

The Board met every month under the chairmanship of Tommy Sopwith. He also chaired another body he had set up, comprising the chief designers of the major companies, which he called the Design Council. This simple but brilliant arrangement enabled him to keep in touch with the various technical developments that move so rapidly in the world of aeronautics, while at the same time watching the general affairs of Hawker Siddeley through chairing the Main Board. He had little to do with day-to-day matters which were handled by Sir Frank Spriggs, the Group Managing Director.

In 1958 plans were afoot to amalgamate Armstrong Siddeley Motors and Bristol Aero Engines with a view to forming a new and more powerful Bristol Siddeley aero engine company that would compete with Rolls-Royce on a more equal footing. It was one of those odd arrangements, typical of the aviation industry, whereby rival firms will sometimes jointly set up a new company.

Sir Arnold Hall was assigned by Sopwith to assess whether or not the amalgamation would be a good idea. The best part of a year was spent looking into every aspect of the possible merger before, in 1958, Hall recommended the proposal to his fellow directors. Discussions at the Hawker Siddeley Board meetings were always short and to the point, and it was rapidly agreed to put

Sir Frank Spriggs, for many years Managing Director of the Hawker Siddeley Group.

Sir Roy Dobson, Managing Director of A.V. Roe and later Chairman of the Hawker Siddeley Group after the retirement of Sir Thomas Sopwith.

The brilliant Sir Arnold Hall, one time professor, government scientist and eventually Chairman of a very diversified Hawker Siddeley Group.

Sir John Lidbury, who became Group Managing Director of the Hawker Siddeley empire when Sir Arnold Hall was appointed Chairman.

Above Sir Sydney Camm, one of the finest military aircraft designers of all time.

Above right Squadron Leader Neville Duke, DSO, OBE, DFC and two bars, AFC, Czech MC, Hawker's Chief Test Pilot (1951-56) who did much of the development flying on the Hunter. In 1953 he broke the World Air Speed record in a Hunter at 727.6 mph.

Right Bill Bedford, OBE, AFC, Hawker's Chief Test Pilot in 1956 who made the first flight in a Hawker P1127 which eventually became the world-renowned Hawker Harrier.

The Hawker Sea Fury was probably the fastest piston-engine fighter to enter production. During the Korean War it gave a good account of itself against Mig 15 jet fighters.

One of Sydney Camm's many masterpieces was the Hawker Hunter, widely regarded as the finest subsonic jet fighter ever built.

In its day, the mighty Avro Vulcan was unmatched in all-round performance by any other heavy bomber in the world.

The Hawker Siddeley Hawk is the late Sydney Camm's very successful advanced trainer/light jet fighter which has been sold in considerable numbers to many countries, including the USA.

Sydney Camm's Hawker Siddeley Harrier remains the only successful vertical take-off and landing fighter in the world. It never ceased to astonish Sir Thomas Sopwith and it was probably his favourite aircraft.

Sir Thomas Sopwith, the genius who led from behind.

Sopwith the Sportsman — shooting ...

... and fishing.

Sir Thomas and Lady Sopwith survey the fruits of their labour. Before this picture could be taken they had to buy a salmon from the local fish shop because one of their catch had been given away before the photographer arrived!

Sir Thomas and Lady Sopwith with another member of the family.

217

Out in the country with Harold Macmillan (left), one-time Prime Minister and later the Earl of Stockton.

A friendly hug from HRH The Prince of Wales.

Amhuinnsuidhe Castle, the Sopwith shooting estate on the Isle of Harris off the north-west coast of Scotland.

The mansion at Tommy Sopwith's Arkengarthdale estate in Yorkshire.

The Sopwith holiday retreat near Hermanus, South Africa.

Compton Manor, the Sopwith family estate where Sir Thomas lived until soon after his 101st birthday.

Sir Thomas, Lady Sopwith, May Sopwith (then in her 90s) and Thomas Edward Sopwith at Compton Manor.

Sir Thomas and Lady Sopwith.

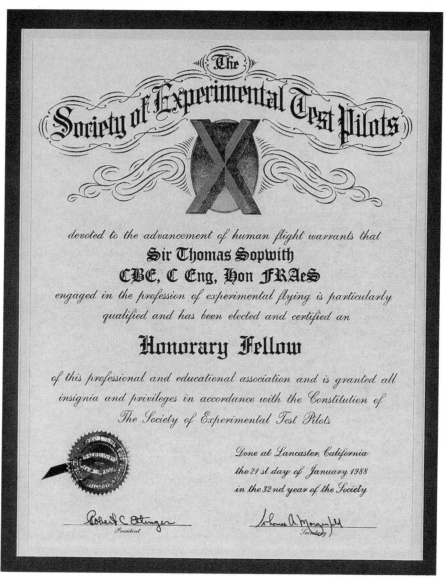

Above left Sir Thomas Sopwith, aged 98, by now totally blind, standing in front of the beautifully restored Sopwith Pup at the Museum of Army Flying. (*Salisbury Journal & Times Series.*)

Left Bill Bedford presents Sir Thomas Sopwith with his Honorary Fellowship of The Society of Experimental Test Pilots.

Above The certificate presented to Sir Thomas Sopwith shortly after his 100th birthday.

Sir Thomas listening to the Sopwith Pup, Hurricane and other Hawker aircraft that flew over Compton Manor on the occasion of his 100th birthday party on 18 January 1988.

in hand the Arnold Hall plan for setting up Bristol-Siddeley Engines Ltd.

The new firm was owned on a fifty-fifty basis by the two parent companies, and Hall was appointed Managing Director while remaining on the Board of Hawker Siddeley. Here again the Tommy Sopwith mystique was evident—he never pushed his views and opinions at these meetings, but there was a quiet pressure that ensured action. By contrast Sir Roy Dobson who ran A. V. Roe was described by Sir Arnold Hall as:

'A "roarer"; a splendid piece of human flesh who threw himself at a problem. Everybody heard about it and "Dobbie" got things done. Sopwith got things done equally effectively in a different way—I never heard the man shout.'

Although he was mainly concerned with the financial health of his massive company, Tommy Sopwith never lost interest in the design process. Often he would buttonhole Sydney Camm at Hawker's and say: 'Come on, Sydney, let's go and see what you are up to'. John Lidbury describes Sydney Camm as: 'A great man—he was terrified of Spriggs but he loved Sopwith'.

The heavyweights at Hawker Siddeley in 1958 were Sir Thomas Sopwith (Chairman of the organization), Sir Frank Spriggs (the Group Managing Director) and Sir Roy Dobson (Managing Director of A. V. Roe in Manchester). Some tension had developed between Spriggs and Dobson over the development of Avro Canada which, at the time, was going well and the relationship degenerated to a stage where Dobson refused to work under Frank Spriggs. There is no doubt that Sir Frank Spriggs was a very able man but something of a closed book, whereas Sir Roy Dobson was quite the opposite—people knew exactly where they stood with 'Dobbie'. Clearly this was an unhealthy situation, and in June, 1958, Sopwith called upon his Board to resolve the matter. Sopwith told the meeting that while, in some respects, tensions could be good for a company the Spriggs-Dobson relationship had got out of hand. He felt that it was time for the long-serving Frank Spriggs to retire. In any case, as he put it to the other Directors, 'Dobbie deserves his turn'.

Frank Spriggs had been with the company for 45 years and was due to retire in a few years time. He left that afternoon, generously compensated, and never came back. Hawker Siddeley may have been a public company with a powerful Board of Directors, but there was never any doubt about who was the boss, and Tommy Sopwith saw to it that Roy Dobson was appointed Group Managing Director in place of Frank Spriggs. On the basis of other people's recollections it seems that the Sopwith-Spriggs relationship was never a very happy one. According to 'Bobo' Sigrist (now Princess Guirey), on a number of occasions during the early days of Sopwith Aviation, Tommy Sopwith sacked Frank Spriggs but her father, Fred Sigrist, always took him on again.

The Canadian enterprise

The transatlantic venture inspired by Roy Dobson could have led to the development of a sound aviation industry in Canada which would have been as much to the advantage of the Canadian people as Hawker Siddeley. Unfortunately, it was not to be and the entire enterprise was destroyed by a mixture of over-optimism and local politics.

During the war the Canadian Government had set up the Victory Aircraft Plant at Malton, Toronto, where Avro Lancasters and other aircraft were built for the Allied war effort. In June, 1945, not many months after the fighting ended, Sir Roy Dobson, acting on behalf of Hawker Siddeley, purchased the factory and set up A. V. Roe Canada Ltd. The staff rapidly grew from 500 to 12,000 and eventually reached a peak of 14,000.

One of the major projects tackled by Sopwith's Canadian enterprise was the supersonic Arrow fighter bomber which was to be powered by a new engine, the Iroquois, being designed and built by another of Hawker Siddeley's Canadian companies. Development of the aircraft and its engine went on apace under the dynamic leadership of Roy Dobson until 1959, when the Government changed and the new regime cancelled the aircraft.

The removal of A. V. Roe's main Canadian project was a serious blow which threatened the very existence of the parent company in England; it was a matter of grave concern to Tommy Sopwith and his Board because vast sums of money had been invested in Canada by Hawker Siddeley. When the problem first emerged Hawker Siddeley tried to hedge its bets by diversifying into other fields. Dobson had developed a liking for heavy industry and, under his influence, the company purchased the massive Canadian Car and Foundry Co at Montreal. It also obtained interests in steel production and coal mines, but these too ran into troubled waters. Drastic action was needed before irreversible damage was caused to the Hawker Siddeley Group. To cut future losses, Dobson immediately got rid of the 14,000 staff employed at A. V. Roe Canada.

Initially, Tommy Sopwith had been in favour of the Canadian venture and had also supported Dobson's heavy industry ambitions. Although it had become a serious drain on Hawker Siddeley's resources, Dobson never really lost faith in the venture and tried to convince the Board that it would gradually improve. But the signs were not good. When Arnold Hall could no longer go along with it, Sopwith was at first inclined to support Dobson, but then he adopted a neutral position. Eventually, Sir Arnold Hall was sent over to disentangle Hawker Siddeley from the worsening situation and there he sold off the various companies.

There are many who regard the cancellation of the Arrow as an act of political madness. Certainly it deprived Canada of an important section of its aircraft industry, cost 14,000 people their jobs and put at risk the entire

Hawker Siddeley enterprise so carefully built up by Tommy Sopwith over a great number of years. The cost of the Arrow project was, however, rising and, although initial tests confirmed that the aircraft was going to meet all of its design objectives, it seemed unlikely that any of the supersonic aircraft would be sold outside the rather limited market of Canada. Whatever the rights and wrongs of the decision to cancel the Arrow, Sopwith and his colleagues were glad to come out of the disaster with the company intact.

*   *   *

Some years later Hawker Siddeley suffered a second blow at the hand of the Canadian Government. When Sopwith and his Board purchased the de Havilland concern in December, 1959, this included de Havilland Canada, a successful company specializing in short take-off and landing (STOL) designs. Possibly inspired by the British Labour Party, the Canadian Government nationalized de Havilland of Canada in 1970, an act from which it never fully recovered. In the 1980s the firm was in such a poor trading position that it had to be sold to Boeing. Looking at the successful track-record of Tommy Sopwith and his many companies, it is interesting to ponder where A. V. Roe Canada and de Havilland Canada might be today had the experts been allowed to manage these potentially highly successful firms.

*   *   *

The purchase of de Havilland also brought with it de Havilland Australia, but here the story is a happier one because it continues trading in the name of Hawker de Havilland as part of the present-day Hawker Siddeley Group. Most articles that have been written about Tommy Sopwith confine themselves to the various Hawker companies, yet he was equally committed to the other large concerns within the group. According to Arnold Hall who naturally knew him well:

'Sopwith was not biased. Yes, he was Hawker-orientated, but he always managed to convey a total equality of esteem to those around him. The other member firms all revered him equally and he never showed any signs of partisanship, despite the fact that he came from the Hawker stable. This was interesting because Spriggs [Sir Frank Spriggs, one-time Group Managing Director] who was also a Hawker man did definitely show Hawker partisanship which was resented by some of the other companies. Then when Dobson [Sir Roy Dobson of A. V. Roe] succeeded Spriggs as Managing Director, the same thing happened—only it was Avro! Sopwith was truly all things to all of us.'

In 1963 Tommy Sopwith was 75 years old and he decided to retire as Chairman, although he was willing to remain on the Board. He felt that Sir Roy Dobson should succeed him as Chairman and the other Directors were happy to respect his judgement. It seems strange that Tommy Sopwith should have formed such a high regard for Roy Dobson because the two men were totally different in so many respects—possibly it was a case of 'opposites attract'. Dobson's promotion to Chairman left the position of Group Managing Director to be filled. A number of senior people were regarded as likely to occupy the now vacant post and it came as a surprise when the relatively young Arnold Hall was appointed. Who would have made the decision? Being a public company one would expect the Directors to discuss such an appointment in committee, but Tommy Sopwith had a talent for making up his mind and winning over his fellow Directors in private discussion. He would stir up an opinion and then act on it.

Arnold Hall got on well enough with Roy Dobson, although at times 'Dobbie' could be difficult to the point of being impossible:

'Dobbie was a man who was hateful and lovable. He would love people for three months and then they were "bloody fools". However, he had a marvellous facility for retrieval. If, on thinking about some incident, he came to believe that he was wrong, he would walk in and say: "Look, I'm the bloody fool".'

Opinions about the late Sir Roy Dobson vary. Some regarded him as a bully who was inclined to throw his weight around, but others who worked more closely with him found the man to be totally uncomplicated if sometimes excessively forthright. In contrast to the quiet and gentlemanly Sopwith, there were times when Roy Dobson could express himself rather forcefully in his pronounced Lancashire accent, but he had an excellent track-record. Furthermore, behind the fierce and at times threatening words was often a heart of gold, and a number of people have good reason to thank him for their rise to high office. In Sir John Lidbury's view:

'I took a very, very good opinion of "Dobbie". He was "Avro's"—and he hated "Hawker's" because it was a competitor. I was then "Hawker's" and when we had the Annual General Meeting, although he was a Group Director and I wasn't (Lidbury was Managing Director of Hawker's at the time and not on the Hawker Siddeley Board) I nearly always ended up sitting at his table and he always got at me. "Hawker's are no bloody good", he used to say, and I used to say the same to him about Avro.

When Sopwith got rid of Spriggs and put Dobson in as Group Managing Director, some of my "unfriendly colleagues" in the group said: "That's the end of you, old boy, because "Dobbie" is now in charge and you know what he thinks of you and Hawker's". A couple of months after he phoned me up and said: "I want to come and see you". He rolled up in my office on a summer's afternoon. He said: "John it's jolly nice to see you. I want you to take over all the aviation interests in the Group". He was supposed to be my enemy!'

Arnold Hall was always impressed by Sopwith's lighthearted manner; even at Board meetings the atmosphere was very relaxed because of his engaging personality. On being appointed Group Managing Director in 1963, he made John Lidbury his deputy. Between them, they tackled an outstanding problem which was a bi-product of the way that Hawker Siddeley had grown since

1935; there were so many separate design teams in the group, each going its individual way, that some form of rationalization was essential.

Naturally, each company, A. V. Roe, Gloster, de Havilland and so on, was proud of its name and the task was going to entail treading on a few toes. Arnold Hall called together the senior executives of all the member concerns and said he did not feel able to run a company which called itself the Hawker Gloster de Havilland Avro Blackburn Armstrong Whitworth Aircraft Co Ltd. It would look silly on the firm's letterhead! He gained the sympathy of those present and the name Hawker Siddeley Aviation was adopted for the new company. It was formed to look after the aeronautical interests of the Hawker Siddeley Group, which by then was rapidly diversifying into other fields.

This was the new organization, embracing all the aviation interests, that Sir Roy Dobson had talked of when he visited Kingston, and John Lidbury was appointed its Managing Director. Behind these important senior appointments, the guiding hand of Tommy Sopwith was always present. He would see to it that the waters ran the way he wanted them to run.

Initially the new company was divided into three divisions, but, over a period of two years, these were slowly merged into one unit. It was a case of gradual integration to avoid loyalty problems as historic firms lost their identity and became totally integrated within Hawker Siddeley Aviation. Strangely, resistance to change was often stronger among overseas' customers than in the UK. For example, the name of de Havilland was highly respected in the United States where the DH 125 business jet had been sold (and continues to sell) in considerable numbers, so much so that the British firm has a large Washington office to handle its affairs in America. But it was years before the Americans would refer to this very successful business jet as the HS 125 (that is, Hawker Siddeley 125).

Diversification

With the full support of Tommy Sopwith, in 1957 Roy Dobson was the prime mover in Hawker Siddeley buying the Brush Group which traded mainly in electrical products and diesel engines. It had been founded in 1879 by an American called Charles Brush, and the firm had pioneered many important developments in electrical engineering. The move might seem rather like a coal mine going into the ice-cream business, but there were sound reasons behind the purchase, not just an ambition to expand.

The infamous Duncan Sandys' paper, which created the impression that missiles were about to take over from manned aircraft, while not taken too seriously by Tommy Sopwith and other elders of the aircraft industry, did have the effect of prompting some of them to ask themselves: 'What if he is right and it is the end of the road for military aeroplanes?'

In that climate diversification seemed the proper thing to entertain and, in later years, it carried on apace under Arnold Hall. One after another Hawker Siddeley bought Crompton Parkinson, Brook Motors, Lister (diesel engines) and a great number of other famous companies in the electrical engineering industry. The motivation behind these acquisitions was not a fear that aviation was dying, far from it. Many take-overs were in progress at the time, vast empires were being established in electrical and non-aviation fields, and Hawker Siddeley felt that if it were to take a share in this business now was the time to act, particularly since the GEC concern was rapidly buying up large sections of the industry.

Having bought the Brush Group and several other concerns, the Hawker Siddeley Board could not leave them in isolation and risk being squeezed out of the market by the fast-growing opposition. It was a case of getting out of non-aviation activities or building up that side of the business to the point where it could hold its own against all comers. Such mergers were a mirror-image of what had happened within the aircraft industry. Large as some of these individual concerns may have been, and the Brush Group was a substantial undertaking, it was unlikely they could survive on their own. Consequently, their future would depend on joining with a much larger industrial group, and few in the world could match the size of Hawker Siddeley.

For reasons mentioned earlier, member firms in Hawker Siddeley Aviation had lost their original trading names under the Arnold Hall reorganizations, but the policy that was adopted with the new industrial acquisitions was to keep the original titles in the interest of brand loyalty. Unlike the aviation companies, the newly-acquired industries were engaged in manufacturing a great variety of totally different products—electric motors, diesel engines, batteries, electric cables, forestry machinery to mention but a few.

During the 1960s Duncan Sandys, a member of Winston Churchill's Cabinet, was pressing the various British aircraft firms to amalgamate. When the response was lacking in enthusiasm, the worthy Minister was not averse to exerting pressure by threatening to confine Government contracts to those who toed the line. To some extent there was logic in his thinking because the growth in size and complexity of post-war aircraft had certainly brought with it a need for large industrial capability. Gone were the days when small teams of men could sketch a new design on an envelope and have it flying in six weeks. Today, some projects are even beyond the capabilities of single countries, let alone companies acting on their own. To a large extent Tommy Sopwith had already taken the steps being championed by Duncan Sandys when he bought the Armstrong Siddeley Development Company in 1936 and formed the Hawker Siddeley Group. But it could be argued that mergers into fewer and bigger units were best encouraged by competition rather than at the end of a politician's shotgun.

It was partly as a result of political pressure that in 1963, when Tommy Sopwith was 75, the Hawker Siddeley Group bought Blackburn and General Aircraft Ltd, an old established firm with its main factory at Brough, near Hull, Yorkshire. Its founder, Robert Blackburn, had set up the company in June, 1914, although his aviation activities actually started five years earlier. For almost half a century his company had designed a great number of aircraft, many of them for use by the Navy, but most of the Blackburn designs were built in small numbers. At the age of 70 Robert Blackburn died while out fishing. The purchase of the company by Hawker Siddeley may have been influenced by political pressure, but there were advantages in taking over Blackburn. It had an engine division which owned the licence rights for a range of Turbomeca gas turbine engines of French design (these were smaller and of lower power than any of the gas turbine engines being produced by British companies at the time). Also its most successful aircraft, the Buccaneer, was in production and it offered scope for development. The Blackburn concern was building it on a 'cost plus' basis and earning only 4 per cent for its efforts. The new management negotiated a fixed price with the Government and then streamlined the manufacturing process to make it more profitable.

Following on the Duncan Sandys' policy of 'merger-mania', by 1960 the UK aircraft industry had reassembled itself into the British Aircraft Corporation, comprising the original companies of Vickers, English Electric, Bristol Aeroplane Co, Hunting Percival, and several smaller units. The other and rather larger conglomerate was the empire that had been built up by Tommy Sopwith, the Hawker Siddeley Group. This embraced Hawker Aircraft, A.V. Roe, Armstrong Whitworth, Blackburn and General Aircraft, de Havilland, Airspeed, Gloster Aircraft, and a number of non-aviation concerns. Short Brothers of Belfast had been nationalized during the war when it failed to deliver its much needed Sunderland flying boats and it remained outside the two combines, as did the Westland helicopter company.

*   *   *

Sir Thomas Sopwith must have been well past his mid-seventies when, one day, John Lidbury asked him how he managed to keep all his irons in the fire and remain as fit and active as a man 25 years younger. He replied:

'I'll tell you my secret, John. You must have lots of hobbies, that is the great thing in life. There's my shooting, my fishing and so forth. The big secret is not to overdo any one of them; and business has always been a hobby to me.'

Tommy Sopwith held to this view throughout his long and active life. In fact, many years after the conversation with John Lidbury someone once asked him why he had involved himself in so many activities—shooting, fishing, power boats, balloons, fast cars, yachting, aeroplanes and high finance. His answer was much the same as before:

'I tried all these things for fun. I should *hate* to be in a business if it wasn't fun.'

Students of heredity may find it interesting to compare Sopwith's advice to Sir John Lidbury and his later comments about 'business for fun' with the following words. They were written, in 1890, by Benjamin Ward Richardson while describing Tommy Sopwith's grandfather, Thomas Sopwith (1803):

Sopwith loved work; with him work was play and play was work, so that he was never for a moment idle; but his method was so quiet and unostentatious that it troubled no one about him.

By 1967 Tommy Sopwith was an active 79 year old. Although he was no longer involved in the day-to-day running of Hawker Siddeley, the firm was still regarded as his brainchild and the Board would often seek his views on radical proposals. In that year, Sir Roy Dobson retired; Sir Arnold Hall became Chairman and Managing Director of the Hawker Siddeley Group, and he appointed John Lidbury as his deputy, a position he held in addition to his duties as Managing Director of Hawker Siddeley Aviation. Although there had been integration on the grand scale, individual companies were expected to stand on their own feet and the local Directors enjoyed considerable autonomy. The Managing Directors of the larger companies were appointed to the main Board. Under the new team, non-aviation activities grew apace as more and more electrical and mechanical engineering companies joined the Hawker Siddeley Group.

Long after Tommy Sopwith had ceased to take an active part in the running of Hawker Siddeley, Arnold Hall would telephone him at Compton Manor and pass on the latest news. Occasionally Sir Thomas would call him and ask: 'Is everything going well?' Because contact was maintained almost to his final days, it is known with certainty that diversification into the electrical-mechanical industry had Tommy Sopwith's full approval. In Sir Arnold Hall's words:

'He was a man whose opinion you always enormously valued; it always had content. It wasn't just a superficial remark. I had great encouragement from him during that period.'

Even after his retirement, Tommy Sopwith's feeling of responsibility towards the Hawker Siddeley Group he had founded never really diminished. It was, after all, his creation and an extension of his unique personality. The spirit of the man was always present within the numerous factory walls.

Nationalization

Not content with the efforts that had been made by the aircraft industry in forming two large but competing groups, when a Labour government took office it went ahead with its stated plans to nationalize the entire British aircraft industry. The policy was to form all the airframe companies into one vast unit. Among the not very rational aims, presented in its *Consultative Document D* of 1975, was the following statement:

To secure the long term economic viability of the industry by giving the new organization the motivation to make the best use of the resources available to it and by engaging the energies and full commitment of its workers at all levels to its success, its vigour and its competitiveness.

It is hard to imagine what was in the mind of the author responsible for those jargonesque words (which sound like a passage from the television series *Yes Prime Minister*). He or she was clearly unaware of Sir Thomas Sopwith's many achievements over the previous 62 years, or what had been attained by his various companies, not to mention those of the rival British Aircraft Corporation. But reason had no part in the 1977 events leading to nationalization. The act was motivated by a political dogma which believed that the State could do things better than people such as Sir Thomas Sopwith. Where was the justification for the Wilson government's determination to take what did not belong to the State? Had not entrepreneurs, such as Sopwith, built successful enterprises that provided jobs for the population, wealth for the country and fair dividends for those who were prepared to risk their money by purchasing shares? Had the British aircraft industry ever let down the nation in times of crisis?

The Government named the new mammoth British Aerospace. It was a blatant act of left-wing political mindlessness which got through the House of Commons by only one vote.

Naturally, the State plunder of the aircraft industry was strongly resented by the various company Directors, most of the shareholders and much of the workforce. Indeed, at a meeting held in the lecture hall of the Royal Aeronautical Society, where the Chairman designate tried without much success to justify the new nationalized aircraft industry, it was clear that they were in a very worried frame of mind. From the questions being asked by members of the audience (many of them key staff from the Hawker Siddeley Group and the British Aircraft Corporation) it was obvious that they were in fear of losing their jobs in the turmoil to come. In the event, Hawker Siddeley lost its UK aviation interests and it is debatable whether or not the shareholders were ever properly compensated. This was a great sadness to Sir Thomas Sopwith who later said:

'Nationalization was unnecessary and counter-productive. Nothing can replace the thrust of free enterprise and the exciting stimulus of private venture.'

Opposition to nationalization was not confined to the Hawker Siddeley Group. Indeed, Sir George Edwards, one-time Chairman of the British Aircraft Corporation recently expressed himself thus:

'I think everyone in the industry regarded nationalization as being irrational and unlikely to help in solving our basic problems; and so I believe it turned out to be. The aeroplanes on which British Aerospace has since prospered, such as the Tornado, saw the light of day in BAC before nationalization. I knew a number of key figures in the Labour Party at that time, and it was pretty apparent that it was dogma and not market forces which brought it about. The battle cry was that the two companies [British Aircraft Corporation and Hawker Siddeley] should be put together and that we were so unco-operative that the only way it could be achieved was to nationalize us. Fortunately for me, I saw it coming and gave up the Chairmanship of BAC over a year before it took place.'

One cannot help but reflect on the damage that was caused to the nation's interests when Sir George Edwards and people like him felt moved to leave the industry they knew so well in order to let the politicians play.

The nationalization saga is taken up by Sir Arnold Hall:

'I was all against it—I resisted it hook, line and sinker and became quite unpopular in the process. Of course, we talked about the possibility of nationalization for years before, because the Labour Party had made it fairly clear at its conferences that if it ever got power it would try to do this thing. To this extent we were always conscious that we could lose aviation if the country went that way.'

At no time during the diversification programme did Arnold Hall and his Directors employ the kind of hostile take-over tactics that have since become fashionable; and in no case was there a forced merger. Nevertheless, having induced a great many non-aviation companies to join the Hawker Siddeley Group, Sir Arnold Hall felt that it was his duty to stay with the company as Chairman after it was divested of all its aviation interests with the exception of Hawker de Havilland which was in Australia and therefore outside the clutches of a British government.

By 1977 aviation amounted to only 25 per cent or so of the group's turnover and, to this day, Hawker Siddeley remains an independent UK-based company embracing firms in a number of countries including Canada, Australia and the USA. There are no fewer than seven battery manufacturers, electric cable factories, firms making railway equipment, others in forestry and agricultural machinery, and electric motor manufacturers, among them one of the largest in America. By 1988 there were 102 companies in the group and it employed almost 43,000 people.

But nationalization had come. The British aircraft industry had been taken under duress from its rightful owners, and the Hawker Siddeley Group,

Tommy Sopwith's soaring eagle, had fallen. In two world wars the German military machine had been unable to destroy Tommy Sopwith's aircraft industry. But where the Germans had failed, a misguided British Government had succeeded.

CHAPTER
11

The Sunset Years

FOLLOWING NATIONALIZATION IN 1977 many jobs were lost in the process of welding together the two large combines. Some may regard this as surprising because job losses are contrary to the aims of the UK Labour Party which has always championed the cause of full employment, even when, in some cases, this is unattainable because a particular industry is in decline. However, in 1985, after a few lacklustre years as a State industry, the Conservatives returned British Aerospace to the private sector. It became a public limited company and a professional Chairman was appointed. Many of the shares were taken up by members of the staff at all levels, and one suspects that this was encouraged to deter any future Labour Government from renationalizing the aerospace industry. It is one thing to deprive the 'shareholding classes' (whoever they might be) of their investments, but hardly a vote-winning exercise to steal from shopfloor workers and junior management who have demonstrated their faith in their firm by putting hard-earned cash into the company.

In its entirety this massive aerospace enterprise, employing more than 130,000 staff, now operates successfully. Nevertheless, the demise of his aviation business continued to rankle with Sir Thomas Sopwith (it could hardly have done otherwise) and when the morning newspaper was brought to him, he would say: 'And what have the bandits done today?'

By the time of nationalization Sir Thomas had been actively connected with the aviation industry for 65 years, and had taken a leading part in a technological progress that had often advanced at breathtaking speed, probably faster than at any other time in the history of mankind. He could look back on the days before stick-and-wire flying machines when ballooning was fashionable and when his sister May had been his constant companion and loyal supporter. When she was over 90, May Sopwith took a long lease on a flat! One day in 1973, about a week or so before her ninety-ninth birthday,

May had been to a hairdressers in London's Mayfair and was on her way to a luncheon party she was giving for some friends in her flat, when the delightful old lady collapsed and died instantly on the pavement. She was in her way a pioneer of early aviation, very much a part of the Tommy Sopwith story, greatly loved by the man himself, and by all who had the pleasure of knowing her.

After Sir Thomas had retired as Chairman of Hawker Siddeley he naturally looked forward, in his remaining years, to enjoying the country activities of which he was so passionately fond, particularly shooting and fishing, a common interest he shared with his wife Phyllis. One might have expected that after the shooting accident that killed his father in 1898, he would have developed an aversion for guns, but the human mind does not always work in that way. However it is interesting that, although at first Thomas Edward shared his father's love of shooting, in later years he turned completely against it and could not bring himself to kill a living creature.

Country pursuits

In addition to Compton Manor, Tommy Sopwith had a home at Hermanus, not far from Cape Town in South Africa. Once a year the Sopwiths went out on one of the Union Castle liners complete with their Rolls-Royce car and chauffeur. Although the sea trip took 14 days each way, they would stay for only four weeks and then come home. During one of its long, unoccupied periods, their holiday home was broken into by a troupe of baboons. They swung from the chandeliers, tore down curtains and left the place as though a hurricane had blown through. The house in Hermanus was eventually sold to the brother of Christian Barnard, the South African heart surgeon.

During one of their South African trips Sir Thomas and Lady Sopwith met a young lady who had just become engaged to The Hon Richard Beaumont of the Northumberland lead mining family. This particular family had a profound influence on the lives of previous Sopwith generations. Richard Beaumont is now Chairman of Purdey's, the internationally-famous London gunsmiths. Because of the ancestral association between the Beaumont and Sopwith families, Sir Thomas loaned Richard Beaumont the book that had been published in 1891 based on the diaries of his grandfather, Thomas Sopwith (1803). At the end of a train journey to Devon, Richard Beaumont had trouble obtaining help with his luggage and, in his haste to remove the cases before the train moved on, he managed to leave the beautifully-bound volume in the carriage. All efforts to trace the book failed and Beaumont was then in the embarrassing position of having to tell Sir Thomas that his prized book, a valuable record of his ancestors, had been lost.

'I was sitting here in this room [at Purdey's] writing "Dear Sir Thomas, the most terrible thing has happened", when at that moment one of the staff came in and said: "Sir Thomas Sopwith wants to see you in the front shop". I walked out and there he was, standing with his hands behind his back. And I said to him: "Sir Thomas the most terrible thing has happened, I've got to tell you . . .", and I didn't get any further than that. From behind his back he produced the book and said: "I think that's what you want. A clergyman's daughter got into your compartment and found it there. As the address is in the front she sent it back to me. Now I think the best thing for you to do is to read it and then, after your wedding in October, will you and your wife come and shoot with me at Compton Manor?" It was typical of his kindness.'

There was also an estate for shooting at Arkengarthdale, near Richmond, Yorkshire, which the Sopwiths only visited once a year and for which a full-time agent was employed to look after their interests. While settling some bills in the estate office one day Sopwith's son Thomas Edward, then a young lad, rushed in and said: 'Daddy can I have sixpence [2½p] for some sweets?' After he had gone, Tommy Sopwith turned to his agent and said: 'That sixpence has just cost me a pound!' Allowing for the top rate of income tax in those days (97.5 per cent) Tommy Sopwith had to earn a pound before he could give his lad sixpence for a bag of sweets!

Until 1961 he also owned Amhuinnsuidhe Castle on the south-west coast of the Isle of Harris, near the northernmost isle in the Hebrides.

Even while active in the Hawker Siddeley Group, he would spend a few of the winter months visiting South Africa, journey to the Hebrides for fishing and deer-stalking and, in the grouse season, go to his place in Yorkshire for shooting. The remaining six or seven months were spent at Compton Manor, near Romsey, Hampshire. With all these enjoyable commitments, it was remarkable that he managed to fulfil his business responsibilities so successfully. Typical of the Sopwith character was an occasion when the butler, who had been with the family for many years and who used to call his boss 'Sir Tom', was ill. The Sopwiths put off the planned South African visit until their old servant was out of danger.

Sir Arnold Hall remembers being invited to join his old chief on the Isle of Lewis along with Hawker Siddeley's Financial Director, J. F. Robertson, a Scot whose father and other relatives had been gamekeepers. Being a keen shot and an excellent fisherman, Tommy Sopwith appreciated Robertson's talents with gun and rod. Although Arnold Hall had done some sea fishing, in such company he was really the odd man out. Despite some coaching by Sopwith, he worked hard at the river without so much as a bite, while Sopwith and Robertson fished out one salmon after another!

Tommy Sopwith often invited his senior staff to join him for a short holiday at one of his estates and, during 1946, Roy Chadwick, Chief Designer at A. V. Roe, Manchester, spent a relaxing time with his parent company boss at the castle on the Isle of Harris. Chadwick returned to Manchester with the first outline sketches of the Vulcan bomber which he had drawn on a copy of *The Sunday Times*. Sadly, it was his last holiday because, soon afterwards, he was killed in the Avro Tudor crash mentioned earlier. The Vulcan project was taken over by Stuart Davies.

At his main residence, Compton Manor, Tommy Sopwith was always the perfect host, inviting old friends for weekends or ex-employees for lunch. He would often greet his regular visitors with the words: 'Welcome home'. He was the personification of the perfect Edwardian gentleman. He had a unique turn of phrase and retained the pre-Great War pronunciation of many words— 'Off', for example, was always 'Orf'.

Whenever he visited his parents at Compton Manor, Thomas Edward used to fly himself in by helicopter. Sir Thomas was never involved in this type of aircraft but he recognized it as a practical vehicle, capable of doing what no others could achieve and his son was always expected to fly him around the estate. He enjoyed these flights enormously and they continued on a regular basis until Sir Thomas's failing sight made the exercise pointless.

Pheasant shooting at Compton Manor is excellent and among those who used to shoot there was Geoffrey Knight, the ex-Vice Chairman of the rival British Aircraft Corporation. Knight used to spend social weekends at Compton Manor which followed a standard routine; the guests would shoot on the Saturday, then Tommy Sopwith would join them for lunch and talk about the old days of aviation. An alert mind, which Sopwith retained to the end of his long life, enabled him to entertain his guests with witty accounts of past events. During his luncheon parties he would introduce a subject, get everyone talking and then sit back and enjoy the conversation. Someone once asked Sir Thomas if Harry Hawker was the kind of man who would have bought a round of drinks in a pub. He replied: 'Harry didn't drink—but I do'. When asked if Hawker smoked, he said: 'No—but I do'. Sir Thomas gave up smoking in 1981, when he was 93.

A measure of the great affection felt for Tommy Sopwith is the number of letters he received whenever his name appeared in the newspapers or on television—many of them came from voices of the past. Typical of the 'do-you-remember?' letters to arrive at Compton Manor on his ninetieth birthday, was one from W. E. Back. It reminded Sir Thomas that shortly after Sopwith Aviation was established at the disused roller-rink in Kingston, Back was interviewed by a then very young Mr Sopwith and Fred Sigrist. After a chat he was taken on the payroll:

'Well do I remember your generous reward to all your employees, when you gave a dinner party one night in Nutalls' large restaurant, with an orchestra and delightful singing by a local young lady who I ultimately married.'

Shades of things to come—Tommy Sopwith was always entertaining people for meals, and his favourite words throughout a very long life were: 'You must come and have lunch'.

There was also a constant flow of letters from complete strangers—housewives with a grandparent who flew Sopwith aircraft in the Great War, others with relations who were Hurricane pilots, navigators, air gunners or wireless operators in Lancasters or other Hawker Siddeley aircraft. Then there were the youngsters, girls as well as boys, who wanted information for school projects. All were answered; none was refused. Another manifestation of Sopwith hero-worship is illustrated by the number of Tabloid, 1½ Strutter, Pup, Triplane and Camel replicas that have been painstakingly built in Britain, America, Australia, South Africa and Canada.

The Sopwiths lived in the grand style and they had a great number of friends, not all of them wealthy by any means. Shooting parties at Compton Manor were widely regarded as the highlight of the season. Among her friends Lady Sopwith was known as 'The Dragon', a name always used good-naturedly and very much enjoyed by her. According to Geoffrey Knight:

'She was a very forthright lady—I can't remember who invented the name—but she loved it. And she was a very, very competent shot and fisherwoman. I sat next to her one night at dinner, years and years ago, when she said to me "Do you know where my pacemaker is Geoffrey?" and I said "No Dragon, I've got no idea". She said: "Well it's this side—see if you can feel it". It was like a sort of flat cigarette tin and I said: "I thought you always had to have them on the right". "No," she said, "not if you shoot from the right shoulder".'

Lady Sopwith had insisted that the doctors fitted her pacemaker where it would not interfere with the way she held her gun. Thus, she remained one of the best women shots in Britain.

During the Farnborough Air Shows it is the practice for the President of the SBAC to invite distinguished guests to his private hospitality chalet overlooking the flying display. One year Sir John Lidbury was President and he invited Earl Mountbatten for lunch. He had for many years been a friend of Tommy Sopwith's and the two men shared a number of interests, particularly fishing. During the lunch Earl Mountbatten turned to John Lidbury and said:

'You know my friend Tommy Sopwith, don't you. How is he at the moment—I haven't seen him lately. And how is the "Dragon"?'

Lady Sopwith's nickname, 'The Dragon', was born of an incident when Tommy Sopwith was running one of his shoots at Arkengarthdale in Yorkshire. They used to issue some of the guests with miniature walkie-talkies so that everyone knew the whereabouts of others in the party. One of the party called the others and said: 'We are just passing the Green Dragon', which was the name of a pub on the edge of the shoot. Lady Sopwith heard this on the radio and, since she was wearing green tweeds, thought they were referring to her. When they assembled again, she looked at her guests accusingly and said: 'What is all this about the Green Dragon?' After the explanations the name stuck.

Given the opportunity Phyllis Sopwith would talk enthusiastically about the important guests who had visited Compton Manor while Tommy Sopwith looked on adoringly. Certainly, some very distinguished and important people had been entertained by the Sopwiths, including HRH Prince Charles and Earl Mountbatten. It is well known that the sailor Earl was larger than life and that, through sheer force of personality, there was a tendency for him to take over whenever he entered a room full of people. Tommy Sopwith took this in his stride. He would sit quietly in a corner, taking it all in as the ebullient Earl went on in his usual interesting manner. On one occasion, John Crampton was summoned to give a presentation on the Harrier before Lord Louis, as the Earl was often known. Part of the presentation included a film of the Harrier in action and Crampton recalls that, while trying to explain the complex aircraft, he was subjected to constant interruptions from Mountbatten. For a long time the Earl was not in favour of the Hawker Harrier because it was regarded by the Royal Navy as a threat to the large aircraft carrier, as indeed it was—the Harrier manages very nicely without need of long flight decks.

At one time, a film company wanted to make a documentary on the life of Sir Thomas Sopwith. The late Kenneth More was retained to do the commentary and conduct some interviews with Sir Thomas sitting by the River Test which flows through the Compton Manor estate. The film was to be illustrated with old film clips as well as modern ones of more recent events. There was a hilarious luncheon when Kenneth More visited the Sopwiths at Compton Manor. More never acted—he was always himself, on and off the screen; few others would have got away with the kind of outrageous remarks he could make in front of ladies when the occasion prompted him and he made a hit with Lady Sopwith. Unfortunately, for financial reasons the film was never made.

There have, of course, been a number of sound and television interviews and in 1989 the BBC screened a documentary, much of it using black and white film made during 1934 and 1937, on the subject of Sopwith's attempts to gain the America's Cup. Commenting on this John Crampton said:

'That is a different man to the man that I knew. There was a man in what you might call his prime, in the 1930s, when he was 46. I met first of all a 75-year old man, and he had entered that stage of life where he had retired, he was living very comfortably and very happily with his beloved Phyllis—and their shooting and their Mountbatten and their Princess Margaret and all this—the stories would flow. Of course I was fascinated by it all. The man of the 1930s was a man I never met. So I can only really reminisce about what you might call the older Sopwith. One has learned a little about what happened in the early days—how he started the company and so on and so forth. One gets the impression that he was probably an extremely fair master to work for but that he didn't suffer fools gladly. You get the decimal point wrong and he probably wouldn't sack you; he probably wouldn't give you any work to do—and there is nothing more awful than that.'

On 18 January, 1978, Tommy Sopwith celebrated his ninetieth birthday and felt that the time had finally come to retire from the Board of Hawker Siddeley, which, by then, had no aeronautical connections in the UK. However, he continued to maintain a close interest in the company he had founded and, although his considerable shareholding was gradually reduced, the founding father was always in the background. Arnold Hall and his colleagues always impressed upon Sir Thomas that he was still wanted.

'It was generally felt that here was an exceptional man, and we wanted him to take an interest in us—the young boys wanted "The Skipper" around. We resolved to offer him, and were glad to find he accepted, the title of Founder and Life President.'

Commenting later on his new title, Sir Thomas said: '. . . I can't retire from that. I don't quite know what the obligations are, but doubtless I'll find out.'

Sadly, in 1978, not long after he was made Founder and Life President of Hawker Siddeley, his wife Phyllis died at the age of 86. The best of us have our weaknesses, and, in the case of Lady Sopwith, she could not bear to hear mention of Tommy Sopwith's first marriage to Beatrix. It was particularly sad that his long friendship with Beatrix's brother 'Sandy' Hore Ruthven (who later became the First Earl Gowrie) gradually came to an end after he re-married. After his wife died, Tommy Sopwith expressed a wish to meet Sandy's grandson, the Second Earl Gowrie (who is Chairman of Sotheby's, the famous auctioneers) and he came to Compton Manor. As he recalls:

'I got to know Tommy Sopwith in a very romantic way, very very briefly, because I knew young Tommy [T.E.B. Sopwith]. And young Tommy flew me down to see the old man in his helicopter because, he said, the old man was very fond of your Great Aunt [Beatrix] and she's never been allowed to be mentioned. And now my Mum [Phyllis Sopwith] is safely dead and everything, he has followed your career and he would love to meet you. And he [Sir Thomas] got me into a corner and he said: "She was a wonderful woman and I adored her you know. And it is so lovely to see you and I knew your father". Then he told young Tommy to look out some photographs of himself and "Sandy"—"Sandy" is my grandfather. Oh I think he was wonderful. I mean he had always been rather a legend because my grandfather used to talk about him a lot; they were very fond of each other.'

After Lady Sopwith died everyone who knew Sir Thomas well felt he would either fade away or take on a new lease of life; there would be no half measures. He was 90 years old, most of his oldest friends had long since departed and his 45 years of happy marriage had come to an end.

The fact that Lady Sopwith sometimes had difficulty in relating to other women must have pained Sir Thomas from time to time. Certainly it was a source of friction between mother and son. According to Thomas Edward Sopwith:

'She was passionately opposed to any lady that appeared in my life, and although up to a point that is understandable, she did, in my view, behave fairly unreasonably about that and it marred our relationship.'

Indeed, it was only after his wife died that Tommy Sopwith really came to know his daughter-in-law, Gina.

The problem was that Lady Sopwith and her son were too much alike to foster a really happy relationship, and although she was an excellent wife, an outstanding hostess and very popular among her friends, according to Thomas Edward Sopwith: 'There were only two totally unacceptable relationships to have with her. One was to be her son and the other was to be her daughter-in-law.'

*   *   *

While entertaining several officials of the Royal Automobile Club for lunch, one of them commented on a large silver trophy which had a decorated lid on it. Sir Thomas explained that, in 1935, the 'King's Cup' for sailing had been presented to him by King George V, but originally there was no lid. It so happens that Lady Sopwith collected antique snuff boxes and very many years later, while walking past a well-known firm of jewellers which enjoyed the Royal 'By Appointment' warrant, there in the window was a snuff box that caught her eye. Inside the shop she decided to buy the little box and getting out her cheque book, there was a discreet cough from the salesman followed by: 'With respect, Madam, we do not normally accept cheques for that amount'. When it transpired that the customer was Lady Sopwith, he immediately handed over the box and then produced the large silver lid to Tommy Sopwith's cup. 'How on earth do you come to have that?' asked Lady Sopwith, and he answered: 'Because when King George bought a number of trophies, including the one presented to Sir Thomas, he said I could keep the lid because he wasn't "bloody well paying for that too!"'

*   *   *

A pioneer of a different kind and an old friend of Tommy Sopwith's was Jimmy Jeffs who is generally regarded as the father of air traffic control in Britain. Long before World War 2 he was developing methods of fixing the position of aircraft by radio, and offering pilots a homing service based upon direction-finding stations so that they could locate the airport in bad weather. Jimmy Jeffs was invited to have lunch at Compton Manor. He was 86 at the time and Tommy Sopwith must have been 97. Before entering the room to meet his old friend, Jeffs was told by the butler how the lunch would proceed.

'There will be just one cocktail before we eat and Sir Thomas has arranged a nice bottle of wine with the meal', he was advised.

The rum-based 'cocktail' was rather like liquid Semtex and it came in a large silver goblet, almost the size of a tumbler. It was, of course, fabulous but there was a lot of it. Jimmy Jeffs later told his son that it almost blew his head off and he was beginning to wilt at the legs. After the two very senior citizens had finished their drinks, Tommy Sopwith turned to his butler and said: 'It's such a long time since I met Jimmy; let's have another one before lunch'. Meals at Compton Manor were always beautifully served and outstandingly prepared. There were usually one or two 'specialities of the house', for example, cheese served with a small heap of powdered Nescafé on the side of the plate. You were supposed to sprinkle the powdered coffee on the cheese before having it on biscuits—the results were worthy of note in the *Michelin Guide*. Of Sir Thomas Sopwith's staff at Compton Manor, Raymond Baxter, the television commentator, once said:

'He attracted a particular type of man and woman, right up to the end. When one was entertained to lunch it was done with quiet devotion; that is the only way I can describe it.'

Being a father late in life meant that Sir Thomas was a very old grandfather by the time his two grandchildren, Samantha and Candida, were grown up enough to appreciate him. Nevertheless, even in his late nineties and past his hundredth birthday, he looked forward to their visits. Candida, the younger girl, was a grandchild he had never seen, for he had lost his sight before she was born.

Sir Thomas Sopwith had an unshakable belief in the importance of aeronautical engineering to Britain. This was expressed by him on a number of occasions, and he once addressed himself on the subject to Mike Ramsden (at the time editor of *Flight International*) in the following words:

'I think it is important for the British to be good at making aircraft. It is important to stay in this business. A lot of people say it costs too much and that it's better to buy from America, but that's a very defeatist outlook. I don't approve of it. True, modern aircraft are very expensive and they take a long time. In the First World War when we thought up a new type, the damn thing was flying in six weeks. Now it isn't flying in six years! . . . I'm glad I lived when I did. But our fathers and grandfathers have all said that before us.'

In his mid-seventies when Tommy Sopwith's eye sight began to decline, it so happens that, about the same time, Sir John Lidbury had a cataract operation which went seriously wrong, resulting in poor sight ever since. The following incident, as recalled by Sir John, is an example of how the human spirit can make light of quite serious afflictions:

'He [Tommy Sopwith] decided to come to the SBAC luncheon for past-Presidents.

He had some sight and could get about. Soon as the lunch was over, he came up to me and said: "Come on, John; you're going to walk me back to the office". I said to him "that's two of us. Do you think you are safe?" and he said: "Oh rubbish, rubbish rubbish. You walk me back". So he and I groped our way through Piccadilly, down St James's—it was the blind leading the blind—I was nearly as bad as he was!'

In addition to cataracts, Tommy Sopwith was suffering from other eye complications and he went into hospital full of hope that, following an operation, his sight would at least be partly restored. Unfortunately, the operation was unsuccessful and this was probably the greatest regret of his life. According to his son: 'The only time I ever really saw him knocked sideways was in hospital afterwards'.

At the age of 96, Sir Thomas's sight was confined to shapes and devoid of all detail, then in the following years it got steadily worse until he was unable even to tell when a photographer had used his flashgun. Sir Thomas never really came to terms with his blindness and it was unfortunate that he did not share his grandfather's interest in music, something that might have brought comfort in his perpetual darkness.

Even in his late nineties people still wanted to interview Sir Thomas. By then his sight had gone and he was rather deaf although that was less of a problem thanks to some particularly good hearing aids. To those who did not know him, such interviews could be a little disconcerting because a question could be followed by a long silence while the interviewer wondered if he had heard what was being asked. In fact, he usually had heard but was determined to be factual and a suitable answer was being carefully prepared in his mind. It was all part of the Sopwith character to think before he spoke.

In general, Sir Thomas did not like being interviewed and he was less than enthusiastic about the television fraternity. He did, however, have a high regard for the television commentator, Raymond Baxter, who was himself a single-engine fighter pilot during World War 2. Raymond had come to know Thomas Edward in the days when he was racing cars and power boats and, through him, he was able to meet Sir Thomas when he was a still remarkably agile man of 75, actively shooting and fishing on a regular basis.

It was when Sir Thomas was approaching his mid nineties that Thomas Edward invited Raymond Baxter to lunch so that they might discuss an idea that he and his wife Gina had in mind. Thomas Edward was mindful of his father's contribution to aviation and his place in history, and he wanted a good recording of him before it was too late. As he put it to Baxter, he feared that:

'He'll topple off his perch one morning. You know how it is. We've got a tremendous archive down at Compton, but would you record some conversations with my father, strictly for the family?'

Raymond Baxter made a number of visits to Compton Manor, completing the recording sessions before lunch so that Sir Thomas could rest in the afternoons. It soon became clear to Raymond that the interviews had great potential for a possible radio programme or, even better, television. However, in the wonderous ways of the BBC the opportunities presented by an interview with Britain's last living aviation pioneer generated little enthusiasm.

Thanks to Aubrey Singer (then Managing Director of BBC Television), a television film was funded out of his 'Exigency Budget'. And, having got the BBC to fund the programme there remained the last important hurdle, that of persuading Sir Thomas who, because of his modest nature, was bound to resist another interview, particularly since this time it was for public viewing. When first approached he said:

'"But I've said all this to you before on that machine of yours" and Raymond explained that this time it was for television so that people could see him. The response was not encouraging. He said "no one wants to look at an ugly old bugger like me". Raymond Baxter could see his brainchild spinning in before it had taken off so he said "Come on Sir Tom, this is very important. You owe this to history. I think of my grandson seeing you on television and it will be like seeing and listening to Napoleon". Sir Thomas was still not convinced and he replied "I'd have preferred it if you had said Wellington".'

In the event Sir Thomas Sopwith did agree and viewers all over the world were able to enjoy the celebrated Raymond Baxter's interview of Britain's last surviving aviation pioneer when he was 96. Technically, the BBC handled the interview with great sympathy. The lighting crew was at pains to minimize the inflamed appearance of the old man's eyes and to avoid directing very bright lights at him which he found uncomfortable. Members of the TV crew, by tradition a hard-bitten breed, had been warned to be on their best behaviour but there was really no need; they recognized the presence of greatness. The programme was made in two morning sessions and, on the second day Sir Thomas, sensing that the young director was ill at ease, turned to him and said:

'I know exactly what you are fussing about, Jonathan. But I'm wearing precisely the same clothes, the same cravat, and I've tied the same knot to the best of my ability, but I can't guarantee that all the spots are in the same place.'

The remark made him an instant hero with the camera crew.

His stories about Charles Rolls and their ballooning days in 1906 were always a source of amusement because he went into so much vivid detail. When asked how he could possibly remember the events of more than 80 years ago, he would say: 'Funnily enough I can remember what I had for lunch with Charlie Rolls on July fifth, 1906, but I've forgotten what I had for breakfast today'. Although he was very fond of the man, Charles Rolls's legendary reluctance to spend money was a constant source of amusement to Sopwith. Tommy Sopwith joined the Royal Automobile Club and the Royal Aero Club in 1906 and he used to recall how Rolls would go into the dining-room at the

Royal Aero Club, order a glass of water, eat the sandwiches he had brought with him and then leave. As a result, the club committee introduced table money; you had to pay sixpence (2½p) to cover the cost of laundry. He also used to talk about the Secretary of the Royal Automobile Club in those days, a formidable character by name of Julian Orde who used to keep the younger members in order, so much so that they called him: 'Orde Gawd Almighty'.

Sir Thomas did not care for the extension that was built onto the original RAC building in Pall Mall, London. He said:

'To my mind, it looked like a bloody great railway station and the whole thing had been turned into an institution in which I wasn't really interested.'

He retired from the Royal Automobile Club around 1912 when he was building up Sopwith Aviation, but in the early 1980s the club made him an Honorary Life Member. When Jeffrey Rose, Chairman of the Royal Automobile Club, went to present him with his honorary membership Sir Thomas's sight was failing and during the lunch a spotlight on the table was directed on his plate in an effort to help him see what he was eating.

Blindness did nothing to dampen Sir Thomas's enthusiasm for Hawker Siddeley, and he was always ready to talk about the highlights of earlier years as well as the current situation. By this stage of his life he was, of course, unable to read, but information was often put on tape for him. Long after nationalization had stripped his great company of its aviation interests he continued to maintain a deep interest in its progress. He found developments in space technology fascinating yet, despite his grasp of advanced aeronautical engineering and the complex requirements of modern fighting aircraft, Sir Thomas never mastered the tape recorder. There were almost daily arguments with his nursing staff because they were unable to convince him that his tape recorder played both sides without first having to rewind the cassette, unless you wanted to find a particular part of the recording. According to Derry Radcliffe, at one time his estate manager and constant guardian, the ritual went something like this:

Sir Thomas: 'What are you doing?'

Nurse: 'I'm putting the tape in, Sir Thomas.'

Sir Thomas: 'It's making a bloody awful noise. Why can't you turn it over and do the other side; have you wound it back?'

Nurse: 'You don't have to wind it back, Sir Thomas, you just turn it over and then play the other side.'

Sir Thomas: 'I don't understand what you are talking about; I think you're wrong. Now start at the beginning and tell me.'

The conversation would go on and on in that vein. Although he was usually the personification of kindness, when he was in the mood for it Sir Thomas would bully his nurses. One of them, Mrs Sally Davis, came to Compton

Manor as housekeeper/nurse at a time when he was 92. He could see a little and they used to go for quite long walks around the grounds, but he insisted on punctuality and there would be trouble if she or any of the other ladies who looked after him were more than a minute late. Punctuality became a way of life with her that remains to this day. He went through a period of being unable to sleep but he refused to take sleeping pills because he said: 'They are habit forming'. (He was almost 99 at the time!)

There was also an occasion when Sir Thomas got stuck in the lift at Compton Manor. One of Sally Davis's colleagues was on duty at the time and the poor woman was frantic at the thought of such an old man being confined in the little cage. To make matters worse Derry Radcliffe had gone back home by this time, so it was in some distress that the lady telephoned him for advice. She was told to contact the maintenance man in the estate office, but he was not to be found so another telephone call was made to Radcliffe. 'Get onto the Fire Brigade; I'm coming back to Compton Manor,' he told her. When Derry Radcliffe arrived, three large fire engines were standing in the drive. By then the maintenance man had managed to remove Sir Thomas's walking stick from the lift door, which had caused the problem by breaking the electric circuit. The little drama had taken best part of an hour, yet the old man took it all in his stride. When finally they got him out the poor lady on duty was there with a glass of brandy, but Sir Thomas said 'You had better drink it; I think you need it more than me'.

Derry Ratcliffe, who was Tommy Sopwith's right-hand man to the very end and came to know him well over a period of 28 years, remembers him for:

'His innate kindness, his generosity—helping people, relations and anybody with a hard-luck tale—he would listen to and probably do something about it sympathetically. He was held in great affection in the village [Kings Somborne]. Although they didn't see very much of him, he was always here as a sort of presence, and he did a lot for the village by subscribing to various things. He was fascinating to listen to—about his career. Then there was his personality; we never tired of listening to him talking.'

Sally Davis, one of the two ladies who shared the responsibility of looking after Sir Thomas, said there were times when he would press his bell at all hours of the day or night and they never knew what to expect. On one occasion the bell rang at three a.m., and Sally Davis went in to see what he wanted. 'Sally,' Sir Thomas said, 'can you remember the name of the ship that sank after the Titanic?'

Even when he was in his late nineties Sir Thomas derived great pleasure from renewing links with his friends of pioneering days, and there was the occasion of 18 July, 1986, when Leslie 'Sam' Cody and his two sons were entertained to tea at Compton Manor. Leslie Cody's grandfather was the legendary Colonel Cody believed by many to be the first to fly an aeroplane in Britain, although there is a school of thought that claims the honour should go to A. V. Roe. However, Colonel Cody was a successful pioneer of man-carrying kites, an early airship was built to his specification, and he flew a number of very large aircraft of his own design which were known among other early pilots as 'Cody's Cathedrals'. Tommy Sopwith often competed against this wonderful character who had invented his own list of aeronautical terms. For example, he called the troublesome magnetos of the day *magnuisances,* and anything electrical was known as *electrickery.*

Shortly before his hundredth birthday it got back to the BBC that Sir Thomas used to listen to Radio 2 and that one of his favourites was a light entertainment programme called *All-Time Greats.* So the BBC advised the staff at Compton Manor that a message of congratulations to Tommy Sopwith would be broadcast the following Sunday. To make sure that the correct station was tuned, Sally Davis was in the room with Sir Thomas. One of the items broadcast was Stanley Holloway reciting his old classic, *Albert and the Lion.* Then the radio presenter said his congratulations and played a recording of a 1920s' song called *Me and Jane in a Plane.* The BBC had obviously tried to find something appropriate for an aviation veteran, but unfortunately the song was unknown to Tommy Sopwith and he told Sally Davis he would have rather had Stanley Holloway.

The talk Sir Thomas gave, on 21 November, 1960, to the Royal Aeronautical Society, entitled *My First Ten Years in Aviation,* had been printed in full in various journals and Derry Ratcliffe recorded this on tape for him so that he might refresh his memory on past events. It helped him answer questions on the history of Sopwith Aviation and H.G. Hawker Engineering when visitors called.

Up to the last weeks of Sir Thomas's life, blindness did not prevent him taking a morning and afternoon stroll, a tall, upright figure on the arm of one of his nurses. He always referred to his nurses as 'My Nannies'. To the very end he could come back with a quick answer and, even on his 'off' days when he might appear to be depressed, a dry sense of humour never deserted him. It was on such a day that Colonel Derry Radcliffe asked: 'What's the matter with you this morning?' to which Sir Thomas replied: 'Oh I don't know—I just feel so old'. In an effort to cheer up the old sportsman, Radcliffe, reminded him he was not so old as his wife's uncle who was 102, to which came the immediate reply: 'Well tell him from me, he is setting us all a bloody bad example'.

*   *   *

British Aerospace now owns the various aircraft factories that once comprised Sir Thomas's aviation empire, but Hawker Siddeley, the electrical-mechanical engineering group that lost its aviation interests in the 1977 nationalization, continues trading under the name he founded. When Sir Thomas Sopwith's hundredth birthday seemed assured, the two companies collaborated in arranging a party for the great man's many friends within the aircraft industry, the RAF, the Army and the Royal Navy. Tommy Sopwith's modesty has already been mentioned. For many years it had been one of his hallmarks, in fact it is often said that he was modest to a fault. If 'fault' is the right word to use, his modesty did not lessen with age. So when the idea of a hundredth birthday party was floated he could not understand why so much fuss was being made and much persuasion was needed before he would agree. According to Thomas Edward, until the birthday party the family had no idea just how highly regarded the legendary Sir Thomas Sopwith was throughout the world.

CHAPTER
12

The Curtain Falls

THE HUNDREDTH BIRTHDAY party was held at Brooklands, scene of Sir Thomas's earliest flying exploits, but it was decided that he should remain at Compton Manor where a small family gathering would be held. Raymond Baxter would be with him and a BBC link-up to the Brooklands party some 48 miles away would enable Tommy Sopwith to hear the speeches and make his reply. Even at the age of a hundred he was proud of his beautiful estate, and it was a source of particular pleasure to him that, among those attending the private party, were four generations of gamekeepers. However, it was only after the persuasion of Raymond Baxter and others that he agreed to appear on television again. When they met Raymond said:

'Sir Tom how nice to see you again.' And the old man replied: 'I wish I could say the same.'

It was his way of reminding Baxter that he was now totally blind.

A number of his old staff were invited to the Brooklands party, including one or two who had worked for Sopwith Aviation. Frank Murdoch, his adviser during the America's Cup races, was present and so was John Crampton, one-time Technical Sales Manager of his beloved Harrier. Then there were the test pilots, many of them household names in the world of aviation—Bill Bedford who made the first flight in a Harrier, Neville Duke who once held the world airspeed record in a Hawker Hunter (a jet fighter that he was the first to fly), Duncan Simpson who did much of the development flying needed to transform the Harrier from a prototype to an efficient fighting machine, and 'Bee' Beamont who, as a young Squadron Leader during the war, was seconded to Hawker's and helped in the development of its formidable Typhoon and Tempest fighters. Sir George Edwards, one-time Chairman of the rival British Aircraft Corporation, sat near his opposite number, Sir Arnold Hall, who became Chairman of the Hawker Siddeley Group in 1967.

Chairing the party was Sir Peter Masefield, a friend of Tommy Sopwith's since the 1930s.

Also present was 90-year old Lord Balfour of Inchrye, a Sopwith Camel pilot who served in the RFC during the First World War, a veteran test pilot of some renown and one time Under Secretary of State for Air. Leading names from the aircraft industry abounded and the Royal Air Force was represented by a number of senior officers, among them Air Chief-Marshal Sir Harry Broadhurst, one-time senior director of such important companies as A. V. Roe, de Havilland and Hawker Siddeley Aviation. In fact, so many of the guests had famous names that it would be easier to describe the occasion as a living 'Who's Who' of British aviation, gathered to celebrate the hundredth birthday of Brooklands' most famous son, Sir Thomas Sopwith.

The party was not, however, confined to the great and famous. Sharing tables with the distinguished and titled were those who worked for Tommy Sopwith in 1920, some of them draughtsmen, others skilled engineers. There were production test pilots, marketing executives and aviation writers among the 166 guests present to honour the great Sir Thomas Sopwith. The BBC link-up to Compton Manor relayed messages from the Queen, the Duke of Edinburgh (in Costa Rica and therefore unable to attend), Charles, Prince of Wales and Prime Minister Margaret Thatcher. Ronald Reagan, President of the USA also sent his congratulations. Among the many letters and telegrams of congratulations was one from the regular customers of the 'Sopwith Camel Bar', conveniently situated at Yibal, in the Omani Desert.

In his hundredth birthday article, published in the *British Aerospace Quarterly* Sir Peter Masefield described his characteristics as 'determination, competence, wisdom, kindliness, sportsmanship, modesty, enthusiasm and good cheer'. Then during his speech at the birthday party, he expanded on the theme:

'Tommy Sopwith, the ever cheerful, ever courteous, ever resourceful, the original press-on type and now the grand old, *young* man of British aviation, one who we hold in such high and affectionate regard. Now all through his life he has shown typically a quiet determination to get things done, not just in a humdrum or an offhand way; instead he has always brought a cheerful competence in regard for detail to everything he has tackled, setting himself clear objectives and then going about them with spirit and goodwill—and I think that characterizes him—spirit and goodwill.

'He has always been a marvellous leader and a wonderful picker of men—the right men for the right job—he has always supported them as members of a happy team.'

One hundredth birthday messages

During the birthday party telegrams arrived at Brooklands from all over the world, some of them conveying messages from royalty and other heads of state. A few were read to the guests by Peter Masefield while 48 miles away Sir Thomas and his family listened over the link-up that had been arranged:

HRH Prince Philip
I am sorry not to be able to join your many friends and admirers gathered at Brooklands to celebrate your hundredth birthday. But I am delighted to have this chance to offer you my congratulations and best wishes on reaching your century. I have many happy memories of shooting those high pheasants of yours at Kings Compton [Compton Manor] and I am thinking of you as we try to round up the wild cocks at the end of the season in Norfolk.

> *Philip*
> *Sandringham*

HRH Prince Charles
I am very sorry not to be with all of you on this unique occasion, but as a long time admirer of Sir Thomas Sopwith and all he stands for in the remarkable story of British aviation I would like to send all at Brooklands my very best wishes for a most successful and enjoyable centennial lunch. I hope that the occasion will serve to emphasise the immense contribution which our highly talented aeronautical engineers continue to make to the aerospace industry and how important it is to this country that we do not waste that brilliant talent by letting it slip away to other countries by default if nothing else. Meanwhile, the part played by Sir Thomas in this period of our national history will always remain as particularly special and renown, for which we can all be immensely grateful to him.

> *Charles*

Among the many telegrams was one from the Chairman of The Royal Automobile Club. It was sent in the form of a mock NOTAM, that is, an official Notice to Airmen of the kind sent by the aviation authorities to pilots when there is a navigational warning, temporary or otherwise. Some years previously Tommy Sopwith had been made an honorary member of the RAC and the wording was as follows:

NOTAM 100-88 URGENT

FROM: THE ROYAL AUTOMOBILE CLUB (AVIATION DEPARTMENT)
      PALL MALL LONDON SW1

TO: ALL AVIATORS

ISSUED: 15th JANUARY 1988

PERIOD OF NOTICE: 24 HOURS FROM 00.01 HOURS, 18 HRS JANUARY 1988

PLACE: COMPTON MANOR, KINGS SOMBORNE

POSITION: 51 03HALF N, 01 30 W

DETAILS: CREATION OF DANGER AREA RADIUS 100 METRES TO 100 FEET

NATURE OF ACTIVITY: 100 YEAR OLD AVIATOR LIKELY TO BE WELL AND
                  TRULY AIRBORNE.
                  EXERCISE EXTREME CAUTION.

ADDITIONAL MESSAGE: CONGRATULATIONS AND THE WARMEST BEST
WISHES FROM THE CHAIRMAN AND THE
COMMITTEE OF THE ROYAL AUTOMOBILE CLUB.

JEFFREY ROSE.

There always had been a constant flow of fan letters at Compton Manor but
the hundredth birthday party, covered as it was by the world press and
television, precipitated hundreds of letters from many countries. Some were
from the eminent or heads of world-renowned institutions, others came from
ex-employees or relations of those long departed this earth. A remarkable
feature of the letters was the way that Tommy Sopwith had captured the
imagination of schoolchildren, girls as well as boys. The youngest to offer his
congratulations was four-year-old Samuel Henry Bompas who got his mother
to write the letter for him, although he signed it himself in inch-high letters.
Young Samuel said:

Dear Sir Thomas,
I saw your aeroplane in the newspaper. I like army and soldiers very much. My first
model aeroplane that Daddy made for me was a Sopwith Pup. My newest aeroplane
we are working on now is a Hurricane. We also made a Spitfire, DH4, Swordfish and
a Henschel.
Did you get seen in the search lights? Did they shoot at you? Did you parachute out
of your aeroplane? What do you like best about flying?
I am four years old. I go to Bickley Parva Nursery School.

Happy Birthday dear Sopwith.
from
       SAMUEL

If four-year-old Samuel Bompas was the youngest to send his congratulations
94-year-old Tom Mapplebeck (he of the Hawker Fury sales to Yugoslavia) and
94-year-old Jim Joel (stepson of Tommy Sopwith's sister Olive) must have
been the oldest.

Other letters came from schoolchildren engaged in projects dealing with
flight, youngsters who were active with ATC Squadrons, adults with no family
or other connections who just felt they had to write and congratulate him on
reaching one hundred years. In many of these letters the same sentiment is
expressed—'your wonderful aircraft saved the British people in two world
wars'—a sentiment with which anyone with first-hand knowledge of Britain's
perilous situation in 1914 and 1939 will readily agree.

Then there were letters from ex-staff or their relatives, such as the one
from Clare Gresham, age 90, who wrote:

You don't know me—and never did—but for over seventy years any mention of 'Tommy
Sopwith' has wakened in me the most lively interest in your career, reviving at the

same time very youthful memories of the happy year I spent as a shorthand typist at Sopwiths in Kingston. There I made many life-long friends and you, Mr. Sigrist and Hawker were our heroes. Now a nonogenarian and nearly blind, you are still mine!

Letters also poured in from the Chairmen of such well known companies as Rolls-Royce, Fairey Group Ltd, Ferranti, Brush Group and many of the firms that supplied the Hawker Siddeley company with materials and so forth. Among many American letters was one from Mr Martin Harwit, Director of the National Air and Space Museum in Washington, USA, one of the finest institutions of its kind in the world. In it he said:

Your personal flying achievements during aviation's early times, and the reputation that the products of your aerospace companies have since won, form a record unmatched in the history of aeronautics. Tens of thousands of aircraft bearing the name Sopwith, Hawker or Hawker Siddeley have for 75 years defended our alliance in war and have shielded us in peace.

There was a letter from The Countess Mountbatten of Burma (daughter of the late Earl Mountbatten) in which she talked of 'family shooting days at Broadlands [the Mountbatten's country home] with you and the dear Green Dragon (always so kind to us)'.

Among the high-ranking officers to write was General Larry D. Welch, Chief of Staff of the United States Air Force. In his letter the general said:

It is a pleasure to offer my congratulations to you on the occasion of the centennial of your birth.

Like aviators everywhere, the United States Air Force remains indebted to you for your many achievements. We salute you, and offer our best wishes on this special occasion.

Sir Thomas Sopwith's marine achievements formed the subject of other letters. One from the Commodore of the Darling Point Sailing Squadron of Queensland, Australia, reminded him of the T.O.M. SOPWITH ENDEAVOUR CUP which he had presented in 1933. It is their 'most prized Trophy'. One Billy de Quincey sent a telegram reminding 'Skipper' that he had been the youngest amateur crew member on his J Class yacht, Endeavour.

A sound in the air, bringing back memories of more than 70 years ago, stirred the family party and the Grand Old Man of British Aviation was led to the steps of his mansion as a First World War-designed Sopwith Pup flew past followed by a Hawker Hurricane of Battle of Britain fame. Then a trio of post-war masterpieces arrived overhead in formation, the Hawker Hunter, Harrier and Hawk—all of them designed and produced by the company Sir Thomas founded and built from small beginnings. Sadly Sir Thomas could no longer see the aircraft flying in his honour, but the sound was music to his ear.

The hundredth birthday party of a man who has been a great sportsman, yachtsman, pioneer pilot and industrialist is, of course, international news and soon it was being flashed around the world. After the party it was reported that Sir Thomas went to bed 'in a state of euphoria'. We can only guess what went through the mind of a man who could look back to the dawn of powered flight as he lay down to rest at the end of what had been an exciting and memorable day.

A few months after the hundredth birthday party A. W. 'Bill' Bedford, one-time Chief Test Pilot at Hawker Aircraft, visited Compton Manor and presented Sir Thomas with an important certificate enrolling him as an Honorary Fellow of *The Society of Experimental Test Pilots*. It is a rule of this organization that recipients must collect their certificates in California. However Bedford was able to persuade them that Tommy Sopwith had been a test pilot of his own new designs in 1913 and, since there had been a slight delay in recognizing the fact, he should not be expected to make the journey from Kings Somborne to California at the age of 100. The accompanying letter from the President of the Society read as follows:

Dear Sir Thomas,

On behalf of the 1,800 members of SETP from 27 countries, it gives me great pleasure to congratulate you on your well deserved award of Honorary Fellowship of our Society. You have excelled on land, at sea, and in the air during a charismatic century of life and your achievements are a fine example to us all of professionalism and tenacity, combined with the rare qualities of being a modest gentleman.

We are all inspired by your outstanding track record, particularly as a famous pioneer aviator and test pilot in the days when flying was an intuitive philosophy of 'hope for the best in the unknown'.

Not content with that, you led the companies which designed and built the top scoring British fighter aircraft in the World Wars I and II, namely the Sopwith Camel (1,294 victories) and the Battle of Britain Hawker Hurricane.

Your Sopwith Tabloid won the Schneider Trophy Race in 1914. You gave the green light to the brilliant V/STOL Hawker P1127, the forerunner of the Harrier of which 750 have been built or ordered. This aircraft flew with operational distinction in the South Atlantic, claiming twenty-eight victories without a single Harrier being lost in air to air combat.

I can only scratch the surface of your spectacular career but be assured you will go down in aviation history as one of 'THE FEW' to whom the free world will always be indebted.

We salute you, Sir Thomas, and thank you. It is a privilege to have you as an Honorary Fellow of our Society. Even this you achieve with charisma, by being our first centenarian! Quite an example for us to follow!

I regret not being able to come from the USA to present this award to you personally, so I have asked Hawker's ex Chief Test Pilot, Bill Bedford, to do the honours on my behalf.

Yours sincerely,
Robert C. Ettinger

What were Sir Thomas Sopwith's likes and dislikes in his old age? According to Lt Col Derry Radcliffe:

'Dislikes: pomposity and anything that he regards as *ersatz* [sham or imitation]. He particularly likes shooting, country pursuits, not horses but very fond of dogs'.

A few weeks before Sir Thomas died, Geoffrey Knight told him of a book that had been written by a wartime fighter ace and, knowing how much he enjoyed such things, arrangements were made to have the complete work read into a tape recorder. Sadly, the old man never had the pleasure of hearing it. Geoffrey Knight and many others are in no doubt that Sir Thomas maintained an interest in aviation developments until the last year or so of his life. Even after modern aircraft had lost their appeal, he was always happy to discuss the ones he knew so well up to the early 1950s.

Towards the end of Sir Thomas Sopwith's long life there were two nurses at Compton Manor and they looked after him around the clock while Colonel Derry Radcliffe kept a keen eye on his wellbeing. On the arm of one of his 'Nannys' he continued taking a short stroll twice a day until the beginning of 1989. His 101st birthday was on 18 January, but he had already caught one of the virus infections that were spreading throughout Britain at the time. Every week without fail his niece, Violet McLean (daughter of his oldest sister Violet) would telephone from her home in Darlington, Maryland, USA. About the time of his birthday, she asked him how he was feeling and he replied 'I feel bloody awful'.

Over the next few days he lost interest in life and stopped taking solid food. Then on 27 January the flame that had blazed so many trails and shone like a beacon, inspired friends and colleagues to unbelievable heights, slowly and peacefully went out. He had been the youngest of Britain's early aviators, he had lived longer than any of his British contemporaries and he was the last of the great aviation pioneers.

*　　*　　*

How did others see Thomas Octave Murdoch Sopwith? One of the earliest written assessments is printed in the Royal Aero Club *Jubilee Book of 1910* which described Tommy Sopwith, then aged 22, in these words:

'A young man of exceptional charm, very fond of a joke, and polished manners. Yet behind this agreeable façade was a penetrating brain, a coolly calculated mind and a power of decision and correct judgement that was rarely, if ever wrong.'

A power of decision and correct judgement—as a young man just one year into his majority the qualities so well described in the *Jubilee Book of 1910* were apparent even then.

A few months after Sir Thomas had died, Thomas Edward Sopwith described his father as:

'A stable, very loyal, very modest man to the point of being self-effacing, which was laudable—unlike the chap that Winston Churchill was talking about when someone once said 'Oh he's very modest' and he replied 'Well he's got a great deal to be modest about'. He was a thoroughly admirable bloke. Nearly all the things that he could be criticized for, funnily enough, had got another side that was admirable. I have, in a sense, criticized him for not supporting me and taking an interest in what I was doing. On the other hand he didn't interfere.'

In the opinion of Sir Peter Masefield:

'He was a great man. First of all, one of the important things about his character was that he was one of the best pickers of lieutenants there has ever been. He never made a mistake in picking the right chap. Then he was a supreme delegator; although he knew what was going on he trusted his chaps and let them get on with it (and this is not always done by some of the captains of industry). He was the power there, he had the authority. No one ever spoke an ill word of Tommy Sopwith, I've never heard anyone say anything, and this, of course, shows greatness because it is so easy to get across people, but he was loyal to all his people, always.'

Frank Murdoch, who ran the Hurricane production line and advised Sir Thomas on his marine activities said:

'I am a tremendous admirer of his and I owe a lot in my lifetime to Tommy Sopwith. He has always struck me as being a wonderful man, a real gentleman. We had quite a bit of fun together. Laterly I have been almost every other month to have lunch with him when he likes to talk about old days.'

Bill Humble, who was a test pilot with Hawker's for eight years and who used to shoot with Sir Thomas described him in words that are so often repeated by others: 'He was a perfect gentleman; a charming character in every respect.'

Sir Arnold Hall, who was Chairman and Managing Director of Hawker Siddeley said: 'He had a constant wit that would bubble along. He was always relaxed, it was always good to be in his company, one always enjoyed it.'

According to John Crampton, Technical Sales Manager for the Harrier who knew Sir Thomas very well during the last twenty-five years of his life:

'He was such an engaging character that those of us who were lucky enough to know him are only too willing to talk about him. Because he was such a man—his modesty, his courtesy, his great sense of purpose, his beautiful speaking voice, not only the beautiful English he spoke but when required he spoke French beautifully too.'

Frank Murphy, OBE, DFC, FRAeS, at one time Chief Production Test Pilot operating from Hawker's Dunsfold Airfield:

'I shall always remember him whether it be on the tarmac at Langley, bringing a 12-year-old son for a trip in the Vega Gull, or on the tarmac at Dunsfold when US generals and senators were viewing the Hunter before purchase for NATO, or picking him up for a Board meeting at Coventry, or after flying at a Farnborough Air Show.

The quick smile and the few friendly words or joke were always there. He would take the time to have a chat with the pilots, not only to ask about progress on the aircraft developments but also on private domestic matters. It was a constant source of amazement to me that he was able to ask technically accurate questions about the Sea Hawk and Hunter development progress and interpolate a query about the health of ones family. It was a unique blend of characteristics—pilot, engineer and astute business man with likeable human being—that made him so universally liked and respected, not to mention the courage to shrug off accidents and reverses and to come back for more. He also had this vast curiosity about what makes things tick.'

Talking of the very fine apprentice training schools operated by Hawker Siddeley's rivals at the various British Aircraft Corporation factories, in particular the one at their Weybridge division, Sir George Edwards recalled that:

'One year we invited the great man, Sir Thomas Sopwith, to come and talk to the lads about his career and especially his days at Brooklands. It was a masterly performance and I suppose he must have been approaching 90. Geoffrey Knight, at the time in charge of Weybridge and Bristol, was chairing the apprentices and I remember saying to him afterwards something to the effect that now the lads had been exposed to that performance, our stock in comparison would go down with a bump and he had better make sure that, from now on, he got speakers we could compete with.'

That was the occasion when Tommy Sopwith told those who had not won prizes not to be downhearted or dismayed because he had only taken one examination in his life and that was for his Royal Aero Club Certificate at Brooklands in 1910. He ended with the words 'I never took another examination again—and look what happened'.

Although he enjoyed a large circle of friends from many walks of life Tommy Sopwith was never what is often popularly described as a 'family man'. In the days when his sisters were alive he hardly ever attended large gatherings with their husbands and children. Indeed, although it was fashionable in Victorian times for families to strike a formal pose while a man hid behind an enormous plate camera and fired magnesium flash powder, the pictures one might have expected to find of Tommy Sopwith with his parents and seven sisters do not seem to exist.

An extraordinary side of Sir Thomas Sopwith's character was that although he obviously enjoyed the good things of life—and his many yachts, succession of Rolls-Royce cars and fine properties bear witness to that—he was not the least interested in money. According to his son:

'From a family financial point of view he couldn't wait to get rid of the responsibility. Money as such never really interested him. The moment I was old enough and was showing an interest in how the family finances should be run he couldn't wait to off-load it. Once a year he waited for us to trot along and give him a rough idea how things were getting on, and for the last fifteen years that was much more a formality than a real briefing.'

Tommy Sopwith's loves were aeroplanes, boats and motor cars in that order. His relaxed, slightly quizical view of life was matched by a determination not to be upset about anything. The 1934 America's Cup, when Vanderbilt behaved badly and the American officials refused to support his complaint, was an example of this rare quality. Discussing the event many years later Sir Thomas said:

'My great regret in life is that I didn't bring home the America's Cup; I really ought to have done and I ought to have been allowed to do it.'

Such is the complex life story of Sir Thomas Octave Murdoch Sopwith that one is left with a feeling of bewilderment that any one person could have achieved so much, even taking into account his very long life. From an early age he displayed a shrewdness which made him successful with stocks and shares and when, over a relatively few years, Sopwith acquired great wealth, he knew how it should be enjoyed. He spent his money freely and gave employment to many hundreds of people in the process. He never showed any signs of ambition or a lust for fame, far from it, because Tommy Sopwith was always at pains to play down his great achievements. Indeed usually he would stand back, allow others to develop the ideas he had originated and then let them take the credit. He never adopted the role of high-pressure tycoon, even when he was chairman of one of the great industrial empires of the world. To him, building up and running a massive industrial concern was something to be enjoyed like sailing, shooting, fishing and all his other activities.

Thomas Edward Sopwith once said of his father that he was always able to recognize when he was at the right place at the right time; then he would act accordingly and build success upon success, but there was much more to Tommy Sopwith than a talent for seizing opportunities. First there is his hundred-and-one years. Doctors will usually say that, if you aspire to old age, select parents who had a long and active life. Tommy Sopwith's remarkable grandfather, Thomas Sopwith (1803), lived until 16 January, 1879; thirteen days past his 76th birthday. That was an above average life-span in those days when so many people never reached their majority. Sopwith's father is no guide because, as previously recorded, he died at the age of only 60 following a shooting accident. Neither did his mother Lydia Gertrude Sopwith (concerning whom few facts are available) live to a great age; she died in September, 1914 at the age of 69 and is buried at Brookwood Cemetery next to her husband, Thomas Sopwith (1838), her own mother (Susan Messiter who lived to the age of 83) and her daughter Rosamond Sopwith.

However Tommy Sopwith's eldest sister Violet reached 91 and May, his supporter and companion during early flying days, lived to within a few weeks of her 99th birthday. May it was who induced him not to smoke while standing near his early and highly inflammable flying machines. In a not very serious moment he once claimed that he gave up smoking at the age of 93 because he thought it might be bad for his health but it seems as though the Sopwith breed was built to last.

The engineering tradition runs continuously through the Sopwith generations from as far back as it is possible to trace while the sportsman in Tommy Sopwith appears to have come from his father who liked his shooting and was a keen fisherman. Although these activities were not pursued by his grandfather, it is in this outstanding man that the seeds of versatility and intellect can be established with certainty. Thomas Sopwith (1803) was a deep-thinking, multi-talented pillar of Victorian society with the urge and determination to embrace knowledge—knowledge on any subject—and record his progress and experiences in beautifully compiled diaries. Clearly Tommy Sopwith inherited much of value from his grandfather including his excellent character; people who came to know Thomas Sopwith (1803), famous and otherwise, regarded him as a man of outstanding good nature, and so it was with Tommy Sopwith. Where his sense of humour came from is less easy to determine although he was brought up in Edwardian times when something of a reaction to strict Victorian codes of behaviour was in progress. He was the master of the short, sharp answer, often with a mischievous twinkle in the eye. An earnest young man, who obviously expected some fortune-making advice, once asked him 'if you had your time over again and could do whatever you liked, in what would you invest your money?' Without hesitation the great man said 'the Roman Catholic Church'.

From the foregoing one can say that when Tommy Sopwith was born on 18 January, 1888, he came into a long living family of talent with strong engineering traditions and a great moral character. His father left him enough money to partake of such sporting activities as fishing, shooting, yachting and ballooning. It is at this point that the word 'luck' may fairly be introduced because he was indeed fortunate to have arrived on this earth at the same time as the internal combustion engine, an essential step towards powered flight, for without it man would never have progressed beyond the balloon. So when he came face to face with the first flying machines the sportsman in Tommy Sopwith left him no alternative but to become involved. The Sopwith engineering tradition made him look for better design and improved constructional methods while the determination to get things done inherited from his grandfather urged him to start his own aircraft factory. These are all compelling ingredients of his unique character.

But how does the Sopwith success story relate to the man himself? There were, after all, other people with engineering talents and the determination to build aircraft but many never progressed beyond a few sheds at Brooklands before fading from the scene, while those who weathered the post-Great War period often failed within a few years, or were taken over by larger concerns.

In the case of Tommy Sopwith his almost psychic ability to pick the right people was matched by a personal charm that made them want to work for him.

In all walks of life there are people of talent who set up a business and perhaps make a good product, yet the enterprise remains small because of the founder's insistence on doing everything himself. Here was Tommy Sopwith's other great strength—an ability to delegate. Having selected his man and got him to join the team he would be told 'don't ask me what you are to do—have a look round, see what needs to be done and do as you think fit'.

If you take these attributes—long life, a sense of humour, engineering flare, intelligence, sportsmanship, a genius with people, a disposition that induced loyalty, a shrewd nose for finance—and mould these into one person it *might* be possible to create another Tommy Sopwith, although the general opinion is that there will never be another one quite like him.

So in coming to the end of this complex story it is perhaps opportune to again quote the words of Sir George Edwards spoken, in his much admired forthright manner, when he addressed those present at Sir Thomas Sopwith's 100th birthday party while the founder of Hawker Siddeley listened at his home, surrounded by his family and a few friends:

'It is jolly encouraging to know that one chap can last through 100 years, most of which was spent in the aviation industry, and still be alright at the end of it. And not only alright but a hell of a lot brighter than a good many of us who profess to be a lot younger. That isn't to say that we are all going to be as bright as that or that we are all going to reach 100. But if one of us can do it then the rest of you lot who are now in your eighties—and the place is littered with octogenarians—just give your mind to it. The only thing I would say is that anyone who has scored 100 runs, the last twenty is the worst. Getting to 80 is relatively straightforward but the last twenty is a right old struggle. So octogenarians give your mind to it and don't let Sir Tom be out there on his own for ever and a day.

'1988 is significant because it is Tom Sopwith's 100th birthday. It won't go down in history as the year in which there was a three-line whip on a private member's afternoon on the Liberal-SDP merger. But there is another occasion that I think is relevant, relevant obliquely because of your tremendous prowess as a sailor. On the 15th July in 1588 the Armada fleet hove off this country and they were defeated by a fleet of which the Vice-Admiral was a young lad named Sir Francis Drake (in this day and age I suspect he would be called Frank Drake). The 400th anniversary, and I don't know the fancy word for describing a 400th anniversary, takes place in July this year. So in one year Tom Sopwith is 100 and the Armada is 400. Now it has been said that the Battle of Britain was Britain's modern Armada, and that could well be right because we don't want to be under any illusions as to what would have happened had we lost. It wouldn't be the SDP that we would be worrying about; it would have been pretty uncomfortable for a lot of us—in fact a good many of us would not be in any position to worry about anything at this particular moment. So, the Armada in July of this year is 400 years old, Sir Tom today is 100 years old and young Frank Drake once delivered himself of a bit of a homily. And if I can remember it I will remind you of it.

'There has to be a beginning of any great matter, but it is the continuing unto the end until it be thoroughly finished that yields the true glory.

'Sir Tom, you finished what you set yourself to do. You are at least ten years away from your own particular end, but by gosh all your old friends here know that you have received the true glory—and bless you.'

Tommy Sopwith's total modesty became public knowledge while he was being interviewed by Raymond Baxter for the widely acclaimed BBC television feature in his 96th year. The last question asked of this pioneer pilot, engineer, sportsman and industrialist on the grand scale was 'what do you consider is the reason for your outstanding success?', to which the great man replied:

'Pure luck.'

Epilogue

AFTER LADY SOPWITH died Sir Thomas spent another eleven years living on his own at Compton Manor and it was eventually decided to put the estate on the market so that he could go to live with his son and daughter-in-law. In the event he died before the plan could materialize but soon afterwards, in fact on 20 April, 1990, Compton Manor was bought by a Mr David Brice.

From the earliest models Sir Thomas Sopwith had owned Rolls-Royce cars throughout his very long life so when he died Thomas Edward Sopwith and his cousin, Derry Radcliffe, thought it would be fitting if they could obtain a Rolls-Royce hearse for the short final journey to the cemetery at King's Somborne, the little Hampshire village but a few miles down the road from Compton Manor. There was a private family service, then he was laid to rest next to Phyllis Sopwith. It was the last chapter in a long, always interesting and sometimes heroic story.

On 12 April 1989 a Service of Thanksgiving for the life of T.O.M. Sopwith, 1888-1989 was held at St Clement Danes, the Central Church of The Royal Air Force situated in The Strand, London. Among those invited to act as ushers were Geoffrey Knight, Raymond Baxter, John Crampton, Derry Radcliffe and Bill Bedford. Some 450 people were there, among them representatives of the British Royal Family. Ex-King Constantine and Queen Anne-Marie of Greece attended and so did Princess Alexandra and her husband, Angus Ogilvy. Many officers of the Royal Navy, Army and Royal Air Force were a reminder of the close link between the fighting services and Tommy Sopwith's companies that had existed since 1913. Yet another link with the past was Lord Kenilworth. In the mid 1930s his family had sold the Siddeley Development Company to Tommy Sopwith. Cecil Lewis, the celebrated author and World War I fighter pilot was there, 92 years old but upright, alert and looking 25 years younger.

The lesson was read by Thomas Edward Sopwith then his older daughter, Samantha recited *High Flight*, the poem written by 19-year-old Pilot Officer John Gillespie Magee of 412 Squadron, Royal Canadian Air Force who was killed in 1941. Through the voice of a ten-year-old child it seemed to take on a new meaning, yet this was not a sad occasion, far from it; Tommy Sopwith had lived 31 years longer than the once expected 'three score years and ten' and throughout his long life there had been many more happy moments than tragic ones. The organ, choir and music in general, always of a very high standard at St Clement Danes, was never better than on this day. The Salon Orchestra of the Royal Air Force played music chosen to reflect Tommy Sopwith's many activities. Before the service there was the *Dambusters' March* by Eric Coates. Sopwith the Sailor was evoked by Vaughan Williams' *Sea Songs, Blow The Wind Southerly* and *Sailing* while his ballooning exploits were remembered by *Up, Up and Away*. After the service we heard Goodwin's *Those Magnificent Men in Their Flying Machines* and this was particularly appropriate because much of the action in the film of that name took place at Brooklands where Tommy Sopwith first became ensnared in aeronautics.

The Address was given by Sir George Edwards and, as usual, he struck the right note. Following an outline of the remarkable Sopwith story, in which he reminded those present that three Sopwiths appear in the *Guinness Book of Records* (Sir Thomas for his quick start and take-off in 1911, son Thomas Edward for powerboat racing and his wife Gina for skiing) he concluded with the words:

'We thank God for putting you on this earth when you did and for allowing you to stay with us for so long. And we give thanks too on behalf of the generations still to come for all that *you* did to enable *them* to live in freedom.'

Appendix I

The History of Brooklands

It was during 666 AD, four hundred years before the Normans invaded Britain, that the Benedictine Abbey of St Peter at Chertsey was founded at Brooklands on the River Wey. Chertsey Abbey continued as a centre of religion and learning for more than 820 years until, in 1538, it fell foul of King Henry VIII. The estate passed into the hands of Sir Anthony Browne, then some years later Queen Henrietta Maria (widow of King Charles I) became the owner.

In 1804 Brooklands was bought by the Duke of York, but, after a few years, it changed hands yet again to be owned for a brief period by a Mr Ball Hughes. In 1829 he sold the property to Lord King of Ockham who left it to his youngest son, the Hon Peter John Locke King. Peter John had a son, Hugh Fortescue Locke King and, eventually, Brooklands came into his ownership. When fate chose H. F. Locke King to be the squire of Brooklands, it smiled graciously upon both motoring and aeronautics.

The 'horseless carriage' burst into rattling life during the second half of the nineteenth century and within a few years of its turn the sport of motor racing appeared on the scene to gather rapidly-growing support from the public. Although other nations were quick to embrace the new motorized carriages, Britain passed laws to repel what the Government regarded as a noisy challenge to the horse; a man with a red flag was required to walk before every motor vehicle. When eventually the politicians were shamed into repealing the red flag law it was replaced by a 20 mph speed limit. It is, therefore, hardly surprising that, in such a climate, motor racing was unlikely to seed in the centre of the British Empire, let alone flourish. During the early 1900s, British drivers who wanted to compete in their cars had to go abroad.

In 1906 motor racing and the development of motor cars were both greatly stimulated when Hugh Locke King transformed his extensive Brooklands Estate into the first purpose-built motor racetrack in the world. To make it bigger and better, two farms owned by the family were included in the overall plan which was on the grand scale. There were banked curves and the ambitious project was completed in only nine months.

The Brooklands race track was opened on 17 June, 1907, and, apart from the Great War period when all motor racing stopped, it was to be the scene of many historic events for the next 32 years. For example, on 24 June, 1914, an Englishman named 'Cupid' Hornsted, driving a 200 hp German Benz, established the world's first land speed record at 124.1 mph measured over two runs in opposite directions. In March, 1921 Count Louis Zborowski won the 100 mile Short Handicap Race at 100.75 mph in his famous car, *Chitty-Chitty-Bang-Bang*. On 7 October, 1935, John Cobb broke the Brooklands' lap record by achieving 143.44 mph in his 450 hp Napier Railton—the list is endless.

From mid 1907 to the outbreak of the Great War in August, 1914, the massive cars of the period came from all over the world to thunder around the track. These were golden days and when motor racing re-started in April, 1920, the old euphoria returned. Few could have believed then that, only 19 years later, another world war would cause the final demise of Brooklands as a racetrack.

The motor car was still a rarity in 1906 but Locke King welcomed the advance of technology and, when European aviation began to flourish, no time was lost in offering hospitality to aviators and their 'flying machines'. In 1909 trees from the centre of the area were removed, the ground was levelled to make a flying ground and the Brooklands Estate Company, encouraged by that great aviation pioneer, Holt Thomas, erected some small hangars which they rented for £10 a month to those experimenting with their frail aircraft.

Brooklands, Hugh Locke King's brainchild, was more than a shrine to motor racing and a valuable testing ground for the motor industry—it nurtured the very foundations of British aviation. The pioneers abounded in varying degrees of financial stability, many of them living from hand-to-mouth, others backed by large industrial concerns. Such historic names as Martinsyde, Roe and, of course, Sopwith, were once written over the doors of the little hangars and workshops inside the racetrack. Then the Great War put an end to motor racing and serious aviation took over completely.

Over a period of more than 50 years many famous aircraft made their first flights at Brooklands. The Australian, Harry Hawker, flew the prototype Sopwith Camel there on 22 December, 1916, and during June, 1928, the great 'George' Bulman made the first flight of a Hawker Hart, a biplane which, in its various forms, was destined to boost the fortunes of its makers and transform the company from a small works into an industrial empire. Even more significant, in as far as its emergence helped save the nation during the Battle of Britain, was Bulman's first flight in the prototype Hurricane fighter on 5 November, 1935. The following year, in fact on 15 June, 1936, the first Wellington bomber flew from Brooklands in the hands of Mutt Summers, a Vickers test pilot.

The last motor race occurred on 7 August, 1939. Inside a month Germany marched into Poland and, on 3 September, Britain and France were at war with the Third Reich. It was the end of the road for motor racing at Brooklands; henceforth all activity would be devoted to aeronautics. Like the Great War when Vickers built more than 1600 S.E.5a fighters and Sopwith Aviation tested its warplanes within the racetrack, history was to repeat itself. At Brooklands Vickers built Wellington bombers, for a long time the mainstay of RAF Bomber Command, while Hawker churned out Hurricane fighters.

Appendix II

T. O. M. Sopwith's Ballooning Log

Date	Balloon	Commander	Start	Finish	Passengers	Distance	Time
						(st.mls)	Hrs/Min
1906 24 Jun	Venus	C. S. Rolls	Chelsea	Near Luton	T. Sopwith A. R. Dresser Mrs Harbord	30	2:15
5 Jly night	Venus	C. S. Rolls	Chelsea	Boston Lincs.	T. Sopwith F. H. Butler	110	8:22
22 Jly	Vivienne III	C. S. Rolls	Crystal Palace	Billericay	T. Sopwith J. M. Jardine	25	2:42
28 Jly	Midget	C. S. Rolls	Reading	Wheathampsted	T. Sopwith	40	2:50
1 Sep *	Venus	T. Sopwith	Chelsea	Kings Langley	J. M. Jardine E. Palmer	25	2:00
2 Sep	Midget	C. S. Rolls	Chelsea	Enfield	T. Sopwith	12	0:52
3 Sep	Padsop	T. Sopwith	Chelsea	Chadwell Heath	A. R. Dresser M. Dresser	?	?
5 Sep	Padsop	T. Sopwith	Chelsea	Laindon	A. Cowburn	26	2:05
8 Sep	Padsop	T. Sopwith	Chelsea	Eynsford	C. Grahame-White	21	2:15
9 Sep	Padsop	T. Sopwith A. Paddon	Chelsea	Haywards Heath	crew only	36	3:30
12 Sep	Padsop	T. Sopwith	Chelsea	Dunmow	May Sopwith	42	4:00
25 Oct	Padsop	T. Sopwith A. Paddon	Chelsea	Horley	crew only	30	2:00
4 Nov **	Padsop	T. Sopwith A. Paddon	Chelsea	Bristol	crew only	120	2:45
11 Nov	Padsop	T. Sopwith	Chelsea	Billingshurst	Stackell	42	4:30
24 Nov	Padsop	T. Sopwith A. Paddon	Chelsea	Epping & North Wield	F. W. Hobdey	23	3:00
? Nov	Padsop	T. Sopwith	Chelsea	Royston	Sprottiswood	?	?

* First flight in command of balloon.
** Flown in a gale at a groundspeed of 60 mph.
   Emergency landing.

Appendix III

Aircraft Designed by Companies under the Chairmanship of Sir Thomas Sopwith

SOPWITH AVIATION LTD

Aircraft Type	Date	Purpose of Design	No built
Hybrid	1912	3 seat general purpose	1
Three-seater	1913	3 seat general purpose	11
Bat Boat	1913	2 seat amphibian	3
Tractor Seaplane	1913	2 seat seaplane	3
Circuit Seaplane	1913	2 seat competition seaplane	1
807 Seaplane	1913	2 seat Naval seaplane	12
Gun Bus	1913	2 seat gun carrier	29
Tabloid	1914	2 seat racer/scout	36
Gordon Bennett	1914	Single seat racer	2
Sociable	1914	2 seat trainer	1
Type C Seaplane	1914	Large torpedo carrier	3
137 Seaplane	1914	2 seat Naval seaplane	1
860 Seaplane	1914	2 seat torpedo carrier	18
Two-seat Scout	1914	2 seat reconnaissance	24
Schneider	1914	Seaplane fighter	137
Baby	1914	Seaplane light bomber	286
1½ Strutter	1915	2 seat fighter	5466
SL. T.B.P.	1915	Harry Hawker's runabout	1
Pup	1916	Single seat fighter	1847
Triplane	1916	Single seat fighter	152
L.R.T.Tr.	1916	Experimental anti-Zeppelin	1
F1 Camel	1916	Single seat fighter	5497
2F.1 Camel	1917	Single seat carrier fighter	250
Bee	1917	Harry Hawker's 2nd runabout	1
B1	1917	Experimental bomber	2

Aircraft Type	Date	Purpose of Design	No built
Cuckoo	1917	Torpedo carrier	233
5F.1 Dolphin	1917	Single seat fighter	1559
2B.2 Rhino	1917	Experimental bomber	2
7F.1 Snipe	1917	Single seat fighter	2103
3F.2 Hippo	1918	Experimental 2 seat fighter	2
2FR.2 Bulldog	1918	Experimental 2 seat fighter	2
Sparrow	1918	Radio controlled flying bomb	1
TF.2 Salamander	1918	Single seat ground attack	c175
8F.1 Snail	1918	Single seat fighter	6
Buffalo	1918	2 seat ground attack	2
Scooter/Swallow	1918	Single seat racer	2
Dragon	1918	Single seat fighter	c200
Snark	1919	Single seat fighter	3
Snapper	1919	Single seat fighter	3
Cobham	1919	Twin-engine bomber	3
Atlantic	1919	2 seat long range biplane	1
Wallaby	1919	7 passenger transport	1
Dove	1919	2 seat sports aircraft	10
Gnu	1919	3 seat light transport	12
Antelope	1920	3 seat light transport	1

Total Sopwith aircraft built by all manufacturers: **18,106**

H. G. HAWKER ENGINEERING CO LTD

Aircraft Type	Date	Purpose of Design	No built
Duiker	1923	2 seat reconnaissance	1
Woodcock	1923	2 seat night fighter	64
Cygnet	1924	2 seat light aeroplane	2
Hedgehog	1924	3 seat naval reconnaissance	1
Danecock	1925	Single seat fighter	15
Heron	1925	Single seat fighter	1
Horsley	1925	2 seat bomber/torpedo	138
Hornbill	1926	Single seat fighter	1
Hawfinch	1927	Single seat fighter	1
Harrier	1927	2 seat bomber/torpedo	1
Hart	1928	2 seat light bomber	989
Tomtit	1928	2 seat elementary trainer	36
Interceptor	1928	Single seat fighter	1
Hoopoe	1928	Single seat naval fighter	1
Hornet	1929	Single seat fighter	1
Fury	1929	Single seat fighter	267
Norn	1930	Nimrod prototype	1
Nimrod	1930	Single seat naval fighter	68

Total H. G. Hawker aircraft built by all manufacturers: **1,589**

HAWKER AIRCRAFT LTD

Aircraft Type	Date	Purpose of Design	No built
Audax	1931	2 seat army co-operation	718
Demon	1932	2 seat fighter	304
Osprey	1932	2 seat naval reconnaissance	138
Hardy	1934	2 seat general purpose, tropical	48
P.V.3	1934	Single seat, 4 gun fighter	1
P.V.4	1934	2 seat dive bomber	1
Hind	1934	2 seat general purpose/bomber	591
Hartbees	1935	2 seat ground support	69
Hurricane	1935	Single seat, 8 gun fighter	15,195
Hector	1936	2 seat army co-operation	179
Henley	1937	2 seat target tug	202
Hotspur	1938	2 seat fighter (gun turret)	1
Tornado	1939	Single seat fighter	2
Typhoon	1939	Single seat fighter/bomber	3,271
Tempest	1943	Single seat fighter/bomber	1,404
Sea Fury	1944	Single seat naval fighter	900
Sea Hawk	1947	Naval jet fighter/bomber	534
Hunter	1951	Jet fighter/ground attack	2,050
P.1127	1961	Vertical take-off fighter	6
Kestrel	1964	Vertical take-off fighter	9
Harrier	1967	Vertical take-off fighter	*c845
Hawk	1974	Advanced trainer/ground attack	*c658

Total Hawker Aircraft Ltd aircraft built by all manufacturers: **c27,126**

*still in production (1990)

GLOSTER AIRCRAFT CO LTD

Aircraft Type	Date	Purpose of Design	No built
F.5/34	1937	Single seat fighter	2
F.9/37	1939	Twin-engine fighter	2
E.28/39	1941	Jet engine testbed	2
Meteor	1943	Twin-engine jet fighter	3,575
E.1/44	1948	Single seat jet fighter	3
Javelin	1950	All weather jet fighter	435

Total Gloster Aircraft Ltd aircraft built by all manufacturers: **4,019**

ARMSTRONG WHITWORTH AIRCRAFT LTD

Aircraft Type	Date	Purpose of Design	No built
A.W. 29	1936	Single engine light bomber	1
Whitley	1936	Twin-engine medium bomber	1,814
Ensign	1938	33-40 passenger airliner	14
Albemarle	1940	Twin-engine glider tug	602
A.W.52G	1945	Experimental flying wing glider	1
A.W.52	1947	Two jet flying wing	2
Apollo	1947	30 passenger turboprop	2
Argosy	1959	4 engine turboprop freighter	76

Total Armstrong Whitworth Aircraft Ltd aircraft built by all manufacturers: **2,512**

A. V. ROE & CO LTD

Aircraft Type	Date	Purpose of Design	No built
Anson I to X	1935	Twin engine trainer etc.	10,315
Manchester	1939	Twin engine heavy bomber	202
Lancaster	1941	Four engine heavy bomber	7,374
York	1942	Four engine 30-54 passenger	337
Lancastrian	1942	13 passenger based on Lancaster	112
Anson 11 to 22	1944	Twin engine light transport	705
Lincoln	1944	Four engine heavy bomber	318
Tudor	1945	Four engine passenger	33
Athena	1948	Advanced turboprop trainer	22
Shackleton	1949	Maritime surveillance	183
Avro 707	1949	Research for Vulcan bomber	5
Ashton	1950	Four jet research	6
Vulcan	1952	Four jet heavy bomber	136
Avro 748	1960	50 passenger turboprop	349
Andover	1961	Military version of 748	31

Total A. V. Roe aircraft built by all manufacturers: **20,128**

A. V. ROE CANADA LTD

Aircraft Type	Date	Purpose of Design	No built
C-102 Jetliner	1949	50 passenger, four-jet	1
CF-100 Canuck	1952	All-weather jet fighter	692
CF-105 Arrow	1958	Supersonic jet fighter	5

Total A. V. Roe Canada aircraft built: **698**

de HAVILLAND LTD

Aircraft Type	Date	Purpose of Design	No built
Trident	1962	3 engine passenger jet	117
125	1962	2 engine business jet	*c750
146	1981	4 engine passenger jet	*c200

Total de Havilland Ltd aircraft built by all manufacturers: **c1,067**

* still in production (1990)

BLACKBURN AIRCRAFT LTD

Aircraft Type	Date	Purpose of Design	No built
Buccaneer Mk 2	1963	Naval low level strike	209

TOTAL AIRCRAFT DESIGNED BY COMPANIES UNDER THE CHAIRMANSHIP OF SIR THOMAS SOPWITH

Name of Designing Company	Total Built in all Factories
Sopwith Aviation Co Ltd	18,106
H. G. Hawker Engineering Co Ltd	1,589
Hawker Aircraft Ltd	27,126
Gloster Aircraft Co Ltd	4,019
Armstrong Whitworth Aircraft Ltd	2,152
A. V. Roe & Co Ltd	20,128
A. V. Roe Canada Ltd	698
de Havilland Ltd	1,067
Blackburn Aircraft Ltd	209

Total production of all types: **75,457**

Appendix IV

Sailing and Motor Yachts Owned by Sir Thomas Sopwith, 1911-1952

Date	Name	Description
1910	MARGERY DAW	18 ton fishing cutter
1911	MARGERY DAW NEVA	as above 166 ton schooner owned jointly with W. Eyre
1912	NEVA	as above
1926	OSPREY DORIS	170 ton diesel yacht 33 ton 12 metre Int. Class sailing yacht
1927	DORIS VITA	as above 340 ton diesel yacht
1929	VITA MOUETTE	as above 12 metre International Class Sailing Yacht
1930	MOUETTE VITA II	as above 502 ton diesel yacht
1932	VITA II SHAMROCK V	as above J Class Racing Yacht (ex-Sir T. Lipton)
1934	ENDEAVOUR VITA III	J Class Racing Yacht (for America's Cup) 752 ton diesel yacht (ex-ARGOSY)
1936	VITA III ENDEAVOUR II	as above J Class Racing Yacht (for America's Cup)
1937	ENDEAVOUR II AAOLA PHILANTE*	as above 471 ton diesel yacht (temporary ownership) 1600 ton ocean going diesel yacht
1938	ENDEAVOUR II PHILANTE ALANNA	as above as above 12 metre International Class Sailing Yacht

Date	Name	Description
1939	ENDEAVOUR II PHILANTE TOMAHAWK	as above as above 12 metre International Class Sailing Yacht
1947	ENDEAVOUR II PHILANTE TOMAHAWK	as above as above as above
1948	LADY HELENA	155 ton ex-Admiralty craft
1949	PHILANTE II	previously the LADY HELENA (as above). Sold in 1952. No further Sopwith boats listed

* PHILANTE is the largest private diesel yacht ever built in the UK.

Appendix V

The Hawker Siddeley Group in 1988

Export Policy and International Sales
Hawker Siddeley International Ltd

Hawker Siddeley Int (China)　　　　Hawker Siddeley Int (Japan) Ltd

Electric Motors and Generators

Brook Crompton Controls Ltd
Brush Electric Machines Ltd
Industrial Controls Division
Fasco Industries Inc (USA)
Consumer Products Division
Thorn Ltd

Brook Crompton Parkinson Motors Ltd
Brook Crompton Parkinson Ltd (AUS)
Crompton Greaves Ltd (India)
Motor Division
Kirloskar Electric Co Ltd (India)
Westinghouse Systems Ltd

Electric Distribution and Controls

Aerospace Avionics Inc
A & M Instruments
Brush Switchgear Ltd
South Wales Transformers Div
Clarostat Mfg Co Inc
Crompton Metermaster
Crompton Modutec Inc
Daytronic Corporation Inc
Elmwood Sensors Inc (USA)
Fasco Controls Corp (USA)
Hawker Siddeley Zambia Ltd
Hawker Siddeley Pwr Eng Ltd
Meters & Instruments Corp
S&S Power Switchgear Ltd

Aluminium Wire & Cable Co Ltd
Brush Fuses Inc
Brush Transformers Ltd
Cable and Plastics Ltd
Connectron Inc
Crompton Parkinson Cables Ltd
Crompton Parkinson Instruments Ltd
Electro Corporation (USA)
Elmwood Sensors Ltd
Hawker Siddeley Dynamics Eng Ltd
Hawker Siddeley Power Eng Ltd
Hawker Siddeley Pwr Transformers Ltd
Mediterranean Power Electric Co Ltd
South Wales Electric Ltd (Zimbabwe)

South Wales Switchgear Ltd

Electrical Specialized Equipment

Crompton Lighting Ltd
Crompton Vidor
Hind Rectifiers Ltd
McKenzie & Holland (NZ)
Oldham France SA
Powertech Inc (USA)
Tungstone Batteries Ltd
Westcode Semiconductors Ltd
Railway Signalling Division

Crompton Stud Welding Ltd
Dimetronic SA (Spain)
KW Battery Co (USA)
Oldham Crompton Batteries Ltd
Power Conversion Inc. (USA)
Safetran Systems Corp (USA)
Unross Batteries Ltd
Westinghouse Brake & Signal Co (Aus)
Westinghouse Cubic Ltd

Westinghouse Signals Ltd

Mechanical Specialized Equipment

CGTX Inc
Dosco Corporation (USA)
Hawker Noyes PTY (Aus)
Hawker Pacific PTY (Aus)
Hawker Siddeley Canada Inc
Canadian Steel Wheel Division
Tree Farmer Equipment Div
HDA Forgings Ltd
Insumat Ltd
Kockums Can-Car Corp (USA)
MC Machinery PTY Ltd
Westcode Inc (USA)
ROC Fluid Power Division

Dosco Overseas Engineering Ltd
Hawker de Havilland Ltd (Aus)
Hawker De H. Victoria Ltd (Aus)
Hawker Siddeley Brackett Ltd
Canadian Steel Foundries Division
Orenda Division
Hawker Siddeley Rail Projects Ltd
Hollybank Engineering Co Ltd
Kockums Can-Car Inc (Canada)
Lister Shearing Equipment Ltd
Tree Farming Equipment Co Inc (USA)
Railway Brake Division
Westinghouse Brakes Ltd

Diesel Engineering

Lister-Petter Ltd
Lister-Petter Ltd (USA)
Onan Corporation (USA)

Hawker Siddeley Power Plant Ltd
Mirrless Blackstone (Stamford) Ltd
Mirrless Blackstone (Stockport) Ltd

Other Trading Activities

Bunnings Ltd (Aus)
Saro Products Ltd

Gardiner Sons & Co Ltd
Invergordon Distillers Holdings PLC

Appendix VI

Existing Sopwith Aircraft

Type	Serial No	Ownership/Location
Antelope	G-AUSS	Mr John Reid, Julia Creek, Queensland.
Baby	N2078	Fleet Air Arm Museum, Yeovilton, England.
Camel	B5250	Arkansas State Museum, Little Rock, USA.
Camel	B5747	Royal Army Museum, Brussels, Belgium.
Camel	B7270	Mr J. Terteling, Boise, Idaho, USA.
Camel	B7280	Krakow Museum, Poland.
Camel	F6314	Royal Air Force Museum, Hendon, England.
Camel	N6812	Imperial War Museum, London, England.
Camel	N8156	Canadian War Museum, Ottawa, Canada.
Camel	*****	US Marine Corps Museum, Quantica VA, USA.
Dolphin	D5329	RAF Museum (not assembled).
Pup	B1807	Mr K. Baker, Keynsham, England.
Pup	N5180	Shuttleworth Trust, Old Warden, England.
Pup	N5182	Royal Air Force Museum, Hendon, England.
Pup	N5195	Museum of Army Flying, England.
Snipe	E6938	Canadian War Museum, Ottawa, Canada.
Snipe	E8100	Cole Palen Collection, NY State, USA.
Snipe	E8102	Canadian War Museum, Ottawa, Canada.
Triplane	N5486	Gagaarin Air Force Academy, Moscow, USSR.
Triplane	N5912	Royal Air Force Museum, Hendon, England.
1½ Strutter	556	Musee de l'Air, Paris, France.
1½ Strutter	88	Royal Army Museum, Brussels, Belgium.

NOTE: In addition to the aircraft listed a number of replicas have been built and are on display in various countries.

Details reproduced by kind permission of Mr L. P. Robinson.

Appendix VII

Hundredth Birthday Messages from Heads of State

WOK1209 LMW6792 PCH0005 P27 BUCK05   17 JAN 1988/1608

                                                    Buckingham Palace
                                                    London
                                                    SW1A 1AA

                                                    17 January 1988

TELEMESSAGE LXP   ROYAL-CARD
SIR THOMAS OCTAVE MURDOCH SOPWITH, CBE.
COMPTON MANOR
KINGS SOMBORNE
STOCKBRIDGE
HAMPSHIRE SO20 6QW

       WE ARE DELIGHTED TO HEAR THAT YOU ARE CELEBRATING YOUR ONE
       HUNDREDTH BIRTHDAY. WE SEND YOU MANY CONGRATULATIONS ON THIS HAPPY
       OCCASION AND OUR GOOD WISHES FOR AN ENJOYABLE DAY.

       ELIZABETH R. AND PHILIP.

☺ Telemessage

17 JAN 1988711605

WOK1200 LMX4747 PCH0002 P27 BUCK02

Buckingham Palace
London
SW1A 1AA

17 January 1988

GREETINGS"B"

TELEMESSAGE LXP
SIR THOMAS SOPWITH
COMPTON MANOR
KINGS SOMBORNE
STOCKBRIDGE
HAMPSHIRE SO20 6QW

WE BOTH SEND YOU OUR VERY WARMEST CONGRATULATIONS AND FONDEST
REGARDS ON THE MEMORABLE OCCASION OF YOUR CENTENARY.

CHARLES AND DIANA.

SANDRINGHAM, NORFOLK

I am sorry not to be able to join your many friends and admirers gathered at Brooklands to celebrate your hundredth birthday, but I am delighted to have this chance to offer you my congratulations and best wishes on reaching your century.

I have many happy memories of shooting those high pheasants of yours at King's Compton and I am thinking of you as we try to round up the wild cocks at the end of the season in Norfolk.

From HRH The Duke of Edinburgh. When he refers to Kings Compton, he does of course mean Compton Manor.

10 DOWNING STREET
LONDON SW1A 2AA

THE PRIME MINISTER   11 January 1988

Dear Sir Thomas,

    I know that you are going to be
100 years old on 18 January and I want
to send you my very best wishes for this
special occasion. What a wonderful milestone
to reach! I hope that you have a very
happy day.

*Denis joins me in sending our
warm regards to you and your family.*

Yours sincerely

Sir Thomas Sopwith, C.B.E. *Margaret Thatcher*

THE WHITE HOUSE

WASHINGTON

Palm Springs

December 30, 1987

Dear Sir Thomas:

I would like to join your family and friends in congratulating you on the occasion of your 100th birthday.

My generation grew up with vivid memories of the heroic pilots in their Sopwith Camels who did so much for our Allied cause in World War I. But the Sopwith name and your many achievements, I am sure, are nearly as well known to my fellow countrymen and women today.

Nancy joins me in wishing you a very happy birthday and many happy returns. God bless you.

Sincerely,

Ronald Reagan

Sir Thomas Sopwith
Compton Manor
Kings Somborne
Hampshire, England

Bibliography

Babington Smith, Constance, *Testing Time*, Cassell.

Birch and Bramson, *Captains and Kings*, Pitman.

Birch and Bramson, *The Tiger Moth Story*, Airlife.

Boyle, Andrew, *Trenchard*, Collins.

Bramson, Alan, *Master Airman, A Biography of Air Vice-Marshal Donald Bennett CB, CBE, DSO*, Airlife.

Brett, R. Dallas, *History of British Aviation 1908-1914*, Air Research.

Gould Lee, Arthur, *The Flying Cathedral*, Methuen.

King, H. F., *Sopwith Aircraft 1912-1920*, Putnam.

Lewis, Peter, *British Aircraft 1809-1914*, Putnam.

Mason, Francis K., *Hawker Aircraft since 1920*, Putnam.

Penrose, Harald, *British Aviation, The Pioneering Years*, Putnam.

——, *British Aviation, The Great War and Armistice*, Putnam.

——, *British Aviation, The Adventuring Years*, Putnam.

Robertson, Bruce, *Sopwith—the Man and his Aircraft*, Harleyford.

Wallace, Graham, *Claude Grahame-White*, Putnam.

Index

Page numbers in *italics* denote photographs.